Powered by Jaguar

The Cooper, HWM, Lister and Tojeiro sports-racing cars

DOUG NYE

D1601887

MOTOR RACING PUBLICATIONS LTD
28 Devonshire Road, Chiswick, London W4 2HD, England.

ISBN 0 900549 56 4
First published 1980

Photosetting by Zee Creative Ltd., Norbury, London SW16.
Printed in Great Britain by The Whitefriars Press Ltd.,
Tonbridge, Kent.

Contents

W. A. 'Archie' Scott-Brown — the great driver.

INTRODUCTION

Ask any enthusiast about Jaguar-powered sports cars and he will immediately picture the classical XK120-140-150 series and the road-going E-Type, plus the Le Mans-winning Cs and Ds. Think a little harder and the subject of this volume will spring to mind; the potent sports-racing cars which used the XK engine, but whose chassis design and production owed nothing more to the famous Coventry marque.

In essence these were the HWM-, Cooper-, Tojeiro- and Lister-Jaguars — in chronological order — which did so much during the 'fifties to enhance Jaguar's reputation beyond the factory's own immediate sphere of influence and interest. While Jaguar's great prize was always Le Mans, and their own sports-racing cars were tailored to that event's requirements, the specialist racers from HWM, Cooper, Tojeiro and Lister were often far more potent performers, and were raced more widely on circuits which today would instantly be banned as 'suicidally dangerous', driven by men whose names were once so familiar in an age of he-man drivers — Stirling Moss, Duncan Hamilton, Peter Whitehead, Peter Walker, Ivor Bueb, and of course the great Archie Scott-Brown, who, in his works Lister-Jaguar, became indisputably the greatest exponent of the type.

Undoubtedly the major works team cars, like the Cs and Ds from Jaguar and the DB3s and DBRs from Aston Martin, have made greater classical impact, and at the time our Jaguar-engined cars were current they were regarded very much as 'specials', of dubious parentage, and rather below the salt. The fact that they could often out-perform their purer bloodstock rivals has only really gained recognition in recent years as historic sports car racing has become so well-supported and one of the major spectator attractions of modern motor racing. Now that Lister-Jaguars are again seen regularly blowing-off the purebred cars from Jaguar itself, Aston Martin, and even Maserati and Ferrari, the time has come to tell their story, and that of others in their class; appealing, big and 'hairy' front-engined sports-racing cars . . . powered by Jaguar.

In assembling pictures to illustrate this book every effort was made to secure shots taken of cars as they appeared originally, in their proper environment and to their correct specification, rather than in their more recent guises as restored or newly assembled cars. I believe that all but two of the photographs date from the heyday of the sports-racing cars and hope that in consequence this book will help to settle many arguments as to the origin and career of individual cars.

D.C.N.

ACKNOWLEDGEMENTS

This whole project started out as a simple and speedy resumé of the Jaguar-powered sports cars' story, but I soon discovered that the slightest scratch on the surface exposed ever deeper and more complicated questions to be asked. For giving so much of their time to providing the answers to these questions I am especially grateful to Messrs George Abecassis, John Cooper, John Tojeiro and particularly Brian Lister. Dick Barton and Don Moore of the original Lister Equipe also provided assistance and encouragement which proved invaluable, as did Stan Sproat of Ecurie Ecosse and Frank Nagel of HW Motors Ltd.

Special thanks also to John Harper, John Coundley, Dr Philippe Renault, John Bekaert, Frank le Gallais, Dick Shattock, Bruce Halford, John B. Blanden, Barry Simpson and John Pearson for giving so freely of their time and knowledge.

I am also extremely grateful for the advice and information supplied by past and present car constructors, owners, drivers and associates including Tony Gaze, Mrs Barbara Heath, Kirk Rylands, Bobby Bell, Stephen Langton, Patrick Head, Jonathan Sieff, Peter Blond, John Bateson, Gil Baird, Austen Nurse, 'Wilkie' Wilkinson, Gil Dickson, Mo Gomm, Len Pritchard, Tim Abbott, Ken Rogers, Geoffrey Marsh, the late Mr John Ogier, Peter Mould, Peter and Terry Moore, Terry Grainger, Ray Fielding, Peter Riley, Malcolm Boston, Jim Diggory, Michael Wright, Peter Gammon, John Horridge, Joel Finn, Peter Bolton, Tom Bleasdale (whose 'Lister-MG' turned out to have been a Lester-MG), Nick Jerromes, David Harvey, Peter Sargent, Jeremy Broad, Frank Webb, Norman Hillwood, Len Hayden, John Michelsen, Chris Drake, Martyn Chapman, David Ham, and last but by no means least Michael Bowler, Editor of *Thoroughbred & Classic Cars* magazine and Lister-Jaguar owner-driver.

On the pure research and journalistic side of this project sincere thanks are due for the supply of photographs and information to Geoffrey Goddard, Denis Jenkinson, Graham Gauld, Duncan Rabagliati, Tony Hogg of the American *Road & Track* magazine, Graham Fleming, Dudley Gahagan, Peter Brockes and Nick Georgano of the National Motor Museum Libraries at Beaulieu, Hants, Quentin Spurring, Editor of *Autosport* magazine and photographer Jeff Bloxham, to Jonathan Wood of *Thoroughbred & Classic Cars,* and to Andrew Whyte — formerly of Jaguar Cars.

Finally, sincere thanks to John Bolster and to publisher Simon Taylor of *Autosport* magazine for allowing his contemporary road tests of these classic sports cars to be reproduced in these pages.

Doug Nye
Lower Bourne, Farnham
September 1980

1

The Jaguar XK engine

You could say that this story began in 1943. At that time the assembly shops at Foleshill, Coventry, where SS-Jaguar cars had been produced immediately prewar, were packed with aircraft fuselage and wing sections destined for the Royal Air Force. Naturally such factories formed prime targets for the *Luftwaffe,* but by 1943 much of its night-raiding effort was spent. The night-time firewatch was still a vital part of Britain's home defence and the Foleshill staff each set aside one night a week for compulsory firewatching.

William Lyons, the artist-industrialist founder of SS and what would become the Jaguar marque, saw these firewatch sessions as a unique and stimulating opportunity for extended design seminars with his leading engineers. He had Sunday night watches scheduled to include himself and engineers Bill Heynes, Claude Baily and Walter Hassan, and while he floated ideas for postwar car body styles and commercial strategy they discussed with him the pros and cons of producing a 'proper' power unit, worthy of the type of cars they were interested in building.

Until the outbreak of war SS-Jaguar had employed what were basically Standard engines fitted with overhead-valve cylinder head conversions and offered in three sizes — a 1,776cc four-cylinder and a choice of 2,664cc or 3,485cc six-cylinder engines. Lyons now visualized engines of his own company's manufacture which were to be more sophisticated and refined and would have the greatest possible scope for further development. Above all he wanted a prestige engine, one which would look good both on paper and in the metal, which sounded right and which 'would go right'. About that he had no reservations. He wanted at least 120bhp and was attracted by the glamour and proven efficiency of the great twin-overhead-camshaft engine once campaigned in Grand Prix racing by Peugeot and their copycats.

His engineers were at first dubious. In those Sunday night sessions they pointed out to him that twin-overhead-cam engines would be expensive to make and almost certainly very noisy — unacceptably so for a long-range high-speed passenger car. They felt confident that they could supply all the power he wanted by simple development of the existing pushrod overhead-valve engine. Their argument was that it would be simpler, cheaper and almost certainly quieter in operation, but Lyons — quite rightly in retrospect — confirmed that he wanted a twin-cam, never mind the problems. He wanted a twin-cam, and only a twin-cam . . . possibly a 2½-litre to power the whole postwar range.

His men consequently set-up shop in a tiny development office at the Foleshill works, and under Bill Heynes as Chief Engineer and Technical Director the world-renowned XK Jaguar engine series was brought to life. Claude Baily, formerly with Morris Engines, was in charge of detail design, while Walter Hassan — former 'Bentley Boy' with massive competition experience and latterly with the Bristol Aeroplane Company — was to take responsibility for test and development of the prototype units.

Lyons' team rapidly became as enthusiastic as their Managing Director, and the initial pilot study, in an atmosphere hardly conducive to anything but war programme work, was for a tiny 1,360cc four-cylinder engine given the serial XF — projects XA to XE having borne no engines as fruit.

The XF was designed primarily to prove the type of twin-cam cylinder-head and valve-gear preferred, but in testing its crankshaft design proved inadequate for the very high revs which would otherwise have been achieved. Bore and stroke had been decided at 66.5mm x 98mm, a hemispherical combustion chamber shape was used and classical 'Ballot-type' valve operation was adopted in its simplest possible form. The head proved a great success, but the design overall was rejected for its inadequate bottom-end and the high cost of tooling and production.

Just after the end of the war in 1945 another route was tried with the XG, which was effectively a conversion of the existing four-cylinder production engine with the head, valve-gear, inlet port design, etc, based on that of the very successful prewar BMW 328. This provided valve operation from a single side camshaft in the block, acting almost directly upon the inlet valves, while cross pushrods and extra rockers controlled the exhausts. They hoped the result would look as good as Mr Lyons wanted, and they chose bore and stroke dimensions of 73mm x 106mm to displace 1,776cc. Unfortunately, testing proved that the BMW-style pushrod valve gear was going to be too noisy for saloon car use since valve-spring pressures would have to be very high for high-speed operation. Gas-flow figures through the vertical valve ports could not in any case compare adequately with those through the experimental XF engine's horizontal ports.

Lyons by this time was totally convinced that his company's new postwar engine line should be designed from scratch without the restriction of using some existing tooling or carry-over parts. Meanwhile, he had acquired all Standard's six-cylinder engine tooling and had had it installed at Foleshill, while Sir John Black of Standard agreed to continue the supply of the 1,776cc four-cylinder power unit, which Black's own concern still required for its new Triumph 1800 models. SS-Jaguar recommenced car production using these prewar engines while Heynes, Baily, Hassan and their team pressed ahead with the all-new engine development programme.

It was decided to replace the three existing Standard-derived engines with a pair of related new designs, one a four-cylinder, the other a 'six' using many common parts. In 1946 test-runs began on the experimental XJ four-cylinder power unit of 80.5mm x 98mm, 1,996cc, and this time they came up with the true progenitor of the legendarily famous XK. What had been a 'whole-range' concept for a 2½-litre engine was now finally abandoned, and by using different cylinder bores the team produced two alternative XJs — the 2-litre four-cylinder and an 83mm x 98mm, 3,182cc six-cylinder. Development proceeded in parallel on both engines with wide-ranging experiments in valve-gear and camshaft-drive systems. Noise from the cam-drive chain was one major problem and oil leaks around the camshafts was another . . .

One of the four-cylinder XJ engines was subsequently loaned to Major Goldie Gardner for installation in his record-breaking MG 'EX135' and using modified pistons and a 12:1 compression ratio it powered the car to a new 2-litre class world record of 176.69mph. In this form the engine developed 146bhp at 6,000rpm, and would rev safely to 'six-five' . . .

Meanwhile, the Jaguar engineering team were well-satisfied with tests of the six-cylinder XJ engine, but realized that American sales success would depend on improved torque. Therefore, the original XF-dictated stroke length of 98mm was increased to 106mm and, with the six-cylinder XJ bore of 83mm, the 3,448cc Jaguar XK engine was born.

Development of an XK four-cylinder continued for some time, but the vibration problems inherent in any 'big-four' always interrupted progress. The larger XK engine was always intended to emerge in a new Mark VII Jaguar

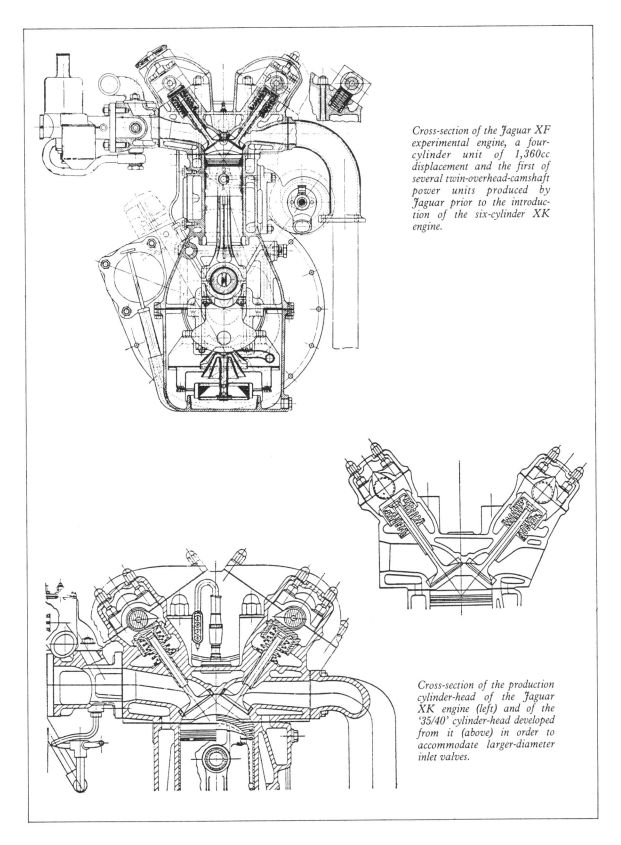

Cross-section of the Jaguar XF experimental engine, a four-cylinder unit of 1,360cc displacement and the first of several twin-overhead-camshaft power units produced by Jaguar prior to the introduction of the six-cylinder XK engine.

Cross-section of the production cylinder-head of the Jaguar XK engine (left) and of the '35/40' cylinder-head developed from it (above) in order to accommodate larger-diameter inlet valves.

saloon and thinking concentrated upon this aim. Lyons appreciated, however, that the twin-cam engine would place a worthy sporting successor to the prewar SS100 within his grasp. He said: '. . . such a car with the XK engine could not fail (provided of course we made no serious mistakes) to become outstanding, as it should easily out-perform everything else on the market by a wide margin, irrespective of price . . .'

Furthermore, a batch of XK-engined sporting cars would prove the engine under the most gruelling everyday conditions before full-scale Mark VII saloon production would commence. Of course, the promotional and prestige value of a brand-new six-cylinder twin-cam sports car was well appreciated. By this time the October, 1948, London Motor Show was rapidly approaching and reputedly in only six weeks the prototype Jaguar XK120 roadster was slammed together. The development shop took an existing Mark V chassis, cut 18-inches from its centre-section, replaced the X-bracing by a single box-section cross-member and narrowed the frame very slightly. With an 8ft 6in wheelbase the result was clad in a striking aluminium bodyshell using exterior panels formed by H.H. Cooke & Sons of Nottingham and mounted on ash under-frames made-up at Foleshill. Lyons had styled the body in less than two weeks from start to finalization. When the London Motor Show opened its doors the public thronged in to see the new Jaguar XK120 Super Sports Open Two-Seater, finished in gleaming bronze and claimed to be capable of the then-staggering road speed of 120mph. Racing car performance was available for £998 basic, the same as the newly-released Mark V saloon.

That release was a promotional masterpiece, staggeringly so. Lyons had envisaged a first-year production batch of around 200 XK120s, with further follow-up batches being put through if demand warranted. But within the first week of the Show response was utterly overwhelming and clearly this car, which had been intended for hand-built production, could not be made in sufficient quantity. Pressed Steel, of Oxford, were buttonholed to tool-up for volume production and ideas to produce a down-market XK100 model with the 2-litre four-cylinder engine were set aside, after a pilot batch of 50 such engines had been produced.

The 3.4-litre six-cylinder XK power unit carried the day, and when factory test driver Ron 'Soapy' Sutton achieved an average of 132.596mph in a carefully choreographed and well-publicized two-way record run on Belgium's Jabbeke Highway in May 1949, the XK120 series' success was virtually assured.

So the Jaguar XK engine came to life. Its all-new block, comprehensively stiffened to carry a robust counterbalanced crankshaft in seven 2¾-inch diameter main bearings, was sub-contracted to Leyland Motors for production. Wet-sump lubrication was circulated by a gear-driven oil pump and the camshaft drive was by duplex roller chain. Valves were placed at 70-degrees to the vertical and the camshafts were chosen to give a 5/16-inch valve-lift, apparently to eliminate the possibility of valves touching should an inexperienced mechanic rotate the camshafts independently while working on the head. In fact the average garage mechanic proved adept very quickly when introduced to the XK engine, and when the Special Equipment XK120 models were released two years after the prototype, new 3/8-inch-lift camshafts still did not produce any notable rash of bent valves caused by careless handling. The cross-flow cylinder-head itself was cast by William Mills, of Wednesbury, Staffordshire, in aluminium rather than the traditional iron, and so was prone to bruising if banged or dropped. But its bare weight of 50lb, when compared with a similar iron head's 110lb-plus, made it more easy to handle in any case, and saved crankcase weight, too, since it did not need the extra beef required to support a 120 per cent heavier iron head. This basic XK engine became known as the 'snail-port' version.

Of course, the engine was every bit the good-looker which William Lyons had required, with two individual-branch exhaust manifolds protruding one side of those twin polished cam-covers and a pair of 1¾-inch SU carburettors on the other. With an 8.0:1 compression ratio the XK engine as released in the XK120 delivered 160bhp at 5,400rpm. On an alternative 7.0:1 compression it

12

Classical design. The XK engine installed in Marsh Plant Hire's ex-Mike Pendleton/Dick Tindell Lister, YCD 422, in 1980, showing off the cross-flow twin-cam head, separate exhaust manifolds and triple twin-choke Weber carburation. This particular car began its career in 1959 with a Chevrolet V8 installed.

gave 150bhp.

In these pages we will be concerned with the XK-powered sports-racing cars which were built outside the Coventry factories by specialists such as HWM, Cooper, Tojeiro and Lister. The story of the C-Type and D-Type factory-built sports-racing cars has often been told, and for our purposes one needs to recap but briefly . . .

In 1950 Jaguar ran three XK120 roadsters in the Le Mans 24-Hours race, the sports car endurance classic which was to become William Lyons' single competition goal in the years to come. These original works racing cars were, in the words of Bill Heynes, 'probably the most standard cars that have ever been run in this race . . .' In his 1960 Institution of Mechanical Engineers paper entitled *Milestones in the Life of an Automobile Engineer* (IME paper 'AD 1/60') Heynes described the cars' careful preparation and the team's good organization but emphasized that no development work had been done to give extra power over the engine supplied to the public, nor to reduce the car's overall weight. The Le Mans engines retained the original 5/16-inch lift camshafts and the moderate valve timing deemed necessary to preserve adequate flexibility in a saloon car. Peak power was as standard, 160bhp at 5,000rpm with a permissible peak speed of 5,500rpm.

After 21 hours of racing the Leslie Johnson/Bert Hadley XK120 was lying third and lapping at 98mph, while Louis Rosier's leading Talbot was strolling around at under 86mph. Unfortunately, the XK120's brakes had wilted, and as the drivers resorted to slowing the car on the gearbox so the production clutch gave out only three hours from the finish. The other two XK120s came home 12th and 15th.

For 1951 the special chassis/special body XK120C, or C-Type Jaguar was developed, and Heynes and his men set out to improve the XK engine's bmep figures at higher speeds and also, if possible, the unit's safe speed range — 'even at the expense of the bottom-end if necessary — but this fortunately was not the case'.

Taking the standard cylinder-head casting with its Harry Weslake-developed porting, they carried out extra port fettling and cut back the inlet valve guide level with the port. The inlet valve was increased 1/8-inch in diameter to provide a larger radius where the port joined the seat, although the actual internal port diameters were increased from 1 7/16-inches to 1½-inches, and from 1¼-inches to 1 3/8-inches, respectively. These modifications improved exhaust valve flow quite considerably, but in his 1953 IME paper *The Jaguar Engine*, Bill Heynes commented: 'It is interesting to note that until the improved inlet port flow was obtained this change gave nothing either on the bench or on the road, and equally the improvement gained by the inlet port change was only partial until the exhaust was also modified . . .'

While the standard valve springs were trouble-free up to 5,500rpm, for racing purposes the same spring was provided with increased free length, permitting bounce-free running up to 6,500rpm. In order to maintain a beefy buttom-end power curve Jaguar retained the standard timing — 10-degrees either side of tdc, 50-degrees either side of bdc. Lift was raised, however, from 5/16-inch to 3/8-inch, simply by eliminating the dwell and raising the cams' top radius.

Solid-skirt pistons with 0.006-inch racing clearances were fitted with MIRA-patent pressure-backed rings capable of surviving continuous operation above 5,000rpm. Carburation was by two 2-inch diameter SUs, replacing the standard 1¾-inch production instruments. In place of the standard air cleaners the XK120C engine used an air collector box, fitting over the carburettor mouths and receiving ducted air from in front of the radiator. The box was left open at its rear-end so there was no ram effect, simply a through-flow of eddy-free air. The induction manifold bore was as production with the entry opened out to match the larger carburettors, while the balance-tube size was increased from 7/8-inch to 1¼-inches.

The engine main- and big-end bearing medium was changed — simply as a precaution — from babbit to Indium-coated lead-bronze, while the crankshaft itself was identical to standard with the extra bearing clearance necessary being allowed on bearing thickness.

An enlarged oil pump had already been fitted to production engines to maintain adequate flow, but for competition use this wet-sump engine design suffered the inevitable problems of oil wash building up at the front-end of the crankcase under braking and at the rear under hard acceleration. Tests revealed that under maximum acceleration in second gear the surface of the oil assumed an angle of 20 degrees to the horizontal, and in first the angle was 30 degrees. Therefore, the oil in the sump had to be trapped somehow to prevent the pump suction being uncovered or the rear main bearing unduly flooded. Excess

XK engine installation in the first second-generation HWM-Jaguar, XPE 2, photographed at HW Motors' Walton-on-Thames workshops in the late-'fifties. HWM used 3.4-litre wet-sump units in the main, with Weslake-modified C-Type heads. Note the small-tube body-support framing outlining the second-generation HWM-Jaguar shape. The Borrani wire wheels were delivered from Italy painted HWM cream.

of oil above the sump baffle was tantamount to over-filling the sump and early engine tests had shown this to cost over 20bhp at speeds over 5,000rpm. To improve the situation in the XK120C engine the sump was deepened and widened slightly and the main chamber at either end of the sump was sealed so that under dip and squat the oil would be trapped in there. The standard compression ratio of 8.0:1 was retained in most instances, though 9.0:1 was employed in the 1951 C-Types, then decreased to 8.5:1 for the 1952 Le Mans cars. Heynes confessed he was opposed to the use of the maximum compression ratio for sports car racing since experience had shown a very wide variation in fuel quality supplied by the organizers of these races. Light detonation from poor fuel, which did not match the compression being used, could easily burn piston crowns. Power output was around 204bhp at 5,500rpm in the 1951 C-Type, allied to 220lb ft torque at 4,000rpm.

Two of the three works C-Types went out early in the Le Mans 24-Hours race that year due to broken oil-delivery pipes. The pipes were formed in steel, and vibration caused crystallization of a flange welded on to them. The third car, shared by Peter Whitehead/Peter Walker, was firmly in the lead at the time these failures occurred, and the Jaguar crews' hearts were in their mouths as a similar failure was confidently expected. However, it didn't happen, and Jaguar won Le Mans.

In 1952 the C-Types returned with a practically identical engine specification apart from the decrease in compression ratio to 8.5:1. Unfortunately, the new long-nosed/long-tailed body style proved to be a catastrophic mistake and the interrupted radiator airflow revealed a water pump defect,creating cavitation, so that steam formed in the eye of the pump and blocked the waterflow completely. As a result the team cars' engines were ruined during practice and all three cars retired in the first hour of the race . . .

For some time Heynes' men had been experimenting with carburettor sets providing one choke per cylinder, and in 1953 they used three twin-choke 40mm Webers for the first time. Again according to Heynes, they gave about the same power at 6,000rpm, but boosted the engine's mid-range considerably from 3,500-5,500rpm — in fact they added about 30bhp between 4,500 and 5,000rpm. This gave a tremendous bonus in acceleration, always at a premium in true road-racing conditions, and peak power in these 1953 engines is recorded as 220bhp at 5,200rpm. They were installed in C-Types fitted with Dunlop disc brakes and using flexible bag-type fuel tanks. They ran faultlessly at Le Mans and were placed first, second and fourth, driven by Tony Rolt/Duncan Hamilton, Stirling Moss/Peter Walker and Peter Whitehead/Ian Stewart, with a production C-Type, Belgian-entered for Roger Laurent/Charles de Tornaco, finishing ninth.

In 1954 the monocoque centre-section D-Type Jaguar chassis was introduced, powered by a dry-sump version of the XK engine. Heynes' team had adopted dry-sump lubrication for their competition cars at long last to solve all the disadvantages involved in having so much surplus oil splashing around inside the wet-sump units. With an oil cooler in the circuit this system allowed the D-Type engine to achieve higher speeds and withstand greater bearing loads, while the sump-depth could be halved and so contribute to a useful saving in frontal area. The two oil pumps, pressure and scavenge, were powered by a cross-shaft which was worm-driven from the crankshaft nose. Of course these racing engines carried no flywheel as such, though they mounted a large torsional vibration damper externally at the front, and the outside circumference of the clutch casing formed the starter ring. The D-Type also introduced an all-new Jaguar gearbox with four speeds, all with synchromesh, replacing the Moss gearbox of the earlier cars.

That year's Le Mans race saw a titanic battle develop between the 3.4 D-Type and the monstrous 4.9-litre Ferrari 375-Plus, driven respectively by Tony Rolt/Duncan Hamilton and Froilan Gonzalez/Maurice Trintignant. The Ferrari could out-accelerate the Jaguar up to 100mph, but around that mark the D-Type's glorious shape, created by Malcolm Sayer, proved to have a marked aerodynamic advantage and the Jaguar could draw away. The Ferrari won a controversial and rainy race by less than two minutes after 24-hours wheel-to-wheel, and a hastily-prepared Belgian production C-Type was fourth, shared by Roger Laurent/Jacques Swaters. It was unfortunate for Jaguar that the 24-Hours was run in continuous rain, for by cooling the Ferrari's brake drums it denied them the advantage they should have had in the dry through the use of Dunlop disc brakes.

This defeat at Le Mans in 1954 convinced Heynes' men that they required more power if they were to stand a chance against the promised Mercedes-Benz attack the following year. To obtain more power without running radical cams (which would rob the engine of bottom-end performance) it was necessary to increase the valve area still further. The only way this could be achieved satisfactorily was to redesign the cylinder-head and alter the exhaust valve inclination from the standard 35-degrees to 40-degrees so that the valve-head would clear the new increased-size inlet. So the Jaguar '35/40' cylinder-head came into being. Its new valve sizes were 2-inches diameter for the inlet and 1 11/16-inch diameter for the exhaust. These valves were operated by still higher-lift camshafts — 7/16-inch — and wider timing enabled Jaguar's engineers to boost power to 270bhp at 5,700rpm, still using the successful 45mm Weber carburettor set-up from 1954. The '35/40' was a pure competition unit, the old faithful 'snail-port' continuing in production.

Of course the 1955 Le Mans 24-Hours was overshadowed by that horrendous accident which claimed the lives of Mercedes-Benz driver Pierre Levegh and over 80 spectators. But the fierce sprint race in the opening two hours had shown Mike Hawthorn's D-Type to be faster on the straights than Fangio's Mercedes-Benz 300SLR, while the German car had an advantage out of the corners owing to its independent rear suspension compared with the D-Type's increasingly outdated and crude live axle. Mercedes-Benz withdrew their surviving cars that night in the wake of the accident. They were leading at the time, but in their final hour's running the Jaguar drivers had noticed they were using their air-brakes much earlier than during the race's opening stages, suggesting all was not well with their drum brakes. Mike Hawthorn/Ivor Bueb subsequently won with their D-Type, supported by the inevitable Belgian Jaguar entry of Jacques Swaters/Johnny Claes, who finished third in a production 'D'.

In 1956 fuel restrictions were applied at Le Mans, which made it difficult for Jaguar to take full advantage of their engines' full potential. Fuel consumption was rigidly restricted, making the most stringent economy all-important with, as Heynes recalled, 'no latitude for fuel wastage that could be produced by flooding or by running on an over-rich mixture. The power developed by the engines showed a slight increase only in the middle ranges, which was effected by slightly modified induction pipe lengths. This year, for the first time, one of the cars was fitted with Lucas petrol-injection . . .'

Unfortunately, Paul Frère dropped his works D-Type at the start of the second lap of the 24-hours grind, spinning into the retaining bank at the Esses and involving Jack Fairman's sister car and de Portago's Ferrari in an accident which put all three out of the race! The third Jaguar, driven by Mike Hawthorn/Ivor Bueb, suffered persistent misfiring during the first seven hours of the race which, combined with repeated pit-calls to investigate the cause, dropped it way down into 22nd place. The car had been suffering the same problem in practice and the engine had been changed on the night before the race in an attempt to clear the fault. The only items not changed were the fuel lines themselves since the intended replacements did not fit well. Eventually, at one pit-stop the cause was traced to a hairline crack in one pipe, which was limiting the pressure in the fuel-injection system. Once the pipe had been replaced the engine came back on song and the car soared back through the field to finish sixth.

Meanwhile, the private D-Type of Ecurie Ecosse had taken the lead driven by Ron Flockhart/Ninian Sanderson, and it won to save Jaguar's reputation. On this occasion a Belgian-entered D-Type was fourth, shared this year by Roger Laurent/Freddie Rousselle.

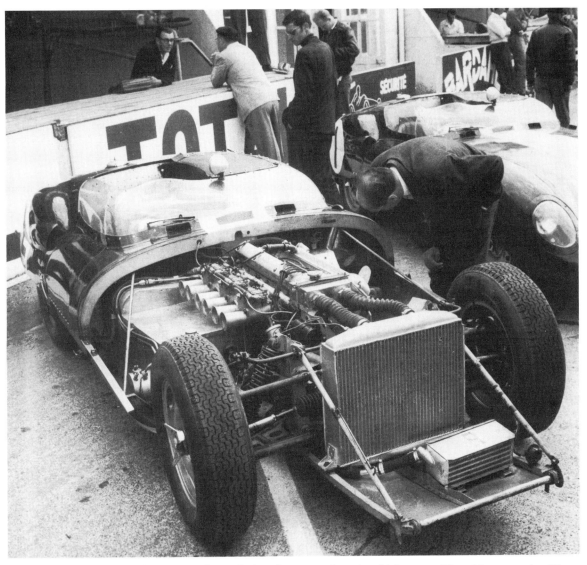

At this point Sir William Lyons decreed that factory racing should be set aside so that the experimental department could become more devoted to production developments. Competition tuning of the basic 3.4-litre XK engine continued to the point where outputs of 288bhp or more were to be expected, and 3.8-litre units were engineered by the factory to give as much as 320bhp in sprint trim.

As early as June 1952, private owner-driver Oscar Moore — we shall be meeting him shortly — had bored-out his own 3.4-litre XK engine to 3,814cc, while almost simultaneously on the West Coast of America, Richie Ginther was sucking his teeth and doing the same thing to a 3.4 for his friend Phil Hill. Briggs Cunningham, also in the USA, was to become a good friend of Jaguar, and when his development adviser Alfred Momo produced a 3.8 the Coventry company began to think maybe such an enlargement was not too marginal to contemplate in safety and reliability terms, and accordingly they produced an enlarged XK in-house.

Whereas early private-owner over-bores of the XK tended to result in cylinder walls cracking through to the water passages, Jaguar's own engine enlargement was, of course, done properly; they inserted wet liners and

The ultimate works Lister-Jaguar engine installation photographed at Le Mans during practice for the 1959 24-Hours race. These were the ill-fated short-stroke 3-litre power units loaned to Lister by the Jaguar factory and destined to break spectacularly during the long grind. Note the Costin-bodied Listers' inflatable passenger-side tonneau cover, cooling intakes in the screen base and webbing-reinforced front wishbones.

modified the block's water passage routing. Mike Hawthorn and Ivor Bueb drove a Cunningham-entered D-Type at Sebring early in 1957, using a full 3.8-litre works engine on fuel-injection, where the PI system had made its own debut on a 3.4 XK the previous year.

To achieve this capacity the unit was first bored-out then linered to 4mm oversize — 87mm as against the standard 3.4's 83mm — which combined with the standard 106mm stroke to displace 3,781cc. On a compression ratio of around 10:1 (Heynes obviously having faith in American fuel), and with 7/16-inch-lift camshafts, 2-inch inlet valves and 1 11/16-inch exhaust valves, this '35/40'-headed engine delivered on the test-bed a peak of 306bhp at 5,500rpm allied to 312lb ft of torque at 4,500rpm.

At the 1957 Le Mans — still very much the apple of Jaguar's corporate eye despite their own works team's withdrawal from the fray — five private D-Types started and all survived to finish first (Flockhart/Bueb, 3.8-litres PI entered by Ecurie Ecosse), second (Sanderson/Jock Lawrence, 3.4-litres, Webers, Ecurie Ecosse), third (Jean Lucas/Jean-Marie Brousselot driving as 'Mary'), fourth (Paul Frère/Freddy Rousselle) and sixth (Duncan Hamilton/Masten Gregory). This memorable occasion saw Jaguar achieve their hat-trick of Le Mans victories, this triumphant record of 1955-57 adding to the C-Type successes of 1951 and 1953 to make it five in all, thereby equalling Bentley's prewar British record.

Then for 1958 the CSI slapped a blanket 3-litre limit on World Sports Car Championship events in an attempt to smother development of such monster cars as the 4.5-litre Maserati 450S V8, which had threatened to become 'too fast for safety' in preceding years.

Jaguar buckled to, and reduced their 3.4-litre XK competition engine to match the new limit, while 'Wilkie' Wilkinson — the well-known Technical Director of Ecurie Ecosse — approached the problem from the opposite direction and enlarged a 2.4-litre XK to a full 3-litres.

Neither of these units was successful, for although they produced just about sufficient power to remain competitive they had lost the larger XK engine's legendary reliability. No D-Type Jaguar would ever again survive 24 hours at Le Mans . . . but one or two 3-litre engines would perform nobly in our 'specials' constructed outside the Coventry works . . .

Jaguar's 3-litre conversion consisted of retaining the original 83mm bore but shortening the stroke to 92mm from 106mm, so achieving 2,986cc. The compression ratio went as high as 10.25:1, while the big 3.8 engine's camshaft lift and '35/40 head' valve sizes were unchanged. Heynes' men retained Weber carburettors and bench-tested their 3-litre unit at 254bhp at 6,300rpm, finding 230lb ft of torque at 5,500rpm.

Ecurie Ecosse, meanwhile, mated the 83mm bore to a short 91mm stroke for 2,954cc, using a 9.17:1 compression ratio, 3/8-inch-lift camshaft and small 1 7/8-inch and 1 5/8-inch diameter inlet and exhaust valves. Also on Weber carburettors, this engine delivered 234bhp at 6,100rpm and 215lb ft of torque at 4,600rpm for a rather more meaty mid-range than top-end performance. In the event the characteristics of these smaller-capacity XK racing engines dwelt unhappily with top-end life. 'Wilkie' Wilkinson recalled how the works engine differed from his own in having a shorter con-rod and a taller piston above the gudgeon pin: '. . . it seemed to me the piston was unbalanced and would tend to cock over in the bore, and in race conditions this seems to be what happened and they broke. I got Laystall to make a special crank for our own engine and used sodium-filled valves and all sorts . . . we had con-rods about half an inch longer than the works', the gudgeon pin was higher in the piston and R.R. Jackson tested the prototype on his dynamometer and ran it for hours trouble-free. But the works engine was more powerful and they talked us into using it and it just wouldn't last . . .'

Later developments included a 'square' Ecosse engine used in their Tojeiro-Jaguar at Le Mans in 1959, while in 1960 the Coventry experimental department produced a fuel-injected alloy-block engine for Briggs Cunningham's Le Mans prototype car, 'E2A'. This unit was more nearly square in bore:stroke proportion than its works predecessors, with dimensions of 85mm x 88mm, to displace 2,997cc. On a 10.0:1 compression ratio this unit featured the high-lift 7/16-inch camshafts and massive 2 3/32-inch diameter inlet valves shoehorned into a modified '35/40' head alongside standard 1 11/16-inch diameter exhausts. Jaguar bench-tested this engine at 293bhp at 6,750rpm with peak torque figures of 234 and 236lb ft at 5,500 and 6,500rpm, respectively.

During still-later development for the Lightweight E-Type, by which time — in 1963-64 — our sports-racing specials were an obsolescent breed, the ultimate XK six-cylinder engine was developed for German Jaguar agent Peter Lindner's Le Mans Lightweight entry of 1964. Run-up on the dyno with a specially-tuned test-cell exhaust system attached, this alloy-block fuel-injected unit mirrored the specification of E2A's plus a new even higher-lift 15/32-inch camshaft. Peak power was recorded as 344bhp at 6,500rpm, with peak torque of no less than 314lb ft at 4,750rpm. Meanwhile a new 'straight-port' head had been introduced in the XK 150S and was adopted by the E-Type and subsequent production models. In the 'sixties it was found that one of these heads with modern valves and timing would give as much if not more power than an expensive wide-angle head . . .

Since that time many tweaks and minor modifications have been carried out by various XK engine specialists producing club-racing power units for myriad E-Types and surviving Listers, HWMs and Cooper-Jaguars running in historic sports car races today. Something between 295 and 315bhp at 6,500rpm on Weber 45DCOE carburettors seems to be the standard, and although that 20-horsepower range may seem wide the standard of chassis preparation and the use of differing exhaust systems in the vehicles concerned tend to compensate greatly for Coventry horses beneath the bonnet.

The heart that beats there provides the central thread which links our story together . . . the story of the Jaguar XK-engined sports-racing cars . . .

2

The first Jaguar-powered specials

In Bath Street, St. Helier, on the Channel Island of Jersey, there's an imposing house furnishing store, the headquarters of F. le Gallais & Sons (established 1825), auctioneers, valuers, estate agents, removal and warehousing contractors and export packers. Frank le Gallais, great-grandson of the company founder, became quite a local celebrity around the war years as he built a series of special competition cars, culminating in one which used the new Jaguar XK six-cylinder engine.

The Jerseyman was quite good. He began driving competitively in 1934 using what was described as 'a £10 stripped-out Chrysler'. He fine-tuned this unpromising device until, in the summer of 1936, it broke its class record at the local hill-climb. There's a story that on one occasion, when the Chrysler was not ready in time for a sprint meeting, le Gallais took the office Ford V8 instead, and still set fastest time of the day!

He ran a GN special powered by a Wolseley Hornet engine and then, in 1938, acquired a straight-eight OM engine which he installed 'in a home-built chassis independently-sprung with Morgan parts at the front and wishbones at the rear, which I built up. I competed in several local events with some success during the summer of 1939, but the outbreak of war put a stop to all motor sport in the island.

'During the course of the occupation of the island my father had the engine taken out of the chassis and stored it in our furniture depository and the chassis remained in a barn on a farm.

'When I returned to Jersey after the war I realized that the OM engine was worthy of a much more sophisticated chassis, but this would take a long time to build so I bought an MG TA chassis and installed a four-cylinder ohc Wolseley 1500 engine that I had got hold of. I made many modifications to this engine with the help of Laystall's and eventually added the Villiers supercharger from the OM. I competed not too unfavourably with this 'special' with competitors who came over from the mainland in 1946 to 1949 . . .

'Amongst those who came from the UK was the late John (George) Dowson who, with the help of Alec Issigonis, had built the Lightweight Special' — a plywood-and-aluminium monocoque single-seater with rubber-band independent suspension. 'Thanks to the great help given me by Alec Issigonis I made up a tubular chassis, fitted modified Citroen front suspension and tried to copy Lightweight Special-type swing-axles with rubber bands. Owing to the large wheels and short swing-axles the roll-centre was too high and the car was very difficult to control. I later scrapped the rear suspension and made up a type of de Dion axle with torsion bars.

'While building the chassis I was persuaded to send the OM engine to England for some modifications, which culminated in long delays and disappointments, and in the meantime news of the new XK Jaguar engine was about . . .

'Through the help and persuasive powers of the local Jaguar agent I got an introduction to Mr Heynes and went to the factory in Coventry to meet him. He was most helpful but made no promises. I continually badgered the local agent and I suppose by persistence, some luck, and the fact of being out of the UK, I got the XK engine!'

Frank le Gallais' postwar mid-engined chassis was welded-up from twin 2½-inch diameter 18-gauge side tubes, one above the other, and cross-braced vertically by welded-on X-pieces. A large 16-gauge cross-member appeared at either end to link these longerons and there were two similar cross-tubes amidships. Citroen front suspension with its torsion bars and brakes was adopted complete, save for the original front-wheel drive-shafts, and including the rack-and-pinion steering. A Riley axle was used at the rear with the half-shafts and tubes removed and Riley brakes fitted on either cheek. Swing-axles were made up *à la* Lightweight Special.

By 1949 the LGS, as this special was christened, was ready to run. Le Gallais had tired of waiting for the XK twin-cam engine to emerge from Coventry and had fitted a 3½-litre Jaguar Mark V pushrod engine to make it mobile. The Jaguar gearbox was installed in unit with the final-drive. Mounting spartan (nose-cone only) bodywork, the LGS-Jaguar ran in several hill-climbs, sprints and sand-races. It climbed Bouley Bay hill in 58.2 seconds and then, towards the end of the year, the XK engine arrived at last via St Helier Motors. It was only the third XK engine to be sold outside the normal production XK120 run and was the first for road-vehicle use, the other two having gone into boats, notably Norman Buckley's *Miss Windermere* record-breaker.

Le Gallais' engine was to feature high-lift cams, stiffer valve-springs and a competition crankshaft damper, but was otherwise standard with 8:1 compression ratio and 1¾-inch SU carburettors.

Frank le Gallais was to campaign his striking mid-engined, rather Auto Union-like special virtually throughout the 'fifties and by 1955 was climbing Bouley Bay in 54.4 seconds and breaking the Guernsey hill-climb record. In 1956 he covered the quarter-mile in 6.8 seconds to average 132mph and lowered the Bouley record to 54 seconds dead. In 1957 he drove the car on the road to the Shelsley Walsh and Prescott hill-climbs on the mainland and set a

The ingenious Jerseyman, Frank le Gallais, taking off at Shelsley Walsh in 1957 in his LGS-Jaguar mid-engined special. Note the square-section tube exhaust stacks, twin rear wheels just beginning to spin and the dented nose, courtesy of British Railways steamship transport.

Frank le Gallais' photograph of his LGS-Jaguar chassis before installation of the engine. Far-forward driving positions are nothing new.

new Shelsley Specials class record. For road use the car was rigged with cycle mudguards and two motorcycle-type silencers mated to the six stub exhaust stacks by flexible tubing. The intrepid le Gallais subsequently reduced his local climb record to 53 seconds, only to see RAC Hill-Climb Champion David Boshier-Jones take his Cooper 1100 up in 52 seconds. The LGS-Jaguar was becoming outclassed and obsolete, and its swansong came in 1958 when le Gallais covered the standing-start half-mile in 21 seconds. At this time the car was reckoned to be capable of accelerating from 0-100mph in 12 seconds, but with the lithe little Coopers now totally ascendant there was little point in proceeding further. Frank le Gallais was getting no younger, and he sold the car through a friend living in Kenya. The car was exported and there it crashed for the first — and apparently the last — time . . .

Meanwhile, as we shall see, many others had followed where the enterprizing Jerseyman had led. In fact one special-builder, Gordon D. Parker of Shorne, in Kent, had accompanied him on the way. As early as May 1946 he had planned to build 'an interesting special', and had bought for £80 a partially burned and engineless N-Type MG Magnette. After stripping the chassis at home he found it was still true and undistorted, and a 1939 2½-litre Jaguar pushrod engine was acquired. Its original mounting plates were replaced by those from an SS1 and a frame cross-member was relocated to match the new engine in unit with an ordinary SS1 gearbox. The standard MG back axle was reckoned not man enough to withstand the new engine's torque and it was replaced by a Standard 20 axle which was modified to accept the original MG tubes. Parker and an engineering friend then machined the Standard half-shafts to fit the original MG hubs. Unfortunately, the Standard axle ratio was found to be far too low at 4.66:1, and while Parker dreamed of a 3.5:1 axle the nearest he could find was one of 4.25:1. The original MG prop-shaft was cut to length and a slightly-modified SS1 radiator was mounted on the frame. The bodywork was modified, placing the scuttle and bulkhead 4 inches further back to clear the larger engine, while overall height was reduced by 2½ inches; these changes meant lengthening and lowering the steering column to match. The whole car was then repanelled in aluminium and by September 1946 it was on the road, a one-ton 2½-litre Jaguar-engined sports car.

Gordon Parker fitted two bucket seats — which he recalled he had bought prewar for 1s 6d (7½ pence) each! — and on its competition debut at Windmill Hill the new Jaguette Special flattered only to deceive with a climb 4.6 seconds slower than Sydney Allard's.

That winter Parker ran the Jaguette trouble-free on the road, and on June 15, 1947, he scored his first victory with it at the Brighton & Hove MC's Storrington speed hill-climb and driving test meeting. The Jaguette went on to prove itself a very reliable and practical special, with distinctly sporting character, and it was reasonably successful in competitive events. Parker adopted a supercharger and reduced weight, allegedly by 400lb, in part by adopting thinner-gauge aluminium sheet for the bodywork. It must have been a lot thinner . . .

Parker, meanwhile, was well ahead on construction of a new Parker special intended to carry a twin-cam Jaguar XK120 engine, and the little Jaguette was sold to Bill Coleman who, in fact, proved far more successful with it.

In April, 1952, John Bolster, Technical Editor of *Autosport* magazine, described Gordon Parker's new Jaguara. It was based on a Buckler multi-tube chassis frame from the Bracknell specialist's works. This structure was welded-up from 17-gauge chrome-molybdenum steel tubes of 1½-inch outside diameter and gave a wheelbase of 8ft, and front and rear tracks of 4ft 4½ in and 4ft 2¼ in, respectively. Front suspension was Dubonnet-type independent from the Vauxhall Velox, mated to Morris Minor rack-and-pinion steering, while at the rear a standard XK120 axle was thoroughly located fore-and-aft by two pairs of superimposed tubular radius rods and laterally by a Watt linkage. Rear springing was by co-axial coil/damper units.

Parker supercharged the XK engine at 9psi by using two Arnott vane-type

Le Gallais on home soil in the LGS-Jaguar bellowing up Bouley Bay hill-climb in Jersey towards the end of this fascinating special's long career.

compressors linked in parallel and driven by triplex roller chains. Provided boost did not exceed 9lb the standard-compression engine would apparently run happily on 80-octane fuel as normally specified at that time for sports car racing.

The new car was completed with a broad separate-mudguard aluminium bodyshell, which enclosed a low-mounted Marston light-alloy radiator in the nose and a 17-gallon fuel tank directly above the rear axle. Lockheed XK120 brakes were fitted within Alfin light-alloy drums front and rear and the all-up weight was reckoned to be around the 17cwt mark.

Parker's new creation was road-registered GDP 1 after his own initials and his main target became the Brighton Speed Trials, although the Jaguara also ran in hill-climbs even though it did not venture on to the race circuits. In 1956 and 1957 the car won the over-3000cc sports car class at Prescott, and on the Madeira Drive standing-start kilometre at Brighton the Jaguara took a hat-trick of sports car FTDs and wins in the supercharged sports car class in 1953-55.

In 1958 Parker and his associate Herbert Kingsbury completed quite a potent single-seater sprint car which they called the HK-Jaguar, this projectile being powered by a 3.4-litre XK engine with the C-Type cylinder-head and two Arnott superchargers, each feeding three cylinders at a maximum boost of 10lb. The new car had a wishbone and coil-spring front-end and coil-sprung de Dion rear, and it came good in September 1961 when Gordon Parker achieved his ambition of setting fastest time of the day overall in the Brighton Speed Trials.

Both the Parker Jaguara and the Jaguette have been owned in recent years by Bob Watkins, of Southampton, and while they and le Gallais' LGS-Jaguar exemplify the amateur special-builder's approach, by 1951 greater developments had begun . . .

Jaguar's own XK120Cs had won Le Mans, and a team and a privateer already hugely experienced in Continental racing looked to the XK engine for motive power. That team was HWM, and the privateer was that no-nonsense character Oscar Moore . . .

3

The HWM-Jaguars

George Abecassis and John Heath did more than any other motor racing people to pioneer the British works teams' way into Europe after World War Two. While the well-intentioned BRM co-operative had become bogged down in its own ambition, bureaucracy and ineptitude, Abecassis and Heath took their HWM team racing virtually on a shoestring, with the accent squarely on practicality, commonsense and a 'we'll race anywhere we can show a profit' mentality.

The initials HWM were drawn from their garage business in New Zealand Avenue, Walton-on-Thames, Surrey, which was called HW — for Hersham & Walton — Motors Ltd. They were Citroen distributors, and dealers in 'serious motor cars', and both were former public schoolboys and rampantly enthusiastic motoring buffs. Abecassis (as English as could be despite his Portuguese surname) had carved himself a considerable reputation as a racing driver prewar and Heath was essentially an engineer — fascinated by the motor car as a technical exercise.

In the mid-'thirties Abecassis had taken a small filling station at Cranford — near today's Heathrow Airport — in order to finance his racing. The Cranford business proved successful and to expand his workshop space he bought another in Southall. His racing budget was still restricted, but in 1937 he bought the remains of the all-independently-suspended Alta single-seat prototype in which Philip Jucker had been killed on the Isle of Man. The car had slammed into a lamp-post at Douglas, and its manufacturer, Geoffrey Taylor, charged George £425, less the price of the wreckage, to rebuild the car as new and deliver it ready-to-run at Brooklands on Easter Monday, 1938.

Abecassis had burst straight into the headlines with his new silver Alta and the car paid for itself in prize and bonus money earned at the Weybridge track, at Crystal Palace and at the Prescott hill-climb. On occasion it humbled the cream of ERA opposition and by 1939 Abecassis was a driver to be feared.

But at Albi that year the Alta's crankshaft broke at top speed and its rear wheels locked, Abecassis was rammed by Leslie Brooke's Brooke Special and both cars were severely damaged.

Meanwhile, John Benjamin Heath had studied motor engineering at the Chelsea College before becoming apprenticed to Talbot in London, then moving to Lagonda for a spell before fetching-up at Packard's London depot, where his cultured good looks made him a natural choice as a salesman. But the 6ft 5in tall sixth Baron Heath (scion of an obscure title bestowed on an ancestor by a grateful Italian Government) preferred greasy-fingered tinkering with cars to smooth-talking while selling them.

In 1937 he left Packard and took a tiny shop frontage at Hersham, close to his mother's home in fashionable St George's Hill, Weybridge, where he was

June 7, 1952. Oscar Moore's newly-completed HWM-Jaguar at its pit during the Ulster Trophy race at Dundrod in which it finished sixth. The distinctive cam-covers of the XK engine are visible together with its twin SU carburettors. Note the separate base for the aero screen, identifying this ex-works 1950 team HWM as the very first prototype car — the three production vehicles which followed it had flaired scuttles with round-based screens attached. The chassis seems to have been retrospectively numbered '3' . . . typical HWM.

living. The shop had just enough room for one car, there was a shed out the back for parts, and the yard in between became his workshop. There, John Heath scratched a happy living, buying and selling, and working mainly on friends' cars.

After a year of this he married Barbara Payne, daughter of the Royal veterinary surgeon who was something of a celebrity in the Weybridge area. He clearly felt his new son-in-law should be pursuing a more respectable profession, and Heath returned to Lagonda at Staines Bridge as an experimental department engineer.

During the war George Abecassis became a heavy bomber pilot in the RAF, rising to Squadron-Leader and flying cloak-and-dagger agent-dropping missions 'never above 300ft' over occupied Europe. In 1944 his unarmed Stirling was shot down and he and his crew were captured. After a few months as a PoW, Abecassis was 'liberated' by the Russians — 'which was a bloody sight worse than being a prisoner of the Germans' — and he finally got home just after VE-day, with a DFC to his name.

John Heath's experimental work at Lagonda kept him out of the services, but once he had completed development on flame-throwers he managed to break out and establish his own small garage within yards of his original shop at Hersham; he called it Halfway Motors. His wife — a competent mechanic in her own right — ran the garage, while Heath and a dozen employees formed a small company known as The Bridge Engineering Works in premises nearby, and produced machine tools for Vickers Aircraft at Brooklands.

Abecassis and Heath had known each other since 1938 and they got together in 1945 and bought the large red-brick Vickers machine shop at New Zealand Avenue, which eventually became HW Motors. Abecassis had tired of his two small garages at Cranford and Southall and wanted to operate nearer his home in the Walton-Weybridge area. Heath kept Halfway Motors briefly, but it was madness to run two garages in the same small town; instead of increasing sales one merely doubled overheads. When Heath sold Halfway Motors, the New Zealand Avenue business became Hersham & Walton Motors Ltd.

Abecassis had quickly returned to racing with his rebuilt Alta single-seater, an ERA and a glorious Type 59 Bugatti, and his exploits soon fired John Heath,

26

who followed his partner's lead with a sports Alta. In 1948 his technical capabilities bubbled over and he created a very special sports Alta streamliner powered by Geoffrey Taylor's four-carburettor ohc engine. Using an Alta chassis, this was the first car built specifically for racing by HW Motors, although even by that time they had immense experience of assembling various sports bodies, chassis and engines — mainly Altas — in bewildering combination. Nothing bought in was ever, ever, thrown away . . .

The streamlined Alta acquitted itself well in the 1948 season, largely in Europe. The partners realized the money-earning potential of racing there, and for 1949 Heath's almost manic energy produced a very intelligently-conceived dual-purpose single-seater/sports-racing car with offset cockpit intended for long-distance and Formula B (2-litre unsupercharged 'F2') racing. It was to use the streamliner's four-cylinder Alta engine mated to an ENV Wilson-type pre-selector gearbox, fitted into a brand-new twin-tube chassis frame. It was called the HW-Alta. John Heath had also experimented by taking his 2-litre ex-Bob (later Roberta) Cowell sports Alta EOY 8, and replacing its front suspension with a transverse leaf-spring IFS system from Standard-Triumph. The actual construction date of this channel-section-chassised car remains obscure, but it would appear that it falls between the streamlined true Alta MPB 77 and the first tube-chassised HW-Alta, which was to be registered NPA 5. In any case, EOY 8, wearing an HW-Alta radiator badge, was to be sold to northern enthusiast Jack Walton and raced by him and later by Peter Bolton and Bobby Pattenden.

The new tube-framed 1949 HW-Alta was the first car actually built from scratch by HW Motors. Its parallel-longeron chassis included three welded cross-members, the foremost of which was a box-section structure fabricated from Anderson shelter scrap steel! Wishbones were made-up to accept proprietary uprights, stub axles and a transverse leaf-spring and Heath adopted his favourite Citroen steering gear. Its back axle was taken from some spares lying in the workshop for a Lagonda Rapier single-seater, and it was located Bugatti-fashion by a single torque-arm and quarter-elliptic leaf-springs.

With Heath's tall, spare figure sprouting high and hunched forward in its spartan Leacroft of Egham bodyshell, the HW-Alta was to become a familiar sight that season. With detachable wings and lights in place it qualified as a 2-litre FIA sports car, and with them removed and a rigid tonneau panel fairing the passenger's side of the cockpit it became a Formula B offset single-seater. It handled excellently and this more than compensated for the unsupercharged engine's modest power output.

Heath inherited victory in the Manx Cup race on the Isle of Man in 1949 and was fifth at Reims in the Formula B *Coupe des Petites Cylindrées*, then came second in the blisteringly hot *Grand Prix de l'ACF*, run for sports cars that year at Comminges. Heath drove the 312-miles there single-handed, and this considerable success made European race organizers sit up and take note of the new name from Britain.

Having proved that HW Motors' entries could not only start European races, but could also survive to finish them in leading positions, the partners discussed running a team of Formula B cars in 1950. They toyed with an idea for a mid-engined car like a grown-up Cooper, using the Alta engine in conjunction with an about-faced Citroen front-drive transmission in the back, but Heath vetoed it on practical grounds — 'If Auto Union had development problems with their resources, what chance do we stand . . .?'

Then Peter Clark, whose team of HRGs had run well at Le Mans in 1949, offered the partners his reserved entries for three cars in the new year's 24-Hours classic. Now it was logical to repeat the dual-purpose HW-Alta recipe of 1949 and four new cars were laid-down at New Zealand Avenue.

The first was built as a trouble-shooter designed in the metal, with the three team cars progressing at most only a day or two behind it.

Heath immersed himself in the project while Abecassis concentrated on running the motor business. The viceless basic layout and front suspension of the HW-Alta was adopted without hesitation, but Heath replaced the original car's live rear axle with a transverse leaf-spring-and-wishbone arrangement to give full independence. An ENV diff was retained, but since that company's pre-selector gearbox was hard to obtain in quantity Heath adopted Armstrong-Siddeley's instead. Geoffrey Taylor undertook to produce four of his twin-cam 1,960cc four-cylinder engines, guaranteeing a minimum of 115bhp.

Abecassis sketched an HW-Alta-like body for the cars, which was built by Leacroft, the Bob Cowell/Gordon Watson-run coachbuilders just up the road in Egham. George simplified Heath's baronial coat of arms to produce a team badge, and the four cars set HW Motors in for about £1,500 each. They were called HWMs.

The first production car was sold to 'Buster' Baring, a racing timber merchant friend, while the three works cars were to be driven by Abecassis himself, young Stirling Moss and Heath, unless suitable rent-a-drivers, or good start money-earning guest drivers, could be attracted. An early disappointment came with the discovery that Le Mans was a prize-money-only race which, of course, was of no interest to the partners whatsoever, and so the 24-Hours was out and they planned instead a full Formula B and open Formula A (F1) calendar. It went well. In a typical European race weekend HWM could earn perhaps £600-£700 start money, and by selling petrol coupons and old racing tyres 'when practically bald at 25 quid a time' this was 'good business . . .' The partners had taken a gamble on young Moss, whose scorching driving style was regarded with intense suspicion by most of the Brooklands-raised British motor racing establishment of that time, and he repaid them fully with brilliant performances. As the sage-green cars followed their gypsy existence through Europe the initials HWM — or *Aarsh-Dooblervay-Emm* as the French commentators rendered them — became honoured and feted wherever they raced.

The cars lacked power, but they handled superbly and did wonders for a country which at that time had zero international motor racing stature. The 1950 season yielded HWM two major victories, three seconds, six thirds, a sensational fastest race lap (by Moss at Caracalla when chasing works Ferraris) and many more minor placings. The two transporters consumed around £500-worth of petrol in 16,000 miles around the Continent, but at the end of that year the three team cars were sold to private owners and HWM as a team emerged that winter showing a handsome profit.

John Heath responded promptly by laying down a team of five true Formula 2 single-seater racing cars for the 1951 season. It was then, against this background of practical enthusiasm, monumental hard work and good old-fashioned wheeler-dealing, that HWM became the first 'proper' marque to throw up a Jaguar-engined sports-racing car . . .

Those dual-purpose 1950 team cars had been sold to the Swiss enthusiast 'Hervé' (Count Jacques de Wurstemberger), who until that time had been racing a very original 1934 MG K3 Magnette, and to Tom Meyer and Oscar Moore in England. Oscar Bernard Moore was 47 at that time and ran a motor and car-hire business in Ballards Lane, Finchley, North London. He had raced a BMW 328 sports car with considerable success since the war and had ultimately converted it into a Formula B single-seater which he called the OBM after his own initials. Now he road-registered his ex-works HWM XMC 34 and raced it throughout 1951 with the original 2-litre Alta engine. Unfortunately, Alta's reputation for rock-solid reliability had always been transparently thin — to put it mildly — and Moore had a lot of trouble.

His sons Terry and Peter vividly recall their late father's phobia for the Alta exhaust system in particular, which repeatedly cracked, split and fell off altogether. Eventually he fed the manifolding straight into a hole cut in one chassis tube and bawled 'Now bloody well fall off . . .!'. Terry Grainger, who has owned XMC 34 since the mid-'sixties, confirms this story with glee, saying the patched-over hole cut in one frame tube is still visible today.

On another occasion Moore amazed the unimpressable Alf Francis (at that time an HWM mechanic, but later to become Moss's famous 'wrench') by whipping out a bent valve, hammering it straight and unconcernedly sliding it back into the Alta engine's head and going racing with it. At the Nurburgring the HWM threw a wheel — a proprietary stub-axle problem which had dogged the works cars in 1950 — as Moore came up behind the pits only half-a-mile or so into his first practice lap. They towed the car back in, repaired the damage overnight and next morning, after another good half-mile, she lost that wheel again! Back in the pits the German officials sought out Mr Moore and asked him to remove his car from the backstretch and reprimanded him for having left it there all night! Not wishing to let them know that the HWM had broken its suspension twice rather than just once, Oscar apologized profusely and was allowed to race and pick up his all-important *startgeld* . . . he was quite a character . . .

Meanwhile, HWM's true single-seaters for 1951 had been produced in similar manner to their 1950 dual-purpose predecessors — a prototype, then a pilot build being progressed just one or two days ahead of the actual team cars. But this time Heath changed his mind between prototype and production, and while the prototype inherited the transverse-leaf independent front suspension of the 1950 dual-purpose cars, the production single-seaters were to adopt MG TD coil-spring IFS. Likewise, the rear suspension of the two types differed, the prototype having a de Dion axle on torsion bars while the team cars employed a de Dion carried on quarter-elliptic leaf-springs.

The first of these team cars showed-up an inbuilt geometry fault which manifested itself by sending Abecassis spinning backwards beneath a concrete barrier at Goodwood in testing prior to the 1951 Easter Monday meeting. The car jammed beneath the barrier with the concrete beam against the back of George's head and he was very fortunate to escape with his life. After suspension modifications Moss won first time out on Easter Monday and the HWM single-seaters went off to war . . .

John Heath concentrated on team management while Moss and Lance Macklin drove regularly, with support from Abecassis (when HW Motors

Later days. The ex-Oscar Moore HWM-Jaguar, XMC 34, shown in the hands of Plymouth motor trader Gerry Scali in the paddock after breaking the Trengwainton hill-climb record in 25.49 secs. Moore fitted the florid front wings and more modern scuttle panel while the quaint little headrest appears to have been a Scali modification. Bruce Halford raced the car in this form at Brands Hatch.

*Denis Jenkinson of **Motor Sport** magazine took this family album photograph of George Abecassis at the wheel of HWM 1 before they shared it in the 1954 Mille Miglia. Here the car is seen at Count Aymo Maggi's castle outside Brescia shortly before the race. The hatch alongside George actually housed the spare wheel; it was not a cockpit door.*

business allowed) and guest drivers like Louis Chiron, Yves Giraud-Cabantous, 'B. Bira' and Harry Schell. George was also driving for the works Aston Martin team at this time, in sports-car events, while the home business made increasing demands on his time.

On August 11, 1951, the HWM team were away with their coil-spring IFS single-seaters when the West Essex Car Club's *Daily Mail* race meeting took place at Boreham Airfield. Abecassis appeared there at the wheel of a makeshift HWM single-seater based upon the discarded prototype chassis with its leaf-spring IFS and torsion-bar de Dion rear-end.

It was a grey, cold and damp day, with incessant rain drenching the featureless Essex countryside. Gabardine macs dripped water and soaked grey flannel trouser legs clung round chilled legs, but still a large crowd braved it all to watch the racing. They saw a diminutive South London motorcycle dealer named Bernie Ecclestone spin away his chances in the 500cc Formula 3 heats and then they watched Brian Shawe-Taylor win the 15-lap *Libre* race in his ERA. Splashing home fourth in that race came George Abecassis, with his makeshift HWM jammed in top gear. He was colder, wetter and more fed-up than any spectator — fed-up with everything, that is, except the new car's handling. 'This', he thought, blowing away the rain which streamed from his vizor, 'would make a damn fine sports car . . .'

Just behind him in the spray that day came Oscar Moore in his older HWM, and he was thinking much the same. That rainy day in Essex saw the start of a mid-'fifties sports car fashion in Britain in which HWM, Cooper, Tojeiro and ultimately Lister were each to build potent sports-racing cars powered by the XK Jaguar engine which could out-perform Coventry's own thoroughbred C-Types and D-Types . . .

At the time of that dank Boreham race meeting in August, 1951, a 3.4-litre wet-sump Jaguar XK engine was already sitting on the floor in HWM's New Zealand Avenue workshops, ready to be fitted into Abecassis' now-obsolete

1949 Grand Prix Alta 'GP No 1'. It was intended for 30-year-old Phil Scragg, technical director of a family textile engineering firm from Macclesfield, in Cheshire. He planned a programme of sprints, hill-climbs and club-races for the car, and although Abecassis — who was quite an artist in his own right — designed and had made an all-enveloping sports body for the old car, Scragg decided he preferred cycle-mudguard open wheels for his type of competition.

He had come to buy the old Alta after shunting his own potent XK120 that May. The car had been prepared for him by Hugh Howarth with a very potent engine with an 8.0:1 compression ratio, modified and highly polished internals, high-lift cams, a lightened flywheel and heavy-duty clutch. It had climbed Shelsley Walsh in 44.1 seconds and Prescott in 51.2 seconds, times which no other Jaguar would approach for some time. Such an engine had seemed just too good to waste and Scragg had considered buying a pure HWM before opting instead for the pensioned-off GP Alta. Its transmission would be much more suitable for the XK's power and torque . . .

HW Motors returned the twin-tube GP Alta chassis to Geoffrey Taylor's tiny works at Tolworth, Surrey, where it was cut-and-shut to reduce the wheelbase to 7ft 10in and then fitted with 'all the latest Formula 2 Alta mods'. A new back-axle capable of withstanding 300bhp was installed, complete with ZF limited-slip differential, and the Alta steering was replaced by HWM's new Morris Minor-derived rack-and-pinion system. A 3.89:1 final-drive was selected, giving a second gear ratio of 7.67:1 and third of 5.28:1. Using 6.50 x 16 rear tyres (with 6.00 x 16s on the front) these ratios represented 70mph and 100mph, respectively, at a trifle over 6,000rpm. Scragg quoted a maximum speed of 140mph in top gear. Leacroft of Egham made the two-seat slipper body, complete with a very practical hood and quickly-detachable full-width windscreen, which would be replaced by aero screens for competition. The spare wheel lived in the tail and *Motor Sport* observed that 'the finish would put many production cars to shame . . .'.

The old GP Alta chassis provided all-round independent suspension by rubber blocks and wishbones and in his first few miles with the car Scragg claimed that he found it very smooth-riding with accurate steering and 'just wonderful' brakes; after the standard XK120's drum-brake system I suspect most things would feel 'just wonderful'. Early on he had some engine trouble, with the XK losing power at high revs, but this was soon corrected and the textile engineer won a scratch race at 61.24mph on the long 1952 club circuit at Silverstone. He preferred sprints and hill-climbs, however, and RPG 418, as the HW-built Alta-Jaguar was registered, was to live a long and low-key life away from international competition.

Meanwhile, Oscar Moore had decided to go up a class for the new 1952 season and he acquired an XK120 engine to replace the four-cylinder Alta unit in XMC 34. A stronger Woodhead transverse leaf-spring was fitted up front, to support the six-cylinder's extra weight, and the standard radiator was reworked to match the larger engine. The original Armstrong-Siddeley pre-selector gearbox was retained since Moore did not share Scragg's pessimistic appraisal of that unit.

The original long-distance tail tank was replaced by a more modest 17-gallon one, allowing the spare wheel to be mounted horizontally ahead of it 'to please those bloody scrutineers . . .'. Moore enjoyed cocking a snook at officialdom by using tiny sidelamps mounted on the front wing stays as his regulation 'headlamps'. Weight distribution of this new HWM-Jaguar was reckoned to be perfect at 50/50 front/rear and the car scaled 17¼ cwt with oil and water, but less fuel.

Moore emerged with the revised car at Prescott in May 1952 and won the over 3-litre sports car class by a fair margin. He embarked thereafter on a series of successful club race and sprint outings, and would allow his son Terry to drive occasionally.

By that time, however, Oscar and his mechanic Stan Harding had delved into the unknown in search of still more power and in Moore's Ballards Lane workshops they bored-out the standard 3,442cc engine to what was quoted at the time as 'a full 3,814cc'. In fact the block was taken out far oversize and then linered down to 4mm oversize at 87mm, while retaining the original 106mm stroke. This gives the same bore/stroke size and displacement as the Jaguar works' own 3.8 engines of later years, whose capacity was 3,780.82cc. It seems, therefore, that the Oscar Moore 3,814cc engine was a product of journalistic miscalculation — whenever I work out the displacement of an 86mm x 106mm six-cylinder it comes to 3,780.82cc . . . just like the works.

Whatever inaccuracies of calculation may have occurred, this was a daring project and apart from the liners showing an unwarranted desire to shift in the block, it paid off. Two 2 3/16-inch SU carburettors were fitted, although Moore said he felt 2-inch would have been better, and the Armstrong-Siddeley transmission was modified because the original Alta engine ratios were considered too closely spaced for the more torquey 'three-eight'.

Moore chose ratios of 3.0:1, 1.81:1 and 1.37:1, and with them he reckoned XMC 34 to be '. . . just about right'. The car used 6.00 x 16 rear tyres against 5.25 x 16s on the front, and Moore ran it first time out in 3.8-litre form in the Ulster Trophy at Dundrod that June; he finished sixth, averaging 10mph less than Piero Taruffi's winning 4½-litre V12 Ferrari ThinWall Special.

On July 10, XMC 34 was in Jersey for the International Road Race and there its owner-driver led the works Aston Martins to beat Reg Parnell in the first heat! Moore then drove very well in the final and lay second behind Ian Stewart's Ecurie Ecosse C-Type only for the engine to throw a rod. At the moment it clattered its way into retirement XMC 34 was leading none other than George Abecassis in his works-entered Aston Martin DB2. George was fascinated by the performance of that antiquated-looking old car which he and his partner had had built 30 months before. He was impressed — and now he knew what to do with that spare single-seater chassis which had been gathering dust in the store at Walton since its one-off race that very wet day at Boreham.

For 1953, Oscar Moore replaced his HWM-Jaguar's pre-selector gearbox with an ordinary manual Moss 'box to save some weight and unnecessary complication. But as the season progressed it became obvious that the car was outclassed by the production C-Type Jaguars then filtering into private hands and running against it in club events. The HWM-Jaguar was sufficiently light to out-accelerate and often out-brake them, but its antiquated body style provided an aerodynamic brick wall at higher speeds, when the C-Types simply roared away. Terry Moore recalls the car as 'a shattering roadie', but as it became obsolescent so Oscar Moore abruptly sold it to West Countryman Gerry Scali (a Plymouth motor trader) and the family's racing days were over. Old XMC 34 has been owned since January, 1966, by Terry Grainger, of Bromsgrove, Warwickshire, who loves it dearly . . .

However, in the middle of that 1953 season the first works HWM-Jaguar made its debut. Abecassis bought back from Scragg the all-enveloping sports body built for his HW-Alta-Jaguar and subsequently rejected, and it was matched to the old Boreham single-seater chassis with an XK engine installed. In fact George had approached 'Lofty' England for a suitable power unit, and recalled that he was offered 'the works team's 3.4-litre C-Type engine which Stirling Moss had used at Le Mans . . .'

Before the body was fitted it had been loaned to Major R.G. 'Dick' Shattock, whose RGS-Atalanta company was producing special chassis, some to be Jaguar-engined, in a tiny workshop behind his Brookside Garage business in Hatchet Lane, Winkfield, near Ascot, Berkshire. Shattock took a mould from the HWM body and contracted the North-East Coast Yachtbuilding & Engineering Co. Ltd of Blyth, Northumberland, to make him a run of glass-fibre bodyshells — apparently the first to be offered to the British motoring public. This RGS-Atalanta body was to be supplied in two sections, with the entire front-end being designed to hinge forward to expose the engine and front suspension. Its price was first advertised as £90 in May, 1953, and by November that year it had risen to £112, but around 100 were sold to enthusiastic special-builders and there was even a hardtop version available. Shattock's slipper-bodied works car, HBL 845, was fitted with a 3.4-litre XK engine late in 1953 and in 1954 it received some added boost in the form of a Weslake-modified C-Type head. In 1955 this machine was rebodied with what were virtually two rear-ends off the original HWM body mould mounted back to back, with flaring tail fins added '. . . to tell which way it's going'. Shattock raced HBL 845 quite successfully in both body guises, and always went especially well in the wet when running on Michelin X tyres. It is interesting to note that the first glass-fibre RGS-Atalanta bodyshell was unveiled to the public before the HWM-Jaguar, from whose body the original mould had been taken, had made its debut.

The single-seater HWM chassis with its transverse-leaf-spring IFS and torsion-bar de Dion rear-end was widened with outriggers to accept the sports body, side-by-side seating and offset controls. It emerged with a wheelbase of 7ft 8in, front track of 4ft 1¾in, rear track of 4 ft 2½in and an all-up weight of around 18½cwt. Enormous dual-circuit Girling drum brakes were mounted outboard, front and rear.

Abecassis recalled that the works' prototype HWM-Jaguar ex-Le Mans engine began life with a high-compression head 'up around 9:1', but they subsequently machined the block and he doubted very much if its final compression ratio was ever assessed. At the time the HWM Formula 2 team was in deep trouble. John Heath had obstinately refused to capitalize on an already excellently handling chassis from 1951 by seeking more powerful engines, and instead had built new cars which did not handle quite so well, which carried too much weight, and which failed to make the most of the Alta-based engines' still modest power output. HWM could no longer match Ferrari and Maserati on the tighter circuits, and in fact they were being out-run there by the lighter Cooper-Bristols, while both Ferrari and Cooper found advantage on the faster courses. HWM's reliability had also slumped and the team's reputation, so hard-won in 1950-51, had thrown-up just one major victory in the 1952 BRDC International Trophy, at Silverstone, after which it had been all downhill . . .

The partners saw the new sports car as a possible attraction for would-be customers while drawing useful revenue from works entries in the sports car races then proliferating around Europe. It could be driven to and from meetings on the road, so saving expensive transport, and the design promised to use up obsolescent single-seater bits. It could hardly look better . . .

Heath examined the XK engine very carefully and became one of the first to

Jack Fairman at Goodwood in Tony Gaze's coil-spring HWM-Jaguar, VPA 8, trying hard and holding the inside line from Bert Rogers' special-bodied Cooper-Bristol. In the background is Colonel Michael Head's white C-Type Jaguar, MDU 212. The registration looks like VPA 9, but contemporary notes record it as VPA 8, a flying stone at Reims having smashed a hole in the plastic number!

George Abecassis enjoyed racing in Sweden and entered his HWM-Jaguar — as he had his ERA in earlier years — in ice-race events and summertime road races, as here at Hedemora. Note the one-man Perspex screen replacing the full-width two-man type as used in the Mille Miglia.

match triple twin-choke Weber carburettors to it, in parallel with works experimental development in Coventry. HWM had run the Italian carburettors on their F2 cars since 1951, and Abecassis recalled how Lance Macklin had first run a set on his Aston Martin DB2 in Italy and came back saying 'the thing went like an absolute bomb'. 'He said "You really ought to try them on the HWMs, old boy", so John did and they were very successful. In fact we then passed the information on to Jaguar, and 'Lofty' and William Lyons were so grateful that that's how we got the Jaguar distributorship we have held ever since!'

The partners called-in Harry Weslake for suitable camshafts, which they subsequently duplicated, and a multi-plate Borg & Beck clutch was coupled-up to a normal C-Type gearbox. An American Halibrand final-drive unit had been obtained from Allard (who were importing them), which featured a pair of quick ratio-changer drop-gears and allowed the prop-shaft to lurk low-down within the chassis. The new body was very neat and functional, all simple curves with a three-intake nose, louvred flanks, a tucked-down tail and an access door on the left side only, the driver's door space being used to house the spare wheel beneath a hinge-out cover.

A few months earlier, the local licensing authority in Southport, Lancashire, had just begun a run of 'HWM' registration numbers and an enthusiastic officer there wrote to HW Motors offering them first shout. 'We were simply mad just to take HWM 1', George said. 'If we'd only thought we would have realized we would be building more sports cars and should have taken 2, 3 and 4 at least...'

So the prototype HWM-Jaguar works car was registered HWM 1, and on June 6, 1953, it was second in its class on its competition debut at Shelsley Walsh hill-climb, near Worcester. Cyril Wick thumped his Allard up the hill first in the over-3,000cc sports car class to record 40.70 seconds then Abecassis made his first run at 41.13. Wick's second climb smashed Peter Walker's existing hill record with the C-Type by clocking 40.45 seconds. Then 'Abby' gritted his teeth in his unfamiliar new car, and recorded 40.64, to leave the Allard as the class-winner.

34

HWM 1 was then prepared to accompany the F2 team to Reims for the French GP meeting on July 4-5, when the single-seater race would be preceded by the Reims 12-Hours for sports cars, starting at midnight on the Saturday and finishing at noon on the Sunday; part of its function seemed to be to ensure that the circuit was liberally covered with rubber and oil in time for the Grand Prix. Happy days . . .

Abecassis was to share the new car with Belgian journalist-driver Paul Frère, who had excelled in the F2 HWMs in previous seasons. According to the local press the car was to be driven by 'Abecassis frères' — the Abecassis brothers — and as the field completed their first lap, hammering through the floodlit pits area with headlights blazing, the fearless 'Abby' was fourth behind Behra's leading straight-eight Gordini, Peter Whitehead's C-Type and Umberto Maglioli's big 4.5 Ferrari. At one-third distance, the green car was running sixth — but not untroubled . . .

The original tail tank was sufficient for home races, but an auxiliary tank had to be squeezed-in alongside the driver and spare wheel for endurance work such as this. It succeeded in unbalancing the car, and on the one left-hand bend at Reims-Gueux the right-rear tyre was fouling the bodywork.

Abecassis had handed over to Frère at about 3am and the Belgian soon realized that the scraping of the body on that tyre was getting worse rather than better as his fuel load diminished. That couldn't be right, and when Paul came in after losing a tyre tread it was found that one of the brackets locating the de Dion axle torque-arm had sheared. It was 5am — Behra's Gordini and Fitch's Cunningham had crashed, and the Maglioli/Carini Ferrari Coupe had been excluded, although it was still ahead of the HWM-Jaguar on the road. In fact when HWM 1 retired it was officially in third place, and had impressed all who saw it . . .

Later that month Abecassis unleashed the new car in the Eastern Counties MC meeting at Snetterton, beating Oscar Moore in a five-lapper for the first-ever HWM-Jaguar 1-2 success and being handicapped out of a later event which Moore won. George passed four cars on the last of the eight laps, but could not improve on seventh place. His fastest lap in 1 minute 58.4 seconds was a new record, at an average speed of 82.09mph.

The following week saw the British GP at Silverstone and there the HWM-Jaguar appeared amongst works Jaguars, Aston Martins and the American Cunninghams in the supporting race. George was sixth fastest in practice, 4 seconds off Parnell's pole-winning pace with the DB3S, but after inheriting that position in the race HWM 1 retired beyond Abbey Curve.

It was quickly revived and driven to France for the sports car Caen GP on July 26 at the Norman city's *La Prairie* horse-race course, where a 2-mile motor racing circuit had been laid out. It was a handicap event over 86 laps with small-capacity cars like the French DB-Panhards covering many miles before the big cars were unleashed. Abecassis had to watch the limit men go by 15 times before he was flagged away and he soon hit trouble as HWM 1 began to wander. The trouble was traced to a lifting tyre tread and he was finally placed seventh, Chancel's Panhard being the popular winner . . .

Back home, on August 22, HWM 1 headed the Le Mans-start line-up for the day-into-night Goodwood 9-Hours race. Abecassis was sharing with Graham Whitehead, Peter's half-brother, and in practice he lapped in 1 minute 43 seconds, a time equalled by Harry Schell's 2-litre six-cylinder Gordini yet 1.6 seconds faster than the Salvadori/Poore Aston Martin and fully *4 seconds* quicker than the works C-Types shared by Rolt/Hamilton and Moss/Walker. Unfortunately, practice times count for little in long-distance racing.

Moss and Ian Stewart (Ecurie Ecosse C-Type) led from the 3pm start with Abecassis third, and the race developed with the C-Type leading Abecassis who, to his delight, was ahead of the works Astons. At 4.45pm he hurried into the HW Motors pit with a rear tyre almost in shreds, and Whitehead rejoined, later to be delayed again due to the wheel-arch tyre-fouling problem. HWM 1's run then ended abruptly as the XK engine's timing chain let go — an uncharacteristic failure.

Repairs were completed in time for the Midland AC's Shelsley Walsh climb the following weekend, and there, in torrential rain, George won his class by over a second, clocking 46.11 seconds and 45.01 seconds on his two climbs, with the car still wearing its additional Goodwood lamps. It was then hurriedly prepared for the RAC Tourist Trophy at Dundrod, in Ulster, but upon arriving for Friday practice Abecassis broke an axle shaft and was unable to start the race, in which he should have co-driven with Lance Macklin from the F2 team.

On September 20, HWM 1 went hill-climbing again, this time at Prescott, near Cheltenham, where Peter Walker's C-Type won the class in 49.69 seconds and Bill Coleman's ex-Gordon Parker Jaguette humbled Abecassis' best of 50.35 by 0.26 second! Oscar Moore's best in XMC 34 was 52.26 seconds, while Frank le Gallais' LGS-Jaguar climbed in 46.44 to win its single-seater class.

HWM and Abecassis always faithfully supported BARC Goodwood meetings with as much enthusiasm as they always avoided Brands Hatch, and for the International there on September 26 Abecassis fielded HWM 1 and dominated the sports car scratch race (ludicrous by modern standards as a mere five-lapper). He won convincingly from Frazer Nashes driven by Ken Wharton and a young dental student named Tony Brooks, who were followed by Duncan Hamilton's C-Type and Graham Whitehead's Aston Martin. George's fastest lap of 1 minute 42.4 seconds represented an average speed of 84.37mph.

Then the car's eventful first half-season ended in the *Coupe du Salon* races at Montlhéry, early in October. Lance Macklin drove it there on the road and pulled into the hilltop circuit's paddock to find Denis Jenkinson of *Motor Sport* at a loose-end and willing to act as 'helper'. Lance qualified on the front row alongside Georges Grignard's big Talbot-Lago and in the race Grignard took an immediate lead from HWM 1, the green car pulling out and rushing up alongside at around 140mph as they slammed past the pits to enter their second lap. Macklin did not reappear. He eventually walked in, explaining that 'the engine simply stopped, I've no idea why . . .'

'Jenks' walked out after the race to find the car abandoned by the trackside. Macklin had gone off in search of company and Jenks thought he'd better investigate HWM 1's ailment. He opened the bonnet to have a poke about and almost immediately spotted that the centre lead to the coil had come adrift; Macklin hadn't looked. So the diminutive motorcycle racer-cum-journalist refitted it, fired-up the Jaguar engine and drove round to the paddock '. . . frightening myself silly in the process by tackling the banking at around 100mph, which was faster than I'd ever driven a car at that time . . . It gave me respect for Macklin, coming round there near peak revs in top!'

The sports-racer had proved itself totally in the partners' eyes and the highlights of that first half-season, like the encouraging early runs at Reims and in the Goodwood 9-Hours, decided Heath and Abecassis that this was the way to go in 1954 when a new 2½-litre Formula 1 took effect and the old 2-litre Formula 2 to which their first cars had been built was to die. Heath had approached Coventry Climax to order a batch of their promised new 'Godiva' V8 GP engines, but the Midlands company was to believe press reports of enormous Italian horsepower from Ferrari and Maserati, and decide not to risk its reputation in Formula 1 at that time. The 'Godiva' engine was not released, and HWM, Kieft and one or two other hopefuls were left high and dry. Had the Climax management just a little more grip on what was going on outside their own patch they would have taken the Continental power claims with a grain of salt — the 'Godiva' could have been competitive.

Heath was left struggling to develop an SU fuel-injected version of the 2½-litre HWM-Alta engine, but very poor outings at Goodwood, Silverstone and Reims (for the French GP) were to be the team's single-seater swansong in races of significance. By the time of Macklin's failure in France, John Heath's interest was centred squarely upon the Jaguar-powered sports cars . . . for he had found a customer.

He was Tony Gaze, an expatriate Australian, then farming at Ross-on-Wye, Herefordshire, who had been connected with HW Motors for several years. He had bought the ex-Abecassis and Heath 2-litre supercharged Alta sports car EJJ

703 in time for his trip home for the Australian summer of 1948-49, and had scored numerous successes with it. Returning to Europe he had then progressed to run a Formula 2 Alta, and in 1952 he bought one of the previous season's HWM works cars. He retired it when the Alta engine's crankshaft broke, and when fellow Australian driver Lex Davison was in Europe in January 1953 to drive a Holden in the Monte Carlo Rally he saw Gaze's HWM and bought it, intending to fit the straight-eight supercharged 2.9-litre engine from his historic Alfa Romeo *Monoposto* (50003), which he had recently rolled at Port Wakefield when a tyre burst.

The single-seat HWM was shipped to Australia for him, but there his men immediately discovered that the twin-tube chassis frame was too narrow to accommodate the Alfa engine's side-slung blowers, and the idea had to be dropped. There was a wrecked XK120 sports car in the garage at the time, and Davison decided to remove its engine and fit that into the HWM instead. While it was shoe-horned into the single-seater he cabled Coventry for some C-Type performance bits. The resultant HWM-Jaguar was completed in time for the Australian GP, in November 1953, but in practice at Melbourne's Albert Park the engine ran its bearings. The mechanics replaced them overnight, but their effort was wasted as blasting sand had been left in the sump during assembly, and immediately after the start of the race the new bearings were ruined.

Meanwhile, Gaze had been racing an ex-works Aston Martin DB3 sports car in Europe and during the Portuguese GP at Oporto he was chopped-off by a local driver and had an enormous accident in which the Aston burned to the ground and from which he was incredibly lucky to escape uninjured. Fortunately he had insured the car and later that year he arrived at New Zealand Avenue with the insurance money and asked Heath to build him a car like HWM 1. ' ''JB'' agreed . . . and said I could run it as part of the HWM works team . . .'

This time the car was constructed around one of the coil-spring IFS, quarter-elliptic de Dion rear-end F2 chassis surviving in storage from 1951, suitably widened with outriggers to accept an HWM 1-like sports body and a Jaguar engine. The car has since been recorded as VPA 9 and indeed that is what the number appears to be on photographs. However, the raised plastic numbers of the time were vulnerable to flying stones, as at Reims, and prior to the 12-Hours race there in 1954 it was noted in the paddock as VPA 8 . . . Closer scrutiny of photographs now reveal that the plastic figure 8 must have been damaged by one of the Marne circuit's notorious pebbles, and it just looked like 9 ever after! Pity the poor historian . . .

A second coil-spring IFS/quarter-elliptic de Dion rear-end HWM-Jaguar was built-up subsequently, apparently for a character from Birmingham named Geoff Mansell, who was to appear in it occasionally in minor sprints and hill-climbs. Abecassis recalls that it was required primarily for public road use, and he subsequently bought it back then resold it to Bob Bodle at Dorchester. This is the car road-registered XPA 748, of which we shall hear more shortly.

While VPA 8 was being assembled, HWM 1's original ex-Scragg aluminium bodyshell was removed and sold to Johnny Marshall, who ran a garage nearby in Feltham. A stack of chassis and running-gear parts accompanied it, which Marshall's men assembled into a car to accept a 5,420cc, 250bhp Cadillac V8 engine and C-Type gearbox, apparently for former Allard exponent R.A.Page. The car scaled only 17½cwt, was road-registered 2 BMF and proved quite quick in Page's hands before he turned to racing a Lotus — which must have seemed as different as night from day — but the non-HWM-built Cadillac could never match the considerable feats of its Jaguar-engined sisters.

Having lost its original body, old HWM 1 was re-shelled with steel panelling to withstand 1,000 miles round Italy in the 1954 Mille Miglia. After his experiences of this race with Aston Martin (whose car had used-up its front dampers within the first 100 miles and subsequently broke its steering and crashed) Abecassis had auxiliary André friction dampers fitted up front to assist the existing Girling piston-type, but although the Mille Miglia was a daunting and important event, for HWM it was just another fixture on their usual crowded calendar.

Early in April, HWM 1 carried Abecassis into third place in two races at Castle Combe, and a week later it boomed round Oulton Park in the

The tall figure of John Heath hunched down in HWM 1's cockpit during the 1955 British GP race meeting at Aintree. Heath drove rarely, mainly when an alternative full-time driver was not available or occasionally 'just to keep my hand in'. His death in the second-generation HWM 1 during the 1956 Mille Miglia was a blow which effectively finished the HWM team's career.

International British Empire Trophy race. This event features prominently in the Jaguar-engined sports-racing cars' story, being purely for sports cars with capacity-class heats deciding grid positions for a medium-distance final. In practice George qualified second, but still 3 seconds slower than Tony Rolt's C-Type on pole, and amongst six C-Types and Sir Jeremy Boles' Aston Martin he finished fifth in his heat, then eighth in the final after his car's drum brakes had succumbed to the course.

Just one week before the Mille Miglia, on April 26, 'Abby' and his sports-racer were at Goodwood for the Easter Monday meeting where they were placed fourth in a handicap, equalling Jimmy (brother of Jackie) Stewart's Ecurie Ecosse C-Type's fastest lap of 1 minute 43 seconds, 83.88mph.

The HWM-Jaguar was then driven down to Italy for the traditional Mille Miglia start in Brescia. For the race Abecassis wanted a passenger 'because it's lonely down in the south if you get stuck . . .' and Denis Jenkinson of *Motor Sport* was to jump at the chance. Twenty-five years later Jenks recalled mechanic Frank Nagel leaning over as he settled happily into HWM 1's passenger seat and growling ominously 'You'll put your comic away above a hundred and thirty . . .'. Frank, still at HW Motors in 1980 as works manager, was bitterly disappointed at not getting the ride — he had been in training for some time!

Jenks recalled: 'The only practice we had was when Abecassis said "Come on, we'll go up and see Count Maggi for tea", and as we reached the *autostrada* he opened it up and it went straight up to 150mph and stayed there all the way! I was shattered . . .'.

Recalling their race afterwards, Jenkinson wrote: 'Dawn had broken and a dull grey sky was overhead as the over-2-litre sports class lined up on the main road out of Brescia . . . We were last in the row of cars; when we had gone, at 6.13 a.m., the organizers could go and have breakfast and the crowds go to sleep. In front of us was Tom Meyer's light green Aston Martin coupe, and as he mounted the starting ramp and was given the signal to start I set my watch to 6.12 and then we drove up onto the ramp. An official gave me our control card that had to be stamped eight times during the next 1,000 miles. Castegnato and Count Maggi, the two most important men in Brescia, the real brains behind the Mille Miglia, were there smiling, and it was 6.13 and we were away . . . In front of us was a solid block of people, but Abecassis had done many Mille Miglias and he just drove straight at them with the speed rising to 80 and 90 mph. When they were petrifyingly close the crowd swayed back to let us pass, and for the next 20 or 30 miles it seemed that we must sweep them down by the hundred, but they always moved aside in time . . . Everyone had had the same trouble, for the number of marks on the road from panic-braking were unbelievable, and every corner showed signs of one of the 373 cars in front of us having had a dodgy moment, with black marks up onto pavements, signs of locking wheels, and so on.

'Once clear of Brescia the road straightened up and "5,000" and more was showing on the rev-counter in top as commonly as the average car shows 50 mph on its speedometer. It was not long before we saw a speck in the distance, that was number 612 and at nearly 130 mph we went past; by now the crowds were thinning out, though the villages and towns were still packed. In Peschiera the crowd were nearly delirious and their attempts to slow us down were fascinating, one man even running straight at us waving a chair. Round the next corner we saw the reason for all this pandemonium. No. 606 was well and truly wrapped round a tree and a quick look at the list stuck on our dashboard showed it to be Farina. I exchanged a wry look with Abecassis just before he opened out and we got back into our 130 mph stride . . .

'Once away from Verona "5,200" came up and after a while I had the feeling of being satisfied with having done 142 mph on the open road and was quite prepared for Abecassis to ease back to a sedate 100 mph, but as far as the eye could see the road ran straight and was completely clear, so there was no reason to ease off and for mile after mile we cruised at 142 mph. Eventually a blind brow necessitated the throttle being eased back and the speed dropped to around 120 mph, but only for a fleeting moment and we were back to our maximum again with nothing but straight flat road in front of us.

'In Vicenza the road was very bad and on one corner we hit a bump which threw us almost onto the pavement, the crowd stepping smartly backwards as one man. Out of the town we accelerated up to three figures and soon realized something was wrong for the car was wandering about at over 120 mph and clearly the big bump in Vicenza had broken something, probably a shock-absorber or part of the rear suspension, for on corners the car was behaving most peculiarly. After a time we became used to the snaking above 120 mph and as there was no one immediately in front of us we had all the road to play with. We had caught 612, 611 did not start, and 610 we had seen by the roadside a long way back. No. 609 was Peter Collins with the works Aston Martin and, now that we could not corner very fast, obviously we could not catch him.

'After Padova a thick mist developed which reduced visibility to less than 100 yards and limited speed to a bare 100 mph and less in places, for the HWM now had a very small safety margin and panic-braking was quite out of the question. This poor visibility continued for more than 15 miles and when it finally cleared the roads were in a very greasy condition. Conditions were not good and we had dropped more than 10 minutes behind our self-imposed schedule and, being unable to motor on full throttle, the engine started to fuss and one cylinder stopped working. This was getting depressing and just after Rovigo the recent floods had washed about two miles of road completely away and a loose cart-track had been built to replace it. Over this the surface limited us to second gear and we took the opportunity of discussing the situation, deciding to continue to the first control at Ravenna, about 30 minutes farther on. Having dropped speed considerably we were re-passed by Meyer in his Aston Martin and we followed him down to Ferrara. It was now raining spasmodically and the roads were like sheets of ice at more than 100 mph, and in addition Abecassis had to cope with a car that was unstable at high speeds. Approaching a fairly sharp right-hand bend we were both suddenly aware that the Aston Martin in front of us was not going to get round it and, sure enough, the front wheels broke away and the car slid straight on. The next few seconds were very full for Tom Meyer while all we could do was to slow down and watch. The car ran along the left bank, bouncing so high that the sump was in full view, missed all the spectators and trees, slid back onto the road, spun gracefully round in front of us, struck a tree with its tail and fell on its side in the ditch at a very low speed. As we passed, the door opened and the passenger O'Hara climbed out and helped the driver out. Thinking very deep thoughts about tyre adhesion we continued on our way.

'Eventually we arrived at the control at Ravenna, had our card stamped and pulled over to our pre-arranged pit. The misfire proved to be something obscure in one of the Weber carburettors, while the damage at the rear was that the complete end of one of the telescopic shock-absorbers had broken off and was quite irreparable. As we were now 20 minutes behind schedule, with no hope of making up any time, only losing more, it was decided to retire . . . For the 200 miles from Brescia to Ravenna we had averaged 87 mph and that was too slow to justify continuing — a solemn thought indeed.'

In retrospect Jenks mused: 'We had retired at the first checkpoint and even then had done the equivalent of a whole season's English club racing. It gave me a proper sense of perspective . . .'. The following year he navigated Stirling Moss in the works Mercedes-Benz 300SLR and they won the Mille Miglia at the all-time record race average of over 97mph.

Back in Britain, on May 15, for the BRDC's annual International Trophy meeting at Silverstone, Abecassis was present and well wound-up in HWM 1, but Gaze's VPA 8 was still incomplete. In pouring rain Abecassis set off fourth after Gonzalez's big 4.9-litre Ferrari 375-Plus. On lap 10 he displaced Stewart's C-Type for third and had lapped at 83.63mph. With four laps to go he nosed out Walker's Ecosse C-Type for second place, and boomed home brilliantly, albeit 50-seconds behind Gonzalez, whose 350bhp Ferrari had simply left

First of the second-generation HWM-Jaguars, registered XPE 2, showing the tapering chassis frame designed by Eugene Dunn, double radius-rod de Dion tube location, sliding-spline half-shafts and tall coil-spring/damper units. Large-diameter steering wheels were preferred. The front suspension featured vertical coil/damper units contained within the wishbones, while the later 1956-built HWM 1 replacement used angled coil/dampers protruding through the upper wishbones.

everyone for dead.

HWM 1 was then shipped to Sweden for the Hedemora races, where Abecassis came home second again behind a big Ferrari — this time the Portuguese Casimeiro d'Oliveira's 4.5. George beat Hamilton's C-Type into third place, and Michael Head won the production sports event in his XK120.

Mrs Mirabel Topham, owner of Liverpool's Aintree horse-race course, inaugurated the new motor racing circuit around its periphery that year, and Tony Gaze was given a drive in HWM 1 since VPA 8 was still not ready and he was feeling restless. Race day was marred by torrential rain and Gaze slithered home fourth behind Hamilton's winning C-Type, Carroll Shelby's Aston Martin DB3S and Jimmy Stewart. They tackled the new circuit anti-clockwise, and the Australian claimed fastest lap and the inaugural Aintree sports car lap record at 2 minutes 23.8 seconds, 75.10mph.

After such a dank day in Liverpool, the South of France beckoned on June 6 when Gaze and Abecassis shared HWM 1 in the Hyéres 12-Hours. Dependent upon whose report you read they either crashed when lying second on the last

Abecassis at speed in XPE 2 at St Mary's, Goodwood, during the 1956 Easter Monday Goodwood meeting in which he finished second behind Moss' Aston Martin. The second-generation HWM-Jaguar body was styled by George with Frank Feeley's Aston DB3S shape in mind.

lap, or were disqualified. In fact both are true. The car was disqualified for an infringement in the pits, but the organizers merely waggled a black flag at green cars in general rather than displayed it alongside the HWM's race number. George was driving and was conscious of much excitement on the pit apron and since the finish was near he thought he had better overtake somebody! He tried to barge ahead of Charles Pozzi — later to become the French Ferrari distributor — but he collided with him and put both cars off the road. 'With one green car and one blue car in the ditch, you can imagine who the French spectators pushed out first . . .'. The HWM-Jaguar had an oil-pipe torn off and Abecassis was towed across the finish line by Charles Brackenbury (sharing an Aston Martin coupe with Nigel Mann), who passed an old pair of overalls out of the window as a tow-rope . . . Great days.

Back at New Zealand Avenue, VPA 8 was nearing completion while HWM 1 was driven on the road to Oporto, in Portugal, for the Sports Car GP there on June 27, but by the time it arrived its clutch was 'shot' and Abecassis didn't last long in the race. Frank Nagel repaired the damage and set-off on the long haul from Oporto to Reims for the 12-Hours and the French GP meeting there on July 3-4.

Gaze's VPA 8 was ready at last, and was taken direct to Reims from Walton, together with the 2½-litre fuel-injected Formula 1 HWM single-seater.

Abecassis was to share HWM 1 with Lance Macklin in the 12-Hours, while Gaze's VPA 8 was to be co-driven by Graham Whitehead. Macklin would drive the F1 car in the Grand Prix in the afternoon.

Unfortunately, the idea of driving the sports cars to meetings was now being taken rather far and by the time Frank arrived at Reims from Oporto with HWM 1 it was pretty well clapped-out and before Thursday practice was over its XK engine had seized a rod on to its crankshaft and burst apart; it was rebuilt overnight by HWM's long-suffering mechanics. Jack Fairman had done some laps in the F1 car in Macklin's absence, while Gaze and Whitehead shook-down their brand-new car.

By late-afternoon on the Saturday the 12-Hours cars were being lined-up in the paddock and at midnight the fearsome spectacle of a Le Mans-type start in darkness took place on the narrow Gueux road. Abecassis brought HWM 1 swishing into the pits after just 10 minutes, and while his mechanics blipped the throttle to investigate there was a dull thud, a metallic clatter and the Jaguar engine fell silent, gushing oil from its holed crankcase. They retired, glad of the start money.

Meanwhile, Tony Gaze and Graham Whitehead began a steady and reliable race in VPA 8, which survived the 12-Hours quite happily and finished seventh, having covered 1,868.27kms (1,160.89 miles) at an average speed of 155.689km/h (96.74mph), sandwiched between the big Fitch/Walters Cunningham and Polensky/von Frankenburg Porsche 1500. Graham's half-brother, Peter Whitehead, won at the wheel of a works D-Type Jaguar — taking its first-ever victory — co-driven by Ken Wharton. They covered over 2,000 kilometres at an average of 168.935km/h (104.97mph).

Of course the new Mercedes-Benz W196 *Strömlinienwagen* made their debut in the Grand Prix race which followed, lapping 20-seconds faster than Macklin could manage in the HWM. It retired after 11 laps with bearing failure — marking the end of HWM's serious single-seater career.

Two weeks later, at Silverstone for the British GP meeting, Abecassis charged as hard as ever with HWM 1 and was third amongst the leaders until Salvadori elbowed him aside, and in his efforts to stay in contention he lost control at Woodcote and spun into a huge puddle at the foot of the safety bank. Gaze ran in midfield in VPA 8 and was classified 22nd after a long stop out at Becketts Corner.

Gaze tasted victory at Crystal Palace, however, when on August Bank Holiday Monday VPA 8 beat Tony Crook's ex-F2 Cooper-Bristol and averaged 68.42mph around the sinuous London circuit. That same day Abecassis was thundering HWM 1 around the Davidstow airfield circuit in Cornwall to win the big-capacity sports car race in dense sea-fog!

On August 15, the two HWM-Jaguars were in Holland for the Zandvoort sports car races, which the KNAC had substituted for a World Championship Grand Prix when Mercedes-Benz announced they would not be taking part. Abecassis had travelled over with Duncan Hamilton, who was running his C-Type Jaguar, and the burly and extrovert former Le Mans winner was fastest in practice and took pole position with George's HWM 1 alongside. In his hilarious autobiography *Touch Wood,* Duncan wrote: '. . . it looked as if George Abecassis and I were faster than anyone else, and over dinner that night we agreed to take things easily and not blow up our engines racing one another. Despite this pact I am not sure that either of us really trusted the other, and Angela' — his wife — 'says the sight of the two of us sitting side by side on the grid casting surreptitious glances at one another was very funny indeed. The flag fell; I departed, George stayed — in letting in the clutch he had sheared the drive-shaft . . .'

Frank Nagel: 'Heath insisted on using as many former F2 2-litre bits as possible in the sports cars and this included the prop-shaft, which really took a hammering. So when Abecassis popped the clutch, determined to beat Duncan Hamilton off the line, that poor tired old shaft just couldn't take it, and it sheared.'

Frank was staying at a small hotel nearby and was left behind to repair the damage and bring HWM 1 home on the road. The daughter of the hotel proprietor had been asking for a ride in the car all weekend, and when he had finally cobbled the prop-shaft together Frank weakened, and agreed. She loved it, booming along the flat Dutch roads in that open cockpit with the slipstream battering around her ears. Frank was demonstrating just how well the big green sports-racer would go when they approached a blind brow and he asked her loudly if the road was straight beyond. She nodded and waved her hand, dead straight, no problem.

At around 100mph HWM 1 blared over the brow to find a roundabout dead ahead and a safe braking point already lost in its wake. Frank Nagel did his best, put her broadside but then the car tripped on the island kerbing and flipped, bouncing and crashing to a halt badly wrecked. The Dutch girl's injuries included a broken arm, which was more distressing than serious, while Nagel had stayed in the cockpit and broke several ribs: 'The boss was very good about it really — he usually is about things like that — and he seemed more concerned that we could be repaired, because he knew the car could be . . . it had been often enough before.'

While these traumatic goings-on surrounded HWM 1, her near-sister VPA 8 had been taken to La Baule, in France, for the sports car handicap GP on the Escoublac airfield circuit. Once again the French organizers handicapped the British cars out of contention, Duncan Hamilton being classified fourth in his C-Type and Gaze sixth in the HWM. The winner was Cornet's DB-Panhard.

Frantic work at New Zealand Avenue repaired HWM 1 again in time to join VPA 8 in the RAC Tourist Trophy, at Dundrod, on September 11. The driver pairings were to be Abecassis/Jim Mayers and Gaze/John Riseley-Prichard, and as Class C starters they had to cover 90-laps of the difficult 7.4-mile road circuit, the same as the 3.7-litre Lancia V6s of Fangio/Castellotti and Ascari/Villoresi, the 3.3s of Taruffi/Piodi and Manzon/Valenzano, the Rolt/Hamilton works D-Type and a pair of C-Types. In short, they had their work cut out, especially since the very quick 750cc DB-Panhards of Armagnac/Laureau and Bonnet/Bayol in Class E had only 67-laps to complete. Even the 3-litre works Astons, the Ferraris and a Jaguar, driven by names like Hawthorn, Collins, Moss, Salvadori and Wharton, had a two-lap start on the over-3-litre cars.

As it happened, almost everybody had trouble apart from the Armagnac/Laureau DB-Panhard, which won on handicap from the Hawthorn/Trintignant Ferrari. HWM 1 went very well to finish fourth overall on distance covered, beaten only by two of the Lancias and the Hawthorn Ferrari, but it fell to 14th on handicap. VPA 8 had an unlucky outing, becoming the first retirement as Gaze abandoned with engine failure.

This was a great disappointment, and in fact worse was to follow. The unfortunate Reims F1 car, using chassis 52/106, had been re-engined with a Jaguar XK unit in similar manner to Davison's down-under conversion of the 1951 car. Duncan Hamilton had driven it into fifth place in the *Libre* race at the Oulton Park Gold Cup meeting on August 7, and in the September International at Goodwood Tony Gaze was entered for another *Libre* event, but he up-ended it in practice. The car was totally destroyed and Gaze went to hospital with severe concussion. In 1976 Tony recalled he had been under medication at the time, the car had a centre throttle pedal, and he simply got muddled up with his feet. Abecassis and Heath were most unhappy — it went right against the grain to write anything off . . . George drove HWM 1 in the Goodwood sports event and finished third behind Salvadori's Ecosse C-Type and Masten Gregory's private 4.5-litre Ferrari.

One week later the circus returned to Aintree for the *Daily Telegraph* International, this time run clockwise. The programme began with a five-lap sprint for production saloons mixed with sports cars and Dick Shattock's RGS-Atalanta-Jaguar led until Page's HWM-Cadillac thundered by, only to spin off almost immediately. Before this misadventure 2 BMF had set fastest race lap at 2 minutes 23.8 seconds, 75.10mph. John Riseley-Prichard drive VPA 8 in the 17-lap main sports car race, but after a dice with Alan Brown's Lotus-Connaught he finished way down the field.

HWM 1 was absent in Sweden at the time, where Abecassis ran the car in the Karlskoga Kannonloppet and led '. . . by such a bloody margin that I just nodded off in the low sun and instead of going round the last corner I just went sailing way past my braking point and ended-up miles off course amongst the trees . . . silly really . . .'

The HWM-Jaguars' first full season had been packed with incident. It had earned the partners quite a considerable sum in start, prize and bonus money, and above all had kept the HWM name to the fore at a time when their single-seater eclipse became total.

Early in 1955, while a new-generation HWM-Jaguar sports car was on the stocks at New Zealand Avenue, John Bolster of *Autosport* was loaned HWM 1

for road test. He cheated a little, using a 4.11:1 final-drive for his acceleration tests and then substituting a 3.48:1 final-drive for maximum speeds, but the figures he obtained remain fairly hair-raising today. The old lady hammered from 0-60mph in just 6.5 seconds, from 0-100mph in 17 seconds and on to 110mph in 20.8 seconds. On the higher back-axle ratio she achieved 77mph at peak revs in second gear, 114mph in third and 145.1mph in top. It was a demanding car to drive fast, but its strong initial understeer could be balanced out on the throttle and the torsion-bar de Dion rear-end provided tremendous traction. The car was stable at high speed, and although at first acquaintance its steering seemed heavy, it was virtually finger-tip sensitive at speed. Having test-driven Gaze's coil-spring IFS VPA 8, Abecassis believed his own transverse-leaf-spring HWM 1 to be far superior, but the new 1955 HWM-Jaguar then being finalized by Heath and his ex-Vickers design engineer Eugene Dunn was to use coil-springs at front and rear.

'Euge' — it rhymes with huge — Dunn's purpose-built sports car chassis was another large-diameter twin-tube affair, arranged this time not parallel, but virtually elliptical in plan form to place one main longeron beneath each of the side-by-side seats. The tubes converged to meet a tubular cross-frame carrying forged double-wishbone front suspension with short coil-springs interposed, while a tall rear frame provided top pick-ups for similar coils suspending the de Dion tube. Outriggers extending from the point at which the main longerons commenced their inward sweep to pick up the final-drive unit, provided twin radius-rod mountings to locate the de Dion tube fore-and-aft. Once again the car used massive Alfin-drummed hydraulic brakes, mounted outboard at front and rear, while Abecassis had designed a handsome new body style, replacing

The scene in HWM's New Zealand Avenue, Walton-on-Thames, workshops in 1957 with what is apparently a hood frame being offered-up on the second-generation HWM 1, and XPE 2 alongside. During their works careers XPE 2 always had its headlights in the wings, HWM 1 its headlights in the nose intake. In the foreground lies Phil Scragg's SPC 982 under construction, revealing a tapering planform twin-tube chassis very unlike the F2 Alta frame it was claimed to be. On the left is what was probably Scragg's ex-Abecassis GP Alta-based HWM-Alta-Jaguar, RPG 418, showing-off its parallel-tube single-seater chassis and uniquely Alta rubber-block-and-wishbone suspension. Presumably parts of 'RPG' were cannibalized to complete 'SPC'.

45

the original simple-curvature slab shape with sweeping voluptuous compound curves, rather like a grown-up Aston Martin DB3S.

While this car was going together, Lex Davison was enjoying some success in Australia with his HWM-Jaguar single-seater. On November 7, 1954, he had won the Australian GP on the 5.7-mile Southport circuit, and the car was undeniably quick, having been timed at 131.7mph on the flying quarter-mile at Bathurst. For the New Zealand International races and the rest of the 1955 season, Davison obtained D-Type engine parts from Coventry, and in the New Zealand GP at Ardmore Airfield, outside Auckland, on January 9, he finished ninth, with some problems. Also running in this race was local man John Horton, driving a two-stage supercharged 1,960cc Alta-engined ex-team 1951 HWM single-seater, which he had bought from Tony Gaze the previous year. It used the last GP Alta supercharger set available from Geoffrey Taylor, and when Gaze had taken it out to New Zealand in January 1954 it had been on loan from the partners '. . . on the express understanding that under no circumstances should he bring it back!'

The team's 1955 season began in March when Abecassis took HWM 1 to Sweden for an ice race at Vesteras. He had been to Sweden ice-racing his ERA just after the war and thoroughly enjoyed it, but this time HWM 1 let him down with final-drive failure and he did not start.

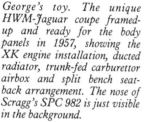

George's toy. The unique HWM-Jaguar coupe framed-up and ready for the body panels in 1957, showing the XK engine installation, ducted radiator, trunk-fed carburettor airbox and split bench seatback arrangement. The nose of Scragg's SPC 982 is just visible in the background.

On April 2, at Oulton Park, Abecassis reappeared for the British Empire Trophy race, qualifying way down the field, but in heavy rain he drove at his forceful best, disputing second place with Hamilton's D-Type towards the end. On the very last lap he was blinded by the Jaguar's spray as they slithered into the right-handed Druid's Corner and the HWM ploughed off along the bank, George eventually pulling the car down to retire on the infield.

At this time the Four Point Garage, of High Street, Feltham, was advertising 2 BMF — their HWM-Cadillac — for sale. It was eventually to be acquired by Dr Pinkerton, who hill-climbed it quite extensively, but by June 1956 it was being offered again, this time by Lockhart's Service Depot, of Dunstable, who

described it as '. . . a competition car of no little potential and a unique road car. There is, however, a technical hitch. The block has been cracked by frost and while a brief course of Wonderweld is doing all that is claimed for it, we are offering the car as it stands at the very low figure of . . .£550'. It sold eventually to New Zealand where, in February 1957, one D. Avery drove it in the New Zealand GP supporting race in which Ken Wharton was killed, and later it reappeared there in the hands of Roly Levis.

Easter 1955 was a busy weekend for HWMs as Abecassis was placed fourth in a *Libre* race and led the 55-miles sports car event for three laps at Castle Combe on the Saturday before the nearside rear tyre lost its tread. On Sunday, at Trengwainton hill-climb in Devon, Gerry Scali drove XMC 34 to set FTD and a hill record in 25.49 seconds. On the Monday, at Goodwood, old HWM 1 was sixth in a five-lap event driven by Abecassis, being led home by two Astons, a Ferrari and a brace of Jaguars.

On May 7, at the BRDC Silverstone International, 'Abby' appeared in the latest HWM — the first of the new-style cars, registered XPE 2. This new chassis and shell were considerably lighter than the original, as well as being far more handsome, and the car's layout improved its balance with the spare wheel now housed in the tail above a rectangular fuel tank instead of alongside the driver.

Abecassis was third away from the Le Mans-type start, chasing the Jaguars of Desmond Titterington and Tony Rolt, but he was rapidly swamped by works Jaguars and Aston Martins and dropped back as the new and unpainted car's water temperature climbed; he retired with overheating after 10 laps. Alan Brown drove the older car and was another early retirement, quoted this time as valve-spring failure.

On May 21, in the first BARC Members' Aintree meeting, the Hon. Patrick Lindsay spun his ex-Tom Meyer 1950 HWM MXK 727, while Phil Scragg took his hill-climbing HW-Alta-Jaguar circuit-racing and was second behind Cyril Wick's ex-Whitehead Cooper-Jaguar Mark I.

John Heath returned to race driving at the Whit Monday Goodwood meeting, handling HWM 1 alongside Abecassis' still-unpainted XPE 2, and while George again struck trouble his partner finished fifth, sandwiched between the C-Types of Peter Blond (soon to drive the HWMs) and Michael Head (about to order a Cooper-Jaguar).

Whit Sunday at Brands Hatch had seen Page's HWM-Cadillac finish fifth behind Scott-Brown's 2-litre Lister-Bristol in the Wrotham Cup, and while the HWM-Jaguars were at Goodwood he was at Crystal Palace, finishing fourth in another Scott-Brown demonstration.

On June 18 Abecassis won two events at Goodwood in XPE 2, setting fastest lap both times with a best of 1 minute 41.4 seconds, 85.21mph. A week later he was at Snetterton for the Eastern Counties 100, where the green-painted XPE 2 ran second, then fell to fourth before spearing straight on into the outside bank at Coram Curve and smashing its front-end. There was some conjecture that a steering arm ball-joint had snapped, but George (suffering facial injuries) dismissed the idea, blaming the accident on his own over-enthusiastic cornering.

HWM 1 was driven in this event by Michael Keen — like Jim Mayers a member of the Monkey Stable team to drive the Walton cars — and he lay fifth early on before a fire broke out in the car's cockpit. He stopped at the pits, the wiring was rearranged and he continued, only to have a second conflagration, quelled this time by the marshals' extinguishers. Page ran 2 BMF, but failed to finish.

Keen bought a second drive from the team in mid-July at the British GP meeting, where he handled the repaired XPE 2, and John Heath sprouted tall out of HWM 1 as they finished poorly, eighth and 12th, respectively.

Geoff Mansell's XPA 748 emerged for the July 24 Prescott hill-climb and was 'slow round the corners and quick up the straights', while Dr Pinkerton had acquired the HWM-Cadillac and spun off into the sand at Orchard Corner on his second run.

At Brands Hatch, on August Monday, Bruce Halford drove fellow West Countryman Gerry Scali's XMC 34 into sixth place, while HW Motors were involved in serious preparation of XPE 2 and HWM 1 for the Goodwood 9-Hours on August 20.

The latest car was to be shared there by Lance Macklin/John Dalton, while Johnny Marshall/Dick Protheroe took HWM 1. At the last moment young Bill Smith — who had made a meteoric rise to fame at the wheel of a C-Type Jaguar — took Dalton's place alongside Macklin, his mother paying for the drive, and they brought the car home fourth, completing 301 laps against the winning Walker/Poore DB3S total of 309. Marshall and Protheroe were eighth in HWM 1 after throwing Michelin tyre treads three times. It was in this race that poor Mike Keen lost his life when his Cooper-Bristol ran off the road, rolled over and over and burned.

One week later, at Oulton Park, XPE 2 was out again, this time entrusted to Franco-American driver Harry Schell, who finished sixth after an unexpected, and as usual with 'Arreee, wildly theatrical refuelling stop. In September, at the Brighton Speed Trials, Angela Brown, daughter of Aston Martin company chief David Brown, drove XPE 2 through the standing-start kilometre in 26.8 seconds to win the ladies' award; in the new year she would become Mrs George Abecassis.

The September Prescott hill-climb found Phil Scragg borrowing HWM 1 to lower the over-3-litre sports class record to 47.40 seconds, but the RAC TT at Dundrod saw no HWM-Jaguar entries although sadly it witnessed the deaths of Bill Smith and Jim Mayers. The former had shown every sign of being a truly great driver in the making — his immense potential was never to be fulfilled.

That same day XPE 2 was being raced at Oulton Park, where Abecassis, recovered from his Snetterton injuries, won two races against meagre opposition and lapped in 2 minutes 5.6 seconds, 79.94mph. Ken Flint's XK-engined E-Type ERA — looking bizarre with 1½-seat bodywork and bicycle mudguards — finished second despite an off-road excursion at the end of the 15-lap USAF Trophy, one of Abecassis' successes.

George won again in XPE 2 at Goodwood, on September 24, without approaching his Whitsun lap times, and the final handicap that day saw Patrick Lindsay start on scratch with his ex-Meyer HWM and roll it on the very last corner. He escaped unharmed and explained that it was his last race in any case; he was retiring to get married. He sold the damaged car for less than the price of its trailer, but missed racing terribly — he took it up again with the famous ERA 'Remus' and was still driving in 1980.

The season ended on a high note for HWM at the Castle Combe International on October 1, where Abecassis won the 20-lap feature event after Salvadori's leading Aston Martin had retired. George just held off Louis Rosier's unusually aggressive Ferrari by a fifth of a second across the line. Third, driving HWM 1 for the first time, was Noel Cunningham-Reid — son of one of the Lascelles family, cousins of the Queen. George saw in him the ability to go far in racing, and was sure that if he could prove himself he could take a place in the works Aston Martin team. He paid for his drive, too! First and third was a great 1955 finale for New Zealand Avenue.

Tony Gaze's VPA 8 had lain fallow all season, but the winter of 1955-56 — which, remember, was summer in Australia and New Zealand — saw the Australian team-up with Peter Whitehead to take a pair of Ferraris down-under for the Kiwi Internationals. Gaze took along the HWM for the supporting sports car races, and Whitehead his latest Cooper-Jaguar Mark II.

At Ardmore, Gaze was third on handicap in VPA 8 behind Moss' Porsche 550 and Whitehead's Cooper, while at Wigram, outside Christchurch, the HWM-Jaguar actually won — much to everyone's surprise as Gaze actually left the Le Mans start in reverse! Reg Parnell had winked at the Australian as they lined-up to run and jump and explained that he had put VPA 8 in gear. 'She's all ready and waitin' for ye . . .'.

In March, VPA 8 appeared at Melbourne's Albert Park circuit, where Gaze won the 150-miles Moomba TT by beating Bib Stilwell's D-Type. The

following weekend it finished third in the Argus Cup — this extended meeting accompanying the 1956 Olympic Games being held in the city — and Gaze then sold the car to Lex Davison. He drove it into seventh place back at Albert Park in November for the Australian TT, and subsequently modernized the HWM's slab shape by fitting one of Paul England's streamlined Ausca bodyshells. The original Leacroft of Egham panelwork was removed and subsequently fetched-up on a Skoda Special. With the glass-fibre Ausca body the old HWM-Jaguar competed in several 1957 events until it was crashed heavily on the public road while being driven home from Templestowe hill-climb by a mechanic. The wreck was taken to Lyndon Duckett's workshop, where the damaged body was removed and scrapped. The remains, with front-end, suspension and road-wheel damage, languished in Duckett's 'shop, unloved and unwanted, until 1974, when old-car enthusiast Gavin Sala acquired them for a reputed A$2,500. Sala traced the original bodywork, amazingly complete and unmodified, on Hugh Guthrie's Skoda Special, in Fairfield, Victoria. Since Sala was engaged on other restoration projects, little work was done on VPA 8 before 1976, when he sold her to Simon Ramsay. As I write the restoration is almost complete.

In mid-February 1956, Abecassis had taken himself off to Sweden for some more ice-racing, this time at Lake Feden, but he was handicapped by the lack of properly studded tyres and could not improve on sixth place in a race won by Gunnar Carlsson's Ferrari with Joakim Bonnier's Disco Volante Alfa Romeo second.

Another new-style car was being completed at New Zealand Avenue at this time, this one differing from XPE 2 in having co-axial coil-spring/damper units which extended through the fabricated tubular top wishbones to pick-up turret mounts, rather than being short springs contained between forged proprietary

Scragg in his potent D-Type dry-sump-engined HWM-Jaguar, SPC 982, during a late-'fifties BARC Aintree sprint meeting — the branch of the sport in which the Macclesfield textile engineer excelled. This car used enormous 13-inch-diameter Al-fin drum brakes and had full-offset Borrani 6½J wire-spoke rear wheels tailor-made to suit. In the 'eighties these original wheels looked so wide they just 'had to be' modern improvements. In fact 'SPC' was a very advanced car, with unequal-length front-wishbone geometry and a split de Dion axle at the rear, though the latter feature was superfluous.

Snetterton, in 1957, with Peter Blond's works HWM-Jaguar leading Graham Whitehead's Aston Martin DB3S and David Shale's ex-Tommy Sopwith Cooper-Jaguar Mark II at Riches Corner. At this stage in its career the hard-raced, often-bent XPE 2 had been refitted with a full-width windscreen.

wishbones as in the '55 car. Other modifications included a vastly enlarged elliptical radiator air intake to cool the D-Type-headed XK engine, and XPE 2's nose section was similarly reworked to produce the ugly gaping maw for which these HWM-Jaguars have since become famous.

On March 27, 1956, before an 8,000 crowd at the 21st BARC Members' Goodwood meeting, Abecassis drove XPE 2 to win handsomely from Head's new Cooper-Jaguar. In the supporting short handicap race, with light fuel load, George really went to town, hurling XPE 2 round in 1 minute 38 seconds, 87.45mph — the fastest race lap ever at a BARC Members' meeting at that time. Again at Goodwood, on Easter Monday, he held off the D-Types without apparent effort and finished a fine second behind Moss' victorious Aston Martin, but he spoiled his day by taking XPE 2 off the road in the closing handicap.

In April, Jack Fairman handled XPE 2 at Oulton Park for the British Empire Trophy, but did poorly, finishing eighth in the heat and only 14th in the final after qualifying at the back of the grid. At Aintree, for the International 200 meeting, Noel Cunningham-Reid returned to the team and brought XPE 2 home fourth amongst good company.

One week later the mighty Mille Miglia was to be run in Italy, and there John Heath was to debut the new car, inheriting the registration HWM 1 from its 1953-built predecessor which had just been sold to garage owner Ray Fielding, of Forres, Scotland.

'JB' had decided to do the Mille Miglia 'just for fun', to fulfil a minor sporting ambition which he had evidently been cherishing for some time. George Abecassis spent ages trying to talk his partner out of the idea: 'John was an enthusiastic driver, but for some years gone by he had only really raced when he had to because we couldn't find anybody else, or maybe a couple of times when he just felt like keeping his hand in. I told him he was going to be out of his depth in such a race as the Mille Miglia. In particular I didn't like the idea of the low-geared steering he had fitted to save fatigue on the mountain passes'.

John Heath's divorced wife, Barbara — he had remarried to a very pretty girl named Laurel Crane some years previously — had been working in the motor trade to help support their two daughters and she met him by chance in a London motor factors. 'Take care', she told him. 'Don't worry', he assured her, although she felt he looked uneasy. 'I've got to go — you know — just to show the flag.'

The evening before the race he sat down in his Brescia hotel room and rewrote his will, just in case, then came the early-morning start and the brand-new HWM 1, with its grille-mounted headlights and race number 545, mounted the ramp, Heath sprouting tall and tense from its cockpit. Promptly at 5.45am he was flagged away into the dawn, in constant, heavy, rain.

He was the first of the final group of 'name' drivers, to be followed by Perdisa, Castellotti, Collins, Taruffi and the Moss/Jenkinson partnership in a Maserati 350S. Rain was teeming down as the HWM boomed out of Brescia and after miles of wet-road racing, as it plumed into the hamlet of Glorie, near Ravenna, its tyres lost adhesion, the tail lurched round into a spin and Abecassis believes the low-geared steering was just too slow for Heath to catch it.

The big car careered quite slowly into a ditch, and then, with its last ounce of impetus, it suddenly reared up and toppled over, to crush its driver. The car looked barely damaged, lying forlornly on its wheels in the ditch as Moss and Jenkinson cascaded by through the rain, but its driver-constructor, who had done so much to put Britain on the motor racing map, had his ribs shattered and he succumbed to lung injuries two days later in hospital.

He was buried in Hersham churchyard, beside his younger brother Jimmy — a Hurricane fighter pilot with the RAF who ironically had died in a motorcycle accident on the A40 before the war had begun. HWM understandably scratched their entries from the Silverstone May meeting, and amid the gloom Abecassis and Angela Brown were married.

Abecassis: 'I decided to retire from driving at that point. We still had a number of racing commitments to fulfil with the season planned and contracts signed, but it wasn't the same without John.'

On May 5, Prescott hill-climb saw the reapparance of the original HWM 1, re-registered YPG 3 by its new owner Ray Fielding, and immaculately prepared in his usual manner. Mike Hawthorn was entered to drive XPE 2 at Goodwood on Whit Monday, but took a Lotus instead, so the trusty Jack Fairman brought the HWM home fourth behind three D-Types.

HW Motors recovered their poise and Noel Cunningham-Reid handled XPE 2 in the Eastern Counties 100 at Snetterton while the damaged HWM 1 was still being repaired. The East Anglian circuit was swept by continuous rain as Les Leston's 1,500cc Cooper-Climax fled into an early lead from Cunningham-Reid and held it for six laps. Then he caught some tailenders in the Esses and in the mix-up Cunningham-Reid saw a gap open-up, slammed XPE 2's great snout into it and emerged as the leader. Leston found he couldn't see a thing past the HWM's bulbous backside and after 10 laps Cunningham-Reid was still ahead, averaging over 84mph and having just lapped at 86.02mph. Leston was pressing very hard, and on lap 14 Cunningham-Reid ran too deep into the hairpin and the big car spun tail-first into the bank, crushing its body quite badly.

By this time HWM's mechanics were adept at straightening-out sports cars, and XPE 2 was available again in time for the Reims 12-Hours on July 1, where Cunningham-Reid was to share her with Leston. They were sixth fastest in practice, Leston clocking 2 minutes 47.5 seconds against Desmond Titterington's pole in the works D-Type at 2 minutes 35.3 seconds.

As the field's headlights flared back through the floodlit pit area three minutes after the midnight start Cunningham-Reid lay fifth behind the D-Types of Bueb, Hawthorn, Flockhart and Titterington, but was quickly caught and passed by Maglioli's Maserati. The car still held sixth place at the end of the first hour, but it was not to last as the XK engine ran its bearings and XPE was retired.

At this time advertisements appeared in the motor-sporting press: 'From July 16 HWM's competitions department offers its comprehensive facilities for race preparation.'

In the British GP meeting at Silverstone Cunningham-Reid shone again in XPE 2, only to lose an exuberant fourth place with a spin at Stowe after soaring through the field. He rejoined sixth and finished fifth, 8 seconds behind Protheroe's Tojeiro-Jaguar.

At this point Cunningham-Reid began racing a new 2-litre Lister-Bristol, but on August 18 he was back behind XPE 2's enormous steering wheel for the flooded *Daily Herald* International at Oulton Park. He qualified on the second row of the grid with a best lap in 2 minutes 01.4 seconds behind a quartet of Aston Martins, Moss' being on pole at 1 minute 58.2 seconds. Cunningham-Reid was a tigerish driver when he felt like it, and in pouring rain he led all the D-Types until the HWM's steering broke, when, after a lurid few moments, he brought it safely to a halt.

The following week he was out again in the car at Shelsley Walsh for the International hill-climb, finishing second in class behind the far more experienced Ray Fielding in YPG 3; 47.06 seconds to the Scot's 47.05 seconds.

It was at this meeting that Phil Scragg made his debut with a brand-new HWM-Alta-Jaguar, sporting his favourite slipper-body/bicycle wing body style and based this time — it was announced — upon a 1952-53 Formula 2 Alta chassis frame. In reality the car seems to have been all new, using a non-parallel twin-tube frame broadly similar to the 'Euge' Dunn sports car design. Modified to accept a D-Type dry-sump engine ('the only one we could ever afford' according to Abecassis) and road-registered SPC 982, this was the last competition HWM-Jaguar to be built at New Zealand Avenue, and it was to enjoy a long if minor-league career which continued into the 'eighties.

That September saw Cunningham-Reid leading at Snetterton before being forced into the pits and leaving Peter Blond's D-Type to win, and then finishing fourth in the 21-lap Goodwood Trophy National event, where Tony Brooks scored his first victory for Aston Martin. In the handicap closing that meeting, Cunningham-Reid was second behind Jock Lawrence's Ecurie Ecosse D-Type.

Prescott was a triumph for the Fieldings, Ray and his wife Doreen sharing YPG 3 to be placed 1-2 in their class, climbing in 49.40 and 51.90 seconds, respectively.

Once again the season ended on a high note for HW Motors as Cunningham-Reid took an immediate lead in the 15-lap RedeX Trophy race at Snetterton, on October 7, and held it all the way to beat the Coopers of Ivor Bueb and Peter Gammon. Archie Scott-Brown was fourth in Bob Dennis' Aston Martin-Jaguar.

By 1957 the old team's effort was almost spent; although HWM 1 was running again alongside XPE 2 their programme was very restricted compared with former years.

First time out at Snetterton, on March 30, Cunningham-Reid became a non-starter after bearing failure in practice, and a week later Duncan Hamilton drove XPE 2 in the British Empire Trophy at Oulton Park and lost a terrific battle with Dick Protheroe's Tojeiro-Jaguar for fifth place. Peter Blond, a cousin of Jonathan Sieff of Marks & Spencer chain-store fame, joined Cunningham-Reid in the HWM-Jaguar team at Goodwood on Easter Monday, Blond running fourth much of the way and finishing fifth in good company. But in May, on the same circuit, Blond pressed too hard in an attempt to beat the handicappers and crashed very heavily at Fordwater, badly damaging HWM 1's front-end.

Just a week later he was out in the other car at Brands Hatch in what, according to *Autosport's* reporter '. . . was obviously going to be a duel to the death between Peter Blond's HWM and Graham Hill in Tommy Atkin's DB3S Aston Martin'.

Graham led the first lap, the HWM's extra power punched Blond clear along the main straight on lap two and 'this, of course, was like a red rag to a bull and

Hill used every trick he knew in making use of his car's slightly superior road-holding'. On the last lap Blond led out of sight behind the trees at Druid's Hairpin and commentator John Bolster remarked: 'Nobody will ever quite know what went on behind those trees!' The Aston burst into sight narrowly ahead and led by the thickness of Graham's moustache only to spin off at Clearways, the last corner, leaving Blond to win for HWM!

He later added a third place in a minor handicap at Oulton Park, and on Whit Monday, at Crystal Palace, Les Leston drove HWM 1 to finish third behind Scott-Brown's new Lister-Jaguar and Graham Whitehead's DB3S. In July, Blond led the opening laps of the big sports car race at the St John Horsfall Trophy Silverstone meeting, finally giving best to Whitehead's Aston and finishing second. Heavy rain marred the British GP meeting's sports car race at Aintree and he was out of luck with XPE 2, but the Vanwall Trophy, at Snetterton, yielded a third place, and on August Bank Holiday Monday he finished fourth in the Kingsdown Trophy at Brands Hatch.

By this time it was abundantly obvious that the old cars were too heavy and too large to be really competitive with the new breed of pure-bred sports-racing cars like the Lister-Jaguar. On September 7, Mrs Jean Bloxam drove one of the HWM-Jaguars to third fastest ladies' time in the Brighton Speed Trials — presumably XPE 2, which her husband Roy was to buy for the 1958 season. At Prescott, Archie Scott-Brown was entered to drive one of the cars, but could not appear at the last moment due to illness in his family, so Phil Scragg drove instead and beat Ray Fielding, while Tony Gaze also ran a Roots-blown HWM single-seater — actually the ex-works/Curtis/Nurse/Brooke 1952 F2 car.

On September 28, both HWM-Jaguars ran at Goodwood, driven without success by Blond and Fairman, and at New Zealand Avenue Abecassis had at last decided to call it a day, to sell the cars and concentrate upon the general motor trade.

He was approached by an impecunious trio of enthusiasts calling themselves Team Speedwell, comprising Whitton garage owner Monty Mostyn, Bill Smith and driver John Bekaert. John recalled: 'The HWM was about the only big sports car you could buy for £1,500. We had a choice of both, I tried them at Brands Hatch and much preferred HWM 1. Harry Weslake was sympathetic and did us a special head for a 3.8 engine and it proved to be a very big, hairy motor car, but bloody good to handle, quite quick and tremendous fun to drive.'

Meanwhile, at the end of September 1957, Ray Fielding had advertised his ex-works HWM 1, now YPG 3, for sale at £1,300 and Bloxam bought XPE 2 to be raced under the banner of his Gerrards Cross Motor Company.

Both late-model cars started the 1958 season inauspiciously. During testing at Goodwood Bekaert '. . . heard somebody say you took the first part of St Mary's at full chat. I tried it and hit the bank at about 130mph! It was all right

Later glory. HWM 1 in its second-generation 1956-originated form dominated its class in 1958 club racing driven by John Bekaert for the amateur Speedwell team. Here at Goodwood's Woodcote Corner John is charging typically hard, lights ablaze.

until one of those Triumph stub-axles broke and then she just went absolutely straight on, just where Moss had his accident, wrote-off the front and broke my left collar bone. Monty threw away the Triumph stubs and machined down some Bentley ones to fit, but it took some weeks to repair the damage.'

At the Easter Monday Goodwood meeting, on April 7, Roy Bloxam went well in XPE 2, while his wife Jean raced her ex-David Brown DB3S Coupe, but at Oulton Park, for the British Empire Trophy the following Saturday, Bloxam crashed his new car very heavily on the opening lap. He was in midfield when XPE 2 broke loose at Lodge Corner and smashed head-on into the outside bank, being halted from probably 60mph in as little as seven feet. Bloxam was knocked cold by the impact, but came round miraculously unharmed apart from shock, some bruises and a gashed leg, while the car was a wreck.

After his early setback John Bekaert simply went from strength to strength in HWM 1: 'It was opposite-lock all the way and I enjoyed every mile I did in that car, although people would always tear past me under braking — really it never had a bad race.' Using its 3.8-litre D-Type engine the drum-braked HWM could not hold the Lotuses on the tighter circuits like Mallory Park and Brands

Hatch, but Bekaert became virtually the uncrowned king of Silverstone club racing. He lived in Chorleywood, naturally drove HWM 1 to and from its races on the open road, and his record for the 40-odd miles from home to Silverstone was 29 minutes. On one occasion he was trapped by the police, entering the 30mph limit on the rural outskirts of Wendover exactly 100mph too fast!

Autosport's club race survey that year commented: 'He also scored successes at Snetterton later in the season but, in general, there was too much uncertainty about the brakes on that car for peace of mind on any circuit; it was also extremely fussy about its tyres' — 35psi all round was the *only* pressure it would tolerate, John recalled — 'and it would accept any excuse to go straight regardless of the attitude of its front wheels. The only man who appeared to be totally unmoved by all this was John himself, and he was driving the thing!' Bekaert combated the car's inherent understeer by hurling it into lurid oversteer and he was always a tremendous crowd-pleaser in what was obviously a very demanding 'man's car'.

In later years the HWM-Jaguars sank into obscurity, or hard-earned retirement. Dick Milne, a friend of Bekaert's, raced HWM 1 in 1959 club events and Alan Mann inherited it in 1960. He remembered it as 'a good car, never any bother, but always a handful as 25 gallons of fuel rushed across that unbaffled tank in the middle of a corner!' He took the Firle hill-climb record with the car and pursued a full programme of club races.

Ray Fielding had sold its 1954 Mille Miglia predecessor YPG 3 to a Dr I. R. Entwhistle, who appeared with it at a Wirral sprint in 1961, and this car subsequently passed to Finchley garage owner Raymond Bowles, who retained it into 1980.

The ex-works/Bekaert/Milne/Mann HWM 1 re-emerged in the 'seventies after a rebuild by Paul Gardner and was used in historic sports car events by Richard Bond. Kirk Rylands bought it from him in 1974, raced it extensively in historic events and also used it widely on the road. Originally he found it 'oversteered like hell, a real beastie, but I had Patrick Head' — engineer son of Col. Michael Head — 'take a look at it and he advised that I fit a thicker front anti-roll bar. I found it wasn't going any quicker, but I was enjoying it a lot more. It's still on drum brakes, it would be quicker on discs, but I think driving the car as it was is what it's all about . . .'

The other late-model team car, the ex-works/Bloxam XPE 2, which had done so much racing, re-emerged in 1968 when Alta enthusiast John Bateson, of Alderley Edge, Cheshire, located it in very poor condition in Manchester. He rebuilt both chassis and engine, tidied the body and used it in sprints and hill-climbs until 1972, when he decided the body required expert attention and had it restored by Derek Whittle of Rochdale. The 3.4-litre D-Type engine and gearbox were in good order and so XPE 2 returned to much of its former glory.

Bateson was in partnership with Anthony Statham at that time in a garage business, and Statham had acquired the ex-Mansell-cum-Lord Lilford/Sir Jeremy Boles/'an RAF officer at Scampton' XPA 748 from one Gerhard Krasner, who had raced it in minor Oulton Park clubbies in the early-'sixties. In fact Krasner took Bateson's ex-Abecassis single-seat Alta (blown-up) in part exchange. Unfortunately, Statham lost control of the HWM-Jaguar in the rain at Silverstone's Maggots Curve and smashed both ends against the bank, folding-up the front so badly that the engine dragged on the roadway when they tried to tow it away! He had the frame straightened by Rubery Owen, and the bits were then sold to Paul Craigen of Henley for restoration. In 1979 he sold the car to John Harper on behalf of Dr Philippe Renault, the Parisian Jaguar collector, and John had the rebuild completed on his client's behalf. This car's frame is interesting in that it features parallel 3-inch-diameter longerons placed 1ft 9in apart, as in the 1951 F2 single-seater chassis, but here they have a 'drop' built-in abaft the front suspension, which was essentially a 1952-53 single-seater frame feature — and those later frames were of 2½-inch tube with extra superstructure trusses and a rigid scuttle hoop to share the load.

Meanwhile, Bateson had sold XPE 2 to Lancastrian enthusiast Hugh Clifford, who moved it on in turn to David Duffy. He fancied a D-Type, and resold the HWM-Jaguar to John Bailey, in whose hands it returned to racing in May 1980 at Brands Hatch.

Down in Australia, the ex-Gaze VPA 8 had a long and chequered career as already related, while Lex Davison's HWM-Jaguar single-seater had a very exciting time. Early in 1956 Davison bought Gaze's latest Tasman Ferrari 4-cylinder and sold the HWM to Arthur Griffiths, of Queensland, who first drove it at Melbourne's Albert Park on March 11, 1956. The following year saw Griffiths sell it to Arnold Glass for a reputed A£2,750 and he was second in it on his debut at the Bathurst 100 that Easter. On August 11, at Mount Druitt, Glass rolled the car but neither suffered serious damage. Werner Grieve bought it for 1958, modernizing its nose and tail and painting the body white (it had always been red in Australia). Grieve retired from races at Fisherman's Bend and Albert Park, but was eighth in the South Pacific Road Racing Championship at Longford, Tasmania. He then traded the car to Leaton Motors, who sold it to Reg Mulligan in 1959, but he crashed it heavily in his first race on the tricky Bathurst circuit and fitted a new body with a lower tail and shortened nose. He never felt happy in the car thereafter and in September 1960 he advertised it for sale at £1,850. John Hough bought it, and in 1961 his best result was fifth in the NSW Road Racing Championship at Bathurst. He traded the car with Dennis Geary in exchange for a Cooper-Maserati, and Geary fitted a Lotus-based GT hardtop body and was second with it in the 1962 Australian GT Championship. It then passed through several hands until, in 1963, it was acquired by Ralph Hough, father of John,. who had been killed in the Cooper-Maserati at Lowood the previous year. He paid £900 for it and used it in sprints, eventually removing the hardtop and using it as an open roadster. Hough finally sold it to a friend named Keith Moran for a token £250 and he sprinted and hill-climbed it in the mid-'sixties and still owned it in the late-'seventies.

One other Jaguar-engined HWM single-seater was built-up in Britain by Rubery Owen/BRM public relations man A. F. Rivers-Fletcher. He bought the ex-Gaze 1957 supercharged sprint car, chassis 52/112, and fitted a Jaguar Mark VII engine into it to mate with the C-Type gearbox. He sprinted and hill-climbed the car for several years, survived a very nasty accident with it at Prescott in 1960, and sold it in 1964 to the Majors Lambton and Chichester, enthusiastic owners of Wiscombe Park hill-climb in Devon. They sold the car in 1979 to John Harper, complete with an original gear-driven-cam HWM-Alta 2-litre engine which Rivers had removed from it to fit the Jaguar, and it passed from him to Roger Williams, collector head of the Wilhire plant company.

Meanwhile, after his retirement from racing, George Abecassis fancied the idea of a road-going HWM-Jaguar Coupe, and one car was built-up from the remaining pieces at New Zealand Avenue, using a Heath-Dunn true sports car chassis-frame. George asked Frank Feeley, Aston Martin DB2 and DB3S stylist, to refine some of his original sketches and supervise construction of a coupe body by Wakefield's of Wentworth. Finishing touches were applied by HW Motors and Louis Giron helped finalize the mechanicals. A 3.4-litre C-Type engine was fitted, equipped with a D-Type head modified by Weslake and using special camshafts intended to improve mid-range torque. It breathed through three Weber 45DCOE carburettors, used a C-Type manual gearbox and the chassis featured coil-spring IFS and a de Dion rear-end, also on coils. Final-drive was 3.54:1, and as the chassis used-up existing parts it pre-dated disc brakes and retained the Alfin drums of the team cars. Maximum power was reckoned to be around 275bhp and ready for the road this striking two-door coupe with its lifting rear screen weighed just over 26cwt. It was completed in the winter of 1960-61 and featured a hinge-down spare-wheel hatch in the tail, electric window lifts and a one-piece hinged-forward engine cover. It was road-registered GPB 5 and resides today in the Philippe Renault collection in France.

One other true HWM used a Jaguar engine, if briefly, this being the ex-Tom Meyer/Lindsay 1950 team car MXK 727, which used an XK in place of the original 4-cylinder Alta unit very briefly in the early-'sixties. It was sold later to HWM-cum-Alta enthusiast John Michelsen, without the XK engine, and in

February 1979 he sold it to dealer Rod Leach, who had its restoration completed to near-original works team trim.

What appeared to be a much cut-about Heath-Dunn frame of dubious provenance came back from Ireland around 1969-70, passed through Hugh Clifford's hands and apparently fetched-up with Don Pither in the south. He sold it to Peter Valentine in Kent, who in 1979-80 built it up with a 9-inch-longer replica of Terry Grainger's XMC 34 body and an XK engine. The frame is virtually identical to the Dunn sports cars'.

Four Alta-chassised HWM-connected Jaguar 'specials' also appeared, including the original John Heath streamliner of 1948, the long-suffering MPB 77. It had been sold ex-works to Tom Meyer, was raced in the early-'fifties by one F. C. Russell and was later bought for £140 from London dealer Danny Margulies by John Michelsen: 'It had a funny V8 engine installed, a side-valve Ford or Studebaker, perhaps, and a mysterious preselector gearbox which was seized. Somebody had fitted a flat front-end to the body and it was just awful. I tucked it away in my garage for years before finally selling it . . .' The car went to Bill Mackie in the Midlands, who built a new body with an unoriginal headrest faring and fitted a 3.4-litre XK engine. He sold it to Jeremy Broad — it went on to Harper in 1979, and in 1980 was owned by Norbert Pinter in France.

The ex-Phil Scragg GP HW-Alta-Jaguar RPG 418 was much cut about and cannibalized, most of the original frame apparently being rebuilt to GP Alta form, while an entity survived in 1980 with C. J. Ball of Woburn Sands, Bedfordshire, and Scragg's later F2 HWM-Alta-Jaguar SPC 982 passed into the classic car dealers' hands in the 'seventies, being owned and raced by Chris Stewart and in 1980 by Chris Drake.

The last of these 'specials' is the most intriguing of them all, and traces its existence partly to the 'Buster' Baring 1950 production HWM chassis No. 3 and Alta engine FB 100. Baring had sold the car to John Brown of Edinburgh, who had driven it occasionally in minor meetings and on at least one occasion had lent it to Ian Stewart — later the leading Ecurie Ecosse driver. Brown sold it to Ray Fielding, who recalled: 'During my ownership I removed the body and engine and replaced the Alta engine with an Aston Martin unit acquired from Paul Emery in exchange for the Alta, which he used in his Emeryson. Part of the same deal was to acquire an ex-Connaught sports car body, which was then fitted to the HWM chassis. This contraption was sold to Peter Gordon of Aberdeen, who eventually sold it to someone in Ireland, where I believe it is now . . .' (in 1980).

'In the same period I bought from a chap called Vincent in the Wigan/Warrington area the ex-Joe Kelly two-stage blown Formula 1 Alta, minus engine. I fitted it with a Jaguar 3.4 engine and gearbox and from memory I used it once at Prescott before a friend by the name of Nestor Douglas thought it would make a nice road car with the HWM two-seater body in place of the single-seater. So, we altered it again and provided him with what he wanted and transferred his cherished number ND 4040 to the car.'

So what appears to be a third of the 1950 HWM team cars with Jaguar power actually has a GP Alta chassis, and in 1980 it was owned by Nick Jerromes at Tardebigge, in the Midlands, complete with rubber suspension and Joe Kelly 'IRA' (Irish Racing Automobiles) lettering scribed on the instrument glasses. Just to confuse the issue, in the mid-'fifties two Irish enthusiasts named Len Earl and Charlie Norton ran what was said to be 'The ex-Joe Kelly IRA' — this being the two-stage blown GP Alta with the original engine replaced by a 2-litre Bristol six-cylinder — 'now fitted with a 3.4 Jaguar XK engine'. They called it the Jirano — J for Jaguar, IRA, and NO for Norton, and the remains of this car are reckoned to exist elsewhere today. The inter-related stories of the Altas, HWMs and HWM-Jaguars still contain some fascinating mysteries, while at New Zealand Avenue, Walton-on-Thames, HW Motors are alive and prospering with both George Abecassis and Frank Nagel still very active; the old team might have died, but the business which spawned it goes on into the 'eighties . . .

4

The Cooper-Jaguars

While HWM was created in an existing and well-established grade of British motor racing, the Cooper Car Company found its feet in a new-fangled and purely postwar development — that of 500cc motorcycle-engined Formula 3.

Where HWM were to go International, to enjoy brief and trail-blazing success and then stumble and fall, the company run by Charles Cooper and his son John progressed logically and sensibly, developing and enlarging its mid-engined design theme in considerable customer car production runs, while their own works cars eventually won the Formula 1 World Championship titles in both 1959 and 1960.

I have related HWM's story here in some depth because it has become so fogged and obscure by the passage of time, but there is little point in examining Cooper's well-known background in such detail. Charles Cooper had in fact served his motor sporting apprenticeship with Kaye Don between the wars. In 1946 he built his first 500cc cars for his son John and for one of his boyhood friends, Eric Brandon. Improved designs emerged each season thereafter, and Cooper's mid-engined chain-drive racing cars were to dominate this type of racing.

Larger 1,000cc and 1,100cc air-cooled twin-cylinder engines were adopted for occasional Formula B, *Libre* and hill-climb events, and a number of small-engined sports cars also emerged from the Surbiton works. In 1952 the front-engined six-cylinder Cooper-Bristol Formula 2 car made its debut and served as a springboard for Mike Hawthorn's leap into the Ferrari GP team in 1953.

That season saw George Abecassis' HWM 1 emerge, as the Walton concern began to put Oscar Moore's ideas to work internationally, and during that same year an Alta-engined Formula 2 Cooper had been ordered and raced by privateer Peter Neild Whitehead . . .

Peter Whitehead was 39 years old at the time, a very wealthy motor racing enthusiast with extensive interests in farming and the wool trade. He had come to prominence prewar driving his own ERA at venues as far apart as Brooklands in England and Bathurst in Australia, where he travelled often on wool trade missions. Postwar, his green-painted privately-owned Ferraris had raced in Formula A and Formula B events throughout Europe, had won the Czechoslovakian GP at Brno and came within an ace of winning the French GP at Reims-Gueux in 1949. He had shared the victorious C-Type Jaguar with Tony Rolt when they won the 1951 Le Mans 24-Hours, and in so doing had underlined his reputation as a smooth and reliable racing motorist with considerable mechanical sympathy if not enormous technical knowledge. His cars were prepared and maintained by full-time racing mechanics at Motorwork Ltd, his own garage in Chalfont St Peter, Buckinghamshire, while he lived at Carters Hill Farm, Arborfield Cross, near Reading in Berkshire. Late in 1953 he had decided to go sports car racing with a car of his own, and he approached Charles and John Cooper and asked them to build him a lightweight counterpart of the C-Type Jaguars he had been campaigning for the Coventry works team, 'to make better use of the XK engine . . .'

This was a new departure for the Surbiton firm. They had never built anything around such a large and powerful engine as the 3.4-litre six-cylinder Jaguar unit. The Cooper-Bristol F2s of 1952-53 had been their first real foray into the world of front-engine/rear-drive conventional racing cars using water-cooled engines, but John Cooper was particularly enthusiastic about Whitehead's proposition and persuaded his reluctant father to let him go ahead.

He laid down a design scheme and watched over draughtsman Owen 'The Beard' Maddock's shoulder while those ideas were set down to scale on paper. Between them they produced an all-new multi-tubular chassis frame in what were to become the best Cooper traditions, using large-diameter steel tubes with long unsupported and unbraced runs, often including quite sharp curves. One wag believed that Cooper didn't own a straight-edge ruler, and that the closest their draughtsman came was an incomplete set of French curves . . . In fact the tube curves in the new big sports car chassis matched those of the external body panels, and so saved the extra complication and weight of tack-on body brackets and subframing. Cooper and Maddock drew on their recent experience with the multi-tubular Cooper-Bristol Mark II chassis frame which they had produced in some quantity that year.

This prototype Cooper-Jaguar Type 33 (or retrospectively the Cooper-Jaguar Mark I) used a frame welded-up from 1½-inch diameter 14 and 16-gauge steel tube with four main longerons curved into typical Cooper half-ellipses and forming the four angles of a central box-section backbone which was to remain unskinned. Similar-size cross-tubes then curved laterally to extend either side of this structure and form oval bulkhead frames around the front and rear of the cockpit area. The driving position was outrigged far to the car's offside with the seat-back just ahead of the right-rear wheel and the pedals were slung just behind the right-front wheel. The passenger's seat position was similarly 'sidecar' on the nearside.

Since he had moved up a league in terms of both power and torque, John

John Cooper at the wheel of his prototype Cooper-Jaguar, supplied to Peter Whitehead's order and seen here in the Silverstone paddock during practice for the 1954 BRDC International Trophy meeting. The shark-mouth radiator air intake beneath the nose section has already been fitted with draught-includers. John looks concerned, while beyond the rear wing is the bearded figure of Cooper draughtsman Owen Maddock and on his left, in the macintosh, the tall spare figure of David Yorke, Whitehead's team manager, later to lead Vanwall and the Essex Wire and Gulf-JW GT40 and Porsche teams.

John Cooper in Peter Whitehead's Cooper-Jaguar Mark I in a later development stage during the summer of 1954 with a transitional nose air intake and top ducted exit for hot radiator air, pictured outside the Surbiton factory.

Cooper felt that he could not rely on his well-proven all-independent suspension system which used simple lower wishbones to locate the lower-end of the wheel hub-carriers, which were then both sprung and located laterally at their upper extremity by transverse leaf-springs. This layout clearly would not be man enough to accommodate a race-tuned 3.4-litre XK engine, and so John adopted upper and lower wishbones, which relieved the transverse leaf-springs — which he retained fore and aft — from lateral-location duties. Instead, the springs were now mounted between widely-spaced pairs of rollers, the centre portion remaining free and so allowing the springs' entire length to be used for suspension purposes, while any tendency to roll was resisted by the twisting action of the roller anchorages upon the spring, to a greater degree than would apply with a conventional central clamp mounting. Armstrong telescopic dampers were used, and steering was by a Cooper rack-and-pinion assembly. Peg-drive Dunlop perforated-disc 16-inch wheels were attached by three-eared knock-off hub nuts, and carried 6.00 and 6.50-section Dunlop racing tyres front and rear. The wet-sump engine was reckoned to deliver about 225bhp and was mounted well amidships in the chassis in unit with the normal C-Type competition gearbox. A short universally-jointed propeller-shaft drove to an expensive chassis-mounted final-drive unit to which John Cooper had applied quite a lot of thought. He had reasoned that there could be quite a useful market for similar all-independently suspended sports cars and had therefore gone to the expense of designing and having made a special magnesium back-axle casing intended to carry an ENV nosepiece and allow the use of IRS in place of the standard C-Type's rather limiting live axle. Bill Heynes of Jaguar was always one to listen to new ideas, and at that time was toying with IRS designs for his own cars. He subsequently showed interest in the Cooper-ENV final-drive and John remembers that it was partly due to Heynes' interest in this magnesium-cased affair that he helped free the supply of competition XK engines. The new final-drive assembly carried short universally-jointed half-shafts powering the rear wheels.

Another new departure was the use of Dunlop multi-pad disc brakes mounted outboard within the road wheels at front and rear and with Plessey servo pump assistance. At a time when the whole car cost probably £4,000 this brake system alone set Cooper in for around £750. The new car had a wheelbase of 7ft 7in (almost identical to that of the new D-Type then being finalized at Coventry) but its track was wider at 4ft 4in and it was competitively light at around 16½cwt — the D-Type's track measuring 4ft 2in at its widest and the car scaling just on 17cwt.

Cooper split the car's 40-gallon fuel load between a large main tank mounted behind the seats above the final-drive and spare wheel and a subsidiary tank slipped beneath the passenger seat. They then clothed the car in a very unusual Porsche-like body in 18-gauge aluminium sheet, each panel being secured by Dzus fasteners and quickly detachable. The design featured a flat drooping tail and curvaceous aerodynamically clean nose beneath which a shark's mouth intake allowed cooling air to pass through a near-horizontal radiator matrix inside. Various deflector vanes were tacked around the trailing edge of the intake to persuade sufficient airstream to enter it. John hoped that this feature would yield an extra 10-15mph top speed and in 1980 — reminiscing in the office of his large garage business at Ferring, in Sussex — he clearly recalled 'that comical system . . . I tested the car extensively on the Dorking Bypass, but it kept getting hotter and hotter and each time we had to make the radiator bigger and bigger until finally we gave up and mounted it behind a proper hole like everyone else . . .!'

Evidently Charles Cooper regarded his son's enthusiasm for this move into the big sports car class with undisguised suspicion: 'The old man was a good engineer, he'd built up a good business making cars we understood, and he didn't want to see me lose it all by making cars we didn't!'

Whitehead's brand-new Cooper-Jaguar made its debut, unpainted, in the wet Silverstone International Trophy meeting of 1954 at which Abecassis in HWM 1 came home second behind Gonzalez's Ferrari 'four-nine'. At that time most of the original shark-mouth radiator system remained intact, although enormous deflector plates had been added underneath. Whitehead drove with his usual careful aplomb, and perhaps quite a lot of caution in the wet, and brought the untried car home ninth.

Later, with the radiator replaced by a conventional arrangement, the car sprayed green and road-registered UBH 292, Whitehead beat the C-Types of

The Whitehead Cooper-Jaguar Mark I in its final form, though yet to be registered UBH 292. This Geoff Goddard shot shows off the 'sidecar' driving position, conventional nose radiator intake and Dunlop disc wheels with centre-lock fixings.

61

The Bertie Bradnack Cooper-Jaguar, later registered PDH 33 after a Mark VIII Jaguar saloon which the Birmingham industrialist had apparently written-off on the Monte Carlo rally, seen here during the 1955 Goodwood 9-Hours race, driven by Tony Marsh, the hill-climb ace. Compared with the Whitehead prototype car, this production model has a thrust-forward lower lip to the nose intake and a reshaped door line alongside the cockpit. The extra lights were fitted for the night section of the Goodwood race.

Col. Michael Head and Bob Berry to win at Snetterton. By June 6 the car was travelling abroad and heading for Hyéres, on the French Mediterranean coast, ready to be shared in the 24-Hours race there by Whitehead and Duncan Hamilton. In *Touch Wood* Hamilton recalled: 'I flew from London Airport to Marseilles where Peter Whitehead met me in his XK120 fixed-head coupe. Although June had only just begun the heat was intense, and the interior of Peter's car was quite insufferable, so hot indeed that we had to take our shirts off. Fortunately, our hotel in Hyéres was beside the sea and we were soon in the water.

'The Cooper-Jaguar had independent suspension on all four wheels and I was most curious to see how it handled compared with the C- and D-Type Jaguars. Arthur Birks had brought the car down to Hyéres and had lost about a stone in the process; the cabin of his transporter had been even hotter than Peter's XK. Peter drove the Cooper first and then handed it over to me. I liked the car, and after three or four laps, during which I got the feel of things, I began to drive fast.

'I was coming down the backleg of the circuit towards the hairpin and had just changed down into third when I either heard a sound or just sensed that something was wrong. I braked, and to my horror, the pedal went down to the floor and stayed there without in any way retarding the car's progress. I changed into second, then first, but it was no good, I was going too fast to get round the hairpin and I could not go through the barricade because it was lined with children. There was only one thing to do. I whipped the wheel round and spun the car. Round and round it went, finally stopping six feet short of, and broadside on to, the flimsy barricade and the children who stood behind it. Not one of them had moved, they had no time; only when I began to spin did they know that anything was amiss. Two very shaken *gendarmes* helped me push the car off the track while the delighted children gathered round. It was not every day that they could examine a racing car at such close quarters . . .'

Hamilton 'phoned Lofty England in Coventry for spares to repair the car,

62

and they were despatched by air, but sadly the aircraft was delayed and they arrived too late to enable the Cooper-Jaguar to race. Hamilton and Peter Whitehead looked after the pit for Peter's half-brother Graham, who was sharing his Aston Martin DB3 with Pat Griffith. Unfortunately, Griffith went off the road avoiding a back-marker and overturned after striking a concrete kilometre post, suffering severe back injuries.

On June 27, the Cooper was running again in the Oporto Sports Car GP at the northern Portuguese port circuit, where Whitehead lay fourth behind the works Lancia V6s driven furiously by Ascari, Villoresi and Castellotti. When the great Ascari's steering failed, seven laps from the finish, P.N. Whitehead (Cooper-Jaguar) inherited a third-place finish, the car acquiring its first international laurel, although having been twice lapped.

Whitehead brought out UBH 292 twice that August, winning at Snetterton from Michael Head's C-Type and Bob Berry's very well-driven XK120 and winning again in Eire at the Curragh army camp circuit, where he took the Wakefield Trophy after Hamilton's C-Type had lost a 13-second lead due to a retaining nut on the end of a half-shaft splitting and leaving the shaft and wheel retained by nothing more than the brake caliper's clasp. As the car was snaking around so Hamilton slowed, Whitehead forged ahead, and the Cooper won from Joe Kelly's locally-entered C-Type. Another local man, Joe Quinn, unfortunately crashed his special during the race and killed himself, two soldier marshals and a spectator, and the Curragh circuit was not to be used again.

At the second Aintree International meeting on October 1, Whitehead was blown-off easily by Archie Scott-Brown's phenomenal 2-litre Lister-Bristol and a week later, at Snetterton, Peter Walker drove the car in a *Libre* event but could not catch the single-seaters.

The new car's maiden season then closed on a much more serious note as, at the end of October, Whitehead took it to Barcelona for the Spanish Grand Prix meeting on the fast Pedralbes public-road circuit. The Formula 1 race was being supported by the Copa Barcelona for sports cars and in practice Whitehead and UBH 292 were second fastest behind Jean Behra's 3-litre Gordini on pole — although a full 5 seconds behind him . . . In the race Whitehead ran in his usual consistent third place for 22-laps until the XK engine uncharacteristically dropped a valve, and that was that.

Two more Cooper-Jaguar Mark I T33s were built with their peculiar saucepan-lid (hopefully) aerodynamic bodyshells and virtual sidecar driving positions and they were sold to northern enthusiasts Bertie Bradnack and Jack Walton. Eventually they were to be registered PDH 33 and UUG 3, respectively, and both were delivered for the 1955 season.

On April 16, Walton drove his new car on the 2-mile Scottish airfield circuit at Charterhall, west of Berwick, in what was to become for many motor racing fans 'Jim Clark Country' and there he finished third behind Scott-Brown's winning Lister-Bristol and Ninian Sanderson's Ecurie Ecosse C-Type. Poor Walton fell seriously ill soon after and died in Harrogate on February 17 the following year.

Meanwhile, the large and jovial figure of Bertie Bradnack, director of Walsall Pressings in the Midlands, shared his Cooper-Jaguar with hill-climber Tony Marsh in the 1955 Goodwood 9-Hours and they soldiered home in 17th place after a terrible time with brakes which wouldn't respond due to servo failure. The car never showed any sign of being competitive with the HWM-Jaguars, never mind the works cars, whatever their type.

In the meantime, Peter Whitehead had ordered a new and much improved Cooper-Jaguar Mark II or Type 38 from Surbiton, and UBH 292 had been sold to 26-year-old Cyril Wick, sales manager of the family Chrome Alloying Company. He enjoyed a season of considerable success with this car in 1955. On May 21 he was second to Phil Scragg's HWM-Alta-Jaguar — having a rare circuit race — at the first BARC Members' Aintree meeting, but on Whit Monday at Goodwood he lost control and ploughed into the sandbanks at Woodcote Corner. Back at Charterhall, on August 6, the veteran Gillie Tyrer drove Walton's UUG 3 and led the 20-lap sports car race, but only briefly, and at the Brighton Speed Trials, in September, Cyril Wick set the sports car FTD at 25.30 seconds for the standing-start kilometre.

Whitehead's new Mark II had made its debut at the Brussels Motor Show in January, where it was displayed with its aluminium body panels removed to show off 'the works'. The basic design of the chassis, suspension and final-drive arrangements were similar to the Mark I, although they had been simplified and tidied-up in detail, but now the car was powered by a full dry-sump D-Type XK engine rated at the normal 'customer' level of 250bhp, with three Weber carburettors. The four-gallon dry-sump oil tank was mounted on the left side of the engine, which was again mounted well back towards the centre of the chassis and canted 8 degrees from the vertical to allow a lower body profile. The virtual backbone formed by the main chassis longerons still enclosed the four-speed-and-reverse gearbox rather tightly, and although the driver's and passenger's seats were still separated quite widely the driver was moved further inboard than in the Mark I and could now enjoy the comforting feeling that perhaps there was a little more metal between him and that waiting tree or telegraph pole . . . However, the far-back engine mounting had pushed the gearbox well to the rear, leaving the gear-change sprouting up somewhere by the driver's left elbow; he had almost to reach behind himself to use it. Nonetheless, the new Cooper-Jaguar Mark II was a handsome-looking beast by any standards, with a far more conventional-looking bodyshell than the Mark I, something like a cross between the robust bulk of the C-Type and the curvaceous elegance of the D-Type . . .

It appears that this prototype car of Whitehead's was never road-registered, but two more T38 variants were built, the second for young Tommy Sopwith, son of Sir T.O.M. Sopwith of aviation and America's Cup yachting fame, and the third custom-made for Col. Michael Head and completed early in 1956.

Tommy Sopwith, of Compton Manor, Kings Sombourne, Hampshire, was 22 at the time and he was to enter his new car under the team name of Equipe Endeavour in honour of his father's 12-metre racing yacht. The car was sprayed dark blue, road-registered YPK 400, and was originally intended to accept nothing so mundane as a Jaguar XK engine — oh no — it was planned for Turbomeca gas-turbine propulsion!

Sopwith wanted to develop this type of power unit for automotive use through his combined motor-industry (he had been apprenticed to Armstrong-Siddeley) and aviation connections. The Turbomeca was being developed in Britain at the time by Blackburn Aviation and John Cooper tailored YPK 400's chassis specifically to this unit and remembers visits to the turbine works to inspect it. Unfortunately, progress was very slow, too slow for Sopwith's ambitious plans, and he eventually bowed to the near-inevitable and simply dropped-in an XK 3.4-litre unit to go racing now. In fact he drove only briefly before deciding (temporarily) to opt out of circuit racing and concentrate merely on sprints and team management, allowing drivers like Reg Parnell to handle the car in his place.

Peter Whitehead, meanwhile, ran his new Mark II car in the BRDC Silverstone meeting on May 7, 1955, without featuring in the results, and on June 12 the car was fully prepared and ready to tackle the Le Mans 24-Hours driven by Whitehead himself — the 42-year-old former race winner — and by his 33-year-old half-brother Graham Whitehead.

The new car could not be expected to cope with the giants from Mercedes-Benz, Ferrari, Jaguar, Aston Martin and Maserati, but the Whiteheads were a steady and reliable pair, and if the Cooper could hold together they stood a good chance of placing well. Unfortunately, that was just too much to ask, and after surviving three hours — completed respectively in 13th, 16th and 14th places — and escaping involvement in the dreadful accidents that day, the XK engine's oil pressure zeroed during the fourth hour and the car was black-flagged for dropping oil on the course. Obviously the Le Mans authorities were extremely nervous by that time, 90 minutes after the Levegh tragedy in the pit area.

Whitehead was out again in his new car on June 25 in the Oporto Sports Car

GP, where he had finished third in the Mark I the previous season. This time he had another reliable run and came home fourth. In the subsequent Lisbon Sports Car GP on that city's Monsanto circuit the Cooper-Jaguar ran as high as third in quite strong company before being forced to slow and eventually retire with gearbox trouble.

In September the big green Cooper-Jaguar reappeared in Britain for the Aintree International, where Ninian Sanderson was victorious in his Ecurie Ecosse C-Type and Whitehead could place no better than fifth. This must have been a considerable disappointment, for the hybrid car was considerably lighter than the C-Type and should have enjoyed a cornering advantage with its simple but effective independent rear suspension system. It could certainly put its power down on the road quite well, but Whitehead, of course, was a reliable endurance racer rather than a short-circuit sprint-race driver.

On September 17 the RAC Tourist Trophy race was run at Dundrod, in Ulster, and once again the Motorwork of Chalfont-prepared Cooper-Jaguar was presented for the Whitehead half-brothers to share. They could hardly hold a candle to the works Mercedes-Benz, Ferrari, Aston Martin and singleton Jaguar entries, but in the opening stages Peter actually battled wheel-to-wheel with the Ferraris of Castellotti and Maglioli and showed rare 'tiger'. This effort used a lot of fuel and the British car was one of the first to make its scheduled stop, Graham Whitehead taking over. But at the 40-lap mark, soon after Peter had retaken the wheel, the big car's lap times abruptly began to stretch from around 5 minutes 10 seconds to 5:51, then to 7:23, and the car was lurching and snaking around the dauntingly narrow country-road circuit like a drunkard. The unbelievable had happened for a Cooper; the chassis had broken and with one suspension shifting around the Whiteheads were forced to retire having completed 44 of the scheduled 84 laps.

Meanwhile, Whitehead had concluded purchase of a special Tasman Ferrari

Ugliest of them all? Colin Murray's repulsive-looking Cooper-Jaguar, UUG 3, in action at Mallory Park on May 26, 1958. It would appear that this car was totally destroyed sometime in the early-'sixties, while PDH 33 went to the USA and its remains form the car raced in the 'eighties by Ken Rogers.

The ex-Peter Whitehead Cooper-Jaguar Mark I was sold to Cyril Wick and then passed to Dick Steed under the registration UBH 292. Here at Goodwood, on Whit Monday 1956, Steed is driving the car he ran the following year in the Mille Miglia, fitted with a full-width windscreen on that occasion to protect the two-man crew. The side scoop apparently fed cooling air on to the dry-sump oil tank.

from Maranello in partnership with Tony Gaze, who had bought a sister car to take part in a joint Tasman racing tour to New Zealand and Australia early in the new year. Gaze was taking his HWM-Jaguar sports car VPA 8 down-under for the supporting events and Whitehead arranged to do the same with his Cooper-Jaguar, taking his ace mechanic Stan Elsworth along to care for the team cars.

The New Zealand GP, first race of the tour, was held at Ardmore aerodrome outside Auckland on January 7, 1956, and after Reg Parnell had blown the engine of his prototype Aston Martin single-seater DB3S in practice, Peter Whitehead loaned him the Cooper-Jaguar for the GP itself.

Stirling Moss won that race in his private Maserati 250F from Gaze and Whitehead in the Ferraris, while Leslie Marr's XK-engined Connaught streamliner — fresh from England and only uncrated at Wellington docks the previous day — was fourth and Parnell fifth, British drivers finishing 1-2-3-4-5. The supporting Ardmore handicap for sports cars was also won by Moss in a Porsche 550 Spyder as he, Whitehead in the Cooper-Jaguar and Tony Gaze in the HWM-Jaguar all started three laps behind the limit men, and according to contemporary reports had 'over 90 cars to pass to come into the lead'. That aerodrome circuit must have been incredibly crowded, but Moss won as he pleased from Whitehead and Gaze.

Amongst the spectators that day was the experienced Australian driver Stan Jones — father of Formula 1 star Alan Jones — and he arranged immediately to buy the Cooper-Jaguar Mark II from Whitehead and have it shipped to Australia, hopefully in time for him to race in the *Formule Libre* South Pacific Championship 100-Miles event at Gnoo Blas circuit, Orange, NSW, on January 31. He sent an employee to New Zealand to accompany the car in the hope of rushing it through customs on its arrival. The idea worked fine, the car was discharged on the day of the race, but since it was a public holiday it could not be road-registered and therefore could not be driven the 165-miles to the circuit. Jones apparently did not have a fast enough tow car available . . .

Formalities had been completed by February 11, however, when Jones made his debut with the big Cooper at Fisherman's Bend, where he won both the

66

Lucas Trophy and a scratch sports car event before retiring in the important Victorian Trophy race.

On March 10, at Melbourne's Albert Park, the Cooper-Jaguar finished second behind Gaze's HWM-Jaguar in the Argus Cup, but fallen leaves and blowing newspapers blocked the radiator air intake during the Moomba TT and Jones pressed-on while the water and oil temperatures soared and eventually the D-Type engine's bearings failed. Whitehead had foreseen debris obstruction as a problem and Elsworth had fitted a grille over the intake for the New Zealand races, but it had since been removed. For the first time in its life the car was now road-registered, carrying the Victorian plates GLP 333.

Immediately after this Melbourne meeting Jones sold the car to John Aldis of New South Wales, who raced it with little subsequent success. In 1958 it was acquired by Ron Philips, and being properly prepared by Ern Seeliger it placed second in the 1958 Australian TT plus the NSW and Victorian Sports Car Championships and was seventh in that year's Australian Grand Prix. In 1960 Philips drove it home second in the Victorian and third in the New South Wales Sports Car Championships.

John Ampt, later to become a familiar Formula Junior driver in Europe, acquired the old Cooper from Philips during 1960, and on September 18 that year he was second in the Victorian Sports Car Championship race. The old car raced on with considerable and continuing success through the early-'sixties and in 1963 it was acquired by Norm Crowfoot, who retired it from the fray after 1964.

There were many rumours amongst enthusiasts concerning the old car's whereabouts in later years until, in 1977, one Dave Robinson discovered that Crowfoot still owned it and it was stored at Lilydale, outside Melbourne. Robinson arranged to buy the car and in the late-'seventies it was being slowly restored to its former glory . . . a genuine ex-Le Mans car.

While Whitehead and Gaze were embarking on their New Zealand trip in December, 1955, Bertie Bradnack's Cooper-Jaguar Mark I PDH 33 had been advertised for sale, offering '3,442cc, Dunlop discs, Webers, four spare wheels and tyres, 3.2, 3.6 and 4.5 diffs . . .' The car was acquired by M.L.Mees, who

The Le Mans Cooper-Jaguar Mark II — Peter Whitehead's unregistered second car — seen here at Dundrod during the 1955 RAC Tourist Trophy meeting, charging hard until sidelined by a most uncharacteristic chassis breakage.

ran it against the new Cooper-Jaguar Mark II of Col. Michael Head and John Ogier's Tojeiro-Jaguar at the Whit Saturday 1956 Snetterton meeting and subsequently won the *Formule Libre* race and was second in the sports car event at Mallory on Whit Monday.

Michael Head's brand-new and unpainted Cooper-Jaguar Mark II was road-registered HOT 95 and had been placed second behind Abecassis' XPE 2 in the March BARC Members' meeting at Goodwood and Head then won at the Sussex circuit in April, beating an Aston Martin DB3S.

The Colonel was military attaché to the British embassy in Stockholm and his road-equipped Cooper was to cover many hundreds of miles in Scandinavia and around Britain and Europe, as had his C-Type Jaguar and competition XK120 before it. He was Irish-born, 44 years old and is remembered as an always charming and courteously dignified military gentleman. On one occasion in Sweden, when witnessing an example of Peter Collins' often hooligan behaviour, his reserve crumpled, and he snorted to everyone in earshot: 'If it were my department, I would confiscate that fellow's passport . . .'. The Colonel died of secondary cancer in 1970. His son, Patrick Head, became a very fine racing engineer and was responsible for the design of the Saudia-Williams Formula 1 cars which were driven by Stan Jones' son Alan to dominate the closing Grand Prix races of the 1979 World Championship season and into 1980.

John Bolster road-tested Head's HOT 95 for *Autosport* magazine and found that with Goodwood short-circuit ratios fitted it could reach 137mph at 6,000rpm in top gear, and would cover the standing-start quarter-mile in 14.8 seconds (0.2 second quicker than the heavier prototype HWM 1).

Cyril Wick had sold his ex-Whitehead 1954 Mark I prototype car UBH 292 to businessman and property-owner Dick Steed. At 25 he seemed a very promising young driver when he acquired the car, and at the Whit Monday Goodwood meeting he brought it home fifth behind Jack Fairman's HWM-Jaguar and ahead of Col. Head's HOT 95. The August Shelsley Walsh hill-climb saw Ken Wharton driving PDH 33 — it would appear — and it passed subsequently to B.C. 'Bernie' Ecclestone of 300 Broadway, Bexleyheath in Kent. The diminutive trained chemist-turned-successful motorcycle dealer and 500cc F3 racing driver had a handsome new body fitted which looked much more like a Whitehead-type Mark II than the original Mark I saucepan lid. Stuart Lewis-Evans, a close neighbour and friend of Ecclestone's, drove the car at Crystal Palace in London, lapping that tight and tricky circuit in a competitive 65 seconds, and it was later advertised for sale in *Autosport* beneath a handsomely retouched photograph. The price of £1,650 was billed as 'less than half its original cost . . .'. While owned by Ecclestone the car had also been driven by dealer Peter Jopp at Brands Hatch, but its subsequent history seems quite thoroughly obscure . . .

The ex-Sopwith Equipe Endeavour car had been sold to 26-year-old David Shale, a Northampton businessman, in time for the 1957 season and he campaigned it in numerous Club and National events, painted red and retaining its registration number YPK 400. For 1958 he sold it to Peter Mould.

The ex-Jack Walton car, UUG 3 — by far the ugliest of them all with a tall full-width road-going windscreen — had been sold after his sad death to Colin Murray for the 1957 season. At 34 he was a garage proprietor from Fleetwood, Lancashire, whose main business involved supplying Pontiac cars to US servicemen based in Britain.

Dick Steed, meanwhile, had been adventurous enough to enter his ex-Whitehead/Wick Mark I in the 1957 Mille Miglia — the race which was the last of this noble series as it was marred by the deaths of 'Fon' de Portago, his passenger Ed Nelson and over a dozen spectators when their works Ferrari burst a tyre at high speed. Steed shared UBH 292 with John Hall. They ran with the start number 520, set off at that time in the morning after Ron Flockhart's Ecosse D-Type with only 10 more runners on their tail, but were out of it before the Rome control; few were surprised at their failure, but it had been a brave attempt . . .

The Whitehead Cooper-Jaguar Mark II in the rain at Aintree on September 3, 1955, when it finished disappointingly far back in a good-quality field. The Mark II's body was much more conventional and attractive than the Mark I's saucepan-lid form, and although still pushed sideways by the backbone members of the multi-tubular chassis, the driving position was better protected.

Michael Head continued his winning ways with HOT 95 into 1957, notably at Goodwood, where the Whitsun meeting saw him beat Peter Blond's Aston Martin DB3S in the 100Kms feature event, and in September he shared fastest lap in the meeting's closing handicap race with Henry Taylor's D-Type. Thereupon the Colonel decided to hang up his crash hat and retire from competition, the pretty white-painted Cooper-Jaguar being advertised for sale from his home 'Woodhambury', in Woodham Lane, Woking, Surrey.

The age of the Cooper-Jaguar, which to be honest had not amounted to very much, was now well and truly over, although Peter Mould raced his ex-Sopwith/Shale car YPK 400 with considerable verve in 1958, finishing hard on the heels of Jimmy Clark's Border Reivers team D-Type on one occasion. This car was by far the widest raced and most successful of its type — the Whitehead Mark II's Australian career excepted — and in later years it was raced in minor English club events by Hugh Chamberlain.

He eventually sold it to the trading partnership of John Harper and John McCartney-Filgate for the princely sum of £837 10s. Harper recalls: 'We met in a pub and haggled all night before finally doing the deal, and then Filgate and I climbed straight into the car and drove it home . . . It was an absolute cracker, a good dry-sump engine, D-Type gearbox, the lot. We did many a race with it . . .'

When the Harper/Filgate partnership split up the latter took YPK 400 with him and sold it eventually to Anthony Hutton, who also raced it extensively in historic sports car events before moving it on to Parisian Jaguar collector and dental surgeon Dr Philippe Renault. He has a very soft spot for the car, chassis number CJ/3/55, as has Harper, who has serviced it for him from time to time. 'I had it here in England for some work and then took it down to a race at Nogaro, deep in the south of France, on the road and it went like a dream, cruising around 130mph most of the time without a sign of any trouble. It was beautiful on all those old French roads, down through Bordeaux, you know. In fact we finally got caught in the rush-hour traffic in Bordeaux and it boiled, so I had to leave it treble-parked and go and sit in a roadside cafe watching the jam

The ex-Whitehead Le Mans Cooper-Jaguar Mark II racing down-under, where Stan Jones, racing driver father of Alan Jones, today's leading Formula 1 driver, achieved considerable success with it. Here, number 42 shows the way to D-Types as well as Lotus, Maserati and Aston Martin opposition.

try to sort itself out . . .'. John has had considerable exposure to all our Jaguar-engined sports-racing cars and recalls the Coopers as 'much under-rated, they incline towards terrible understeer, but were super tools, even the Mark I felt a really solid, stable, dependable kind of racing car . . .'

Colonel Head's HOT 95 was raced by David Chamberlain in British club events in 1959 before falling into neglect and disrepair in the early-'sixties. The pile of bits were owned by Michael Wright, who ran a garage at Much Wenlock, in Shropshire, at the time, and he eventually sold them to former Lister-Jaguar racing mechanic John Pearson 'for a hundred quid'. They passed through Harper's hands to Gordon Chapman, in Birmingham, who rebuilt the old car very nicely indeed and it later passed to Renault and on to Roland Urbain in France. The old car is chassis CJ/2/55, despite its later completion than the Sopwith machine.

Of the Mark I cars the only firm storyline is that of UBH 292, the original prototype ex-Whitehead/Wick/Steed car, which John Harper bought in the mid-'sixties from one Henry Pearson in Huddersfield, for £475. Unfortunately, John virtually destroyed the car in an ugly accident at Castle Combe in 1966: 'I'd been working on it way into the night before the race and like a twit rushed off to Castle Combe and just forgot that Quarry Corner comes after that blind brow. It was plain driver error, I came over the brow flat and there was no way I could get round. The car spun and went into the bank absolutely backwards at about 80mph. I was lucky it was a Cooper really, because it had an absolutely flat bulkhead behind the cockpit extending from the floor right up into that headrest, and when we hit the bank I hit that bulkhead so hard I cracked six vertebrae *and* my sternum and bruised my lungs so I thought I'd given up breathing for good and all. If it hadn't been for the support given by that panel I think I'd have been a goner for sure . . .'

He subsequently sold the remains of the car to an enthusiast at Keele, up on the M6, some three years after the accident, and eventually bought them back — virtually untouched — from a third party in London in the mid-'seventies. He then had the car laboriously rebuilt to its original form and it now resides in France with Michel Gosset.

John recalls that one of the other two Mark Is was reportedly destroyed in an accident at Brands Hatch very early in the 'sixties, and he certainly bought a batch of mechanical parts apparently from a defunct Cooper-Jaguar at one time, '. . . including multiple-pad calipers and four D-Type rear discs, which is what the Cooper-Jags used all round . . .'.

The other car, either the smart ex-Ecclestone PDH 33 (which seems very likely) or the ex-Murray UUG 3 (which, since he dealt with US servicemen, must also be a candidate) was bought back from the USA by classic car dealer Chris Renwick for Bill Meredith-Owens, founder of the Stratford Motor Museum, and he in turn sold it to Ken Rogers of Radlett, Hertfordshire, who began racing it in historic sports car events in 1979 after a long Harper rebuild.

In this way five of the six Cooper-Jaguars live on into the 'eighties . . .

5

The Tojeiro-Jaguars

Both the Tojeiro and Lister marques originated in the Cambridge area. John Tojeiro and Brian Lister knew each other quite well and both began racing at an amateur level around 1950. John 'Toj' — moustached, bespectacled, 'a quiet, nice, man' — drove an MG TA fitted with a lightweight body, while the burly Brian Lister handled a Morgan 4/4 before progressing to a Cooper-MG.

Tojeiro was unhappy with his production MG's handling, and so set-to with a minimum of equipment to build a new all-independently suspended chassis to accommodate the car's well-developed engine. Tojeiro had quite a wide-ranging engineering background. Prewar he had been apprenticed to a company producing refuse trucks, and the war years found him serving primarily on aero-engine maintenance with the Fleet Air Arm training scheme in Canada.

He now set himself up working single-handed in a tiny shed behind the Hardwick Arms Garage at Arrington, a tiny village near Little Gransden, which is just outside Cambridge. At one time the Hardwick Arms pub there was run by Eric Winterbottom, a great racing enthusiast and amateur driver who was to lose his life after crashing a Frazer Nash in the 1951 RAC TT at Dundrod. (By that time he had become mine host of the Albert Hotel in Kingston, a popular meeting place for members of the burgeoning 500 Club.)

At the time Tojeiro went to work on his special chassis, the Hardwick Arms Garage was being run by Vin Davidson, and while John essentially worked alone, 'we put our heads together on some aspects of the design . . .'.

The prototype Tojeiro chassis emerged as a robust twin-tube frame with main longerons in 16-gauge T45 steel linked by a central cross-member of similar material. Each end of the H thus formed was then closed by 12-gauge sheet-steel boxes which carried Cooper-like independent suspension using high-mounted transverse leaf-springs to locate the top of each hub-carrier, while its foot was carried by the apex of 3/8-inch T45 tube wishbones. Tojeiro adopted Morris hubs, Morris Minor rack-and-pinion steering, an ENV hypoid back-axle assembly, Girling dampers and Turner cast-alloy wheels.

Before it could be completed Chris Threlfall had appeared on the scene asking if he could buy it. After this sale a number of other customers were expected and Tojeiro decided to offer alternative sizes of Alfin-drummed hydraulic brakes for subsequent frames, dependent upon what engine the customer intended to use.

His little shed at Arrington became something of a minor Mecca for East Anglian racing enthusiasts, and several of them placed orders. Threlfall's original prototype ran a Wolseley-MG engine with considerable success, and proved capable of what was at that time 'phenomenally good cornering'. Tojeiro No. 2 was completed for Brian Lister with a twin-cylinder JAP air-

All the Tojeiro-Jaguars were very attractive sports-racing cars at some stage during their long careers. Here at Goodwood, late in 1957, Jack Brabham handles the second of the John Ogier-prompted cars, the wire-wheeled lengthened-wheelbase variant which Ogier himself wrote-off at Stapleford soon after.

cooled engine. Chris Sears commissioned a Lea-Francis-powered model and Lionel Leonard bought another frame as the basis of his Leonard-MG. Sears' 1½-litre 'Leaf' engine had worked wonders in his chain-gang 'Nash, but for John Tojeiro the breakthrough was heralded by the appearance on his doorstep of Cliff Davis . . .

Frederick Clifford Davis was a rakish, heavily-moustached 35-year-old motor trader from London's Shepherds Bush. He inclined to lurid extroversion, favoured loud checked shirts and was a tigerish club racing driver. He had used a Lionel Leonard-produced 1,500cc Cooper-MG during 1952 and became a consistent 1,500cc class winner in it. The car's polished aluminium bodyshell followed the lines of the contemporary Pininfarina-styled Ferrari 166/212 Barchetta, and David had it road-registered JOY 500. Now he had been impressed by the handling of Threlfall's Tojeiro and since he wanted an additional car to attack the hitherto dominant Frazer Nash Le Mans Replicas in the 2-litre class, he commissioned John 'Toj' to build him a suitable machine for 1953 — using the Bristol six-cylinder engine. The new car was completed around one of the successful twin-tube, all-independently suspended chassis frames, and was fitted with a polished aluminium body similar to JOY 500's. Davis registered it LOY 500 and instantly became the scourge of British 2-litre class racing, consistently out-performing cars of much larger capacity and more thoroughbred pedigree along the way . . . Everyone sat up and took note of John Tojeiro's engineering and while he claimed that credit should go to the driver, Cliff Davis believed the car 'wasn't half bad . . .'.

The Hurlock family, owners of AC at Thames Ditton, were certainly impressed, and they bought manufacturing rights to the twin-tube design from Tojeiro and it formed the basis of their AC Ace sports roadster which was released (Barchetta copy body style and all) at the 1953 Earls Court Motor Show, showing just how quickly some branches of the motor industry could operate in those days . . .

Cliff Davis raced LOY 500 into 1954 with continuing success, and that season saw John Fiander and bearded Allan Moore both making their names in British club racing with Tojeiro cars. In 1955 Percy Crabbe joined them and

Tojeiro was building de Dion rear-suspended cars and finding considerable custom for his very limited production. Vin Davidson had gone to AC when they had acquired rights to the original twin-tube chassis design, and in 1954 John had formed Tojeiro Automotive Developments Ltd to continue production and to handle contract development work for other concerns.

Meanwhile, John Ogier, a prosperous Essex farmer who raced and sprinted a black Jaguar XK120 for fun, decided that a lighter and better-handling chassis could make the most of his reliable and powerful XK engine. He discussed the idea with John Tojeiro and readily agreed to sponsor construction of a lightweight D-Type-eater.

By this time, TAD were established in a small light-engineering works at Barkway, Royston, in Hertfordshire and the first Ogier-sponsored Tojeiro-Jaguar was completed there in time for the late-season races of 1956. John Toj was building his cars virtually as a two-man band with Bernard Pitt, 'who was my employee, but we worked so closely and so long together that the relationship was virtually that of two friends with a shared enthusiasm . . .'. Tojeiro had designed a multi-tubular spaceframe chassis with coil-and-wishbone front suspension and a coil-sprung de Dion rear-end located by parallel radius-rods and a bronze central slide block. 'That chassis which we used for the first Jaguar car was intended originally for a six-cylinder Bristol engine. I had wanted to build a more advanced and rigid frame, even though AC were happy for me to continue with the twin-tube type, and when John Ogier came along we decided to put the XK engine into this new spaceframe'.

In fact two similar Bristol-engined spaceframe cars were completed, one selling to Percy Crabbe and the other to popular A.P.O. 'Bert' Rogers, who christened his 'SunPat Special'. Tragically, he lost control of it on the first lap of the 1956 Easter Monday Goodwood sports car race and was killed as it overturned at Lavant Corner. John Tojeiro was deeply shocked, for this was one of those silly fatal accidents in which the car was barely damaged, and it was in fact sold and continued its racing career.

Ogier's Tojeiro-Jaguar was completed with the compact — in retrospect alarmingly short — wheelbase of 7ft 3in and a track of 4ft 2in. Tojeiro did all the tube-fitting and joint-welding himself and initially an XK engine of about 200bhp in C-Type tune was fitted, but then quickly replaced by a full 250bhp 3.4 wet-sump unit with D-Type '35/40' cylinder-head. In this trim the car was described as the Tojeiro-Jaguar Mark II. A four-speed Moss gearbox drove to the chassis-mounted Salisbury ZF limited-slip final-drive, and rear disc brakes were mounted inboard on the drive-shafts. They lacked Jaguar's own optional servo-assistance. Tojeiro looked at the contemporary D-Type and Aston Martin body shapes and styled an aluminium shell which was made for him by the Panelcraft company in London which had bodied Cliff Davis' cars. The end result looked reminiscent of a lean and hungry D-Type, with a streamlined headrest, ballooning front fenders and a rather too large elliptical radiator air intake in the nose. The new car was registered 7 GNO.

He conducted the initial testing and rapidly decided that over 200bhp in an aerodynamic sports car weighing only 15½cwt was a world away from his relatively vintage XK120 production sports car. In 1976, when Ogier was Chairman of Ogle Design and unfortunately about to lose his life in a road accident, he told me: 'I was just getting too old for that type of car, and Dick Protheroe was another Jaguar enthusiast who could drive quicker than I could. We called him in . . .'.

Wing-Commander Protheroe was 34, a V-bomber force pilot from Seaford, Sussex, and a man with several seasons' experience of tuning and racing XKs. John Ogier raced his XK120 quite extensively early in the 1956 season while the new car was being completed by Tojeiro and Bernard Pitt, and he gave it its debut race in a Jaguar handicap at Snetterton on May 19, 1956, finishing unplaced.

Ogier was out in the car again at Snetterton on June 17 for the Eastern Counties 100, running fourth behind Cunningham-Reid's leading HWM-Jaguar, Leston's 1,500cc Cooper-Climax and Peter Blond's D-Type in the early

Ivor Bueb in the third Tojeiro-Jaguar, the car loaned to Ecurie Ecosse from new, on its debut in the sports car race supporting the 1958 British GP at Silverstone. This very pretty car used a body styled by artist Cavendish Morton and produced by Mo Gomm of Byfleet. It was relatively successful. Ecosse practised this car for the TT that year, but withdrew it due to ill-handling and tyres fouling the bodywork.

stages, only for a steering arm to snap on the 13th of the scheduled 37 laps. He brought the big car safely to a halt, but began to feel convinced that he really was too old for this sort of thing . . .

Dick Protheroe appeared behind the wheel of 7 GNO in the 25-lap unlimited-capacity sports car race supporting the British GP at Silverstone, on July 14. He qualified eighth fastest for the Le Mans-type start with a lap time of 1 minute 55 seconds compared with Moss' pole time of 1 minute 47 seconds with a works Maserati 300S. Protheroe took to the car like a duck to water, revelling in its phenomenal straight-line speed. Tojeiro had, however, lost the excellent cornering characteristics of his earlier designs, and although Protheroe initially lay fifth behind Hamilton's famous D-Type OKV 1, and by the third lap had passed the former Jaguar works driver, he could not hold off Cunningham-Reid's HWM and after spinning wildly at Abbey Curve — which is always a nasty experience — he surrendered his fourth place on lap nine. Rain began to fall, Cunningham-Reid slithered off course, and the Tojeiro-Jaguar slammed by to regain the fourth place in which it finished, though lapped by Moss' victorious Maserati and Salvadori's second-placed Aston Martin.

Ogier reappeared in the car for the Vanwall Trophy Snetterton meeting later that month, finishing second to Salvadori's Gilby Engineering-entered 2-litre Maserati in the *Formule Libre* 10-lapper. On August Bank Holiday the Tojeiro ran at Crystal Palace, where the intrepid Dick Protheroe displaced Tom Kyffin's Aston Martin DB3S at the end of the opening lap and led the remaining six to win comfortably at an average speed of 68.68mph on this most unsuitable circuit for such a demanding motor car. He also set fastest lap in 1 minute 10.4 seconds, 71.08mph. Cliff Allison won the August Trophy feature race in his Lotus 11, clipping 1.6 seconds off the Tojeiro's best time, with a 2-litre-smaller engine.

On August 18, 7 GNO raced in the torrential downpour which characterized the *Daily Herald* International at Oulton Park. Protheroe qualified 12th on row four of the starting grid with a best practice lap of 2 minutes 08.4 seconds against Moss' Aston Martin pole time of 1 minute 58.2 seconds. Such a disparity looks laughable by modern standards, but fields were much more varied 25 years ago; that's just the way motor racing was 'in the good old days' . . . The race was best forgotten by the Tojeiro crew, for Protheroe ran unhappily in seventh place among 17 starters and failed to finish as the car continually threatened to get away from him.

The following week saw Ogier taking it into a straight-line event for which it was eminently well-suited, setting BTD at the Ramsgate Speed Trials in 14.59 seconds. He retired the car from the big September National at Goodwood, soon after winning the unlimited sports car class in the Brighton Speed Trials from the HWM-Jaguars of Cunningham-Reid and Abecassis. His 25.36 seconds for the kilometre compared with their figures of 25.91 and 26.62 seconds, respectively.

John Bolster was loaned the car at the end of the year for an *Autosport* road and track test. He collected it from London's Steering Wheel Club and found it very tractable in city traffic. But John 'Toj' had warned him that he was unhappy with the car's roadholding and Bolster quickly discovered that its rear suspension was apparently going solid under cornering load and hiking the tail out into violent oversteer. Evidently the de Dion tube had insufficient travel and was hitting its stops. Neither did the brakes inspire much confidence, for without a servo they were 'lacking that reserve of power which one appreciates on a very fast car . . .'.

Clearly the leap from 2-litre cars and less to a full-blooded 3½ had not come easily, and in retrospect John Tojeiro was to observe: 'I suppose at that time we were really trying to do too much with too little, just the two of us actually building the cars and trying to be jacks of all trades and ending-up by being masters of none. But when the cars were well-maintained and properly set-up for good drivers they did have their share of success'.

Ron Flockhart in the fourth Tojeiro-Jaguar, the machine specially commissioned by Ecurie Ecosse and purpose-built for the Le Mans 24-Hours race in 1959. Here, locking over for Tertre Rouge corner on the Sarthe circuit, Flockhart leads Graham Hill's Porsche, a DB and a Porsche, but RSF 301 was already in overheating trouble with Ecosse's 'square' 3-litre XK engine.

75

There was no doubting the original 7 GNO's straight-line speed. At Silverstone in the GP meeting it had been timed at 127.66mph on the Hangar Straight, that figure only being bettered once, by Moss's Maserati, at 128.22mph. Bolster's timing revealed it as the fastest car tested to that time by *Autosport,* touching 50mph in first, 84mph in second, 122mph in third and a massively exciting 152.5mph in top. While a Ferrari Daytona of the 1970s could accelerate from 0-60mph in a mere 5.4 seconds the 'Toj' could equal those figures in 1956. One hundred miles per hour came up in 12.6 seconds from rest and 120mph in only 16.8! But to preserve a sense of perspective, remember the American *Road & Track* magazine's timing of a 1974 Ferrari 312B3 F1 car at just 2.4 seconds 0-60mph . . .

Early in 1957, the prototype Tojeiro-Jaguar was advertised for sale at £2,500, but Ogier subsequently changed his mind and retained it to join a new model as a works team for the new year. John 'Toj' and Ogier formed a new Tojeiro Car Company to enter the cars, while Ogier became a shareholder and director of Tojeiro Automotive Developments Ltd, but still bought and paid for the cars built for him, just as a regular customer. The Tojeiro-Jaguars were to be prepared at Rob Walker's Pippbrook Garage in Dorking, Surrey, by former Connaught chief mechanic Les Wilson. Meanwhile, Richard Utley was instrumental in establishing a production line of 1,100cc Climax-engined Tojeiro sports cars at Mo Gomm's Byfleet premises — better-known for their competition car bodybuilding. Tojeiro was also involved in the Britannia quality GT car projected by Acland Geddes, while a small GT of his own was also mooted, using a body styled by the artist Cavendish Morton. 'We were really trying to do too much with too little . . .' indeed.

The new 1957 Tojeiro-Jaguar had a 3-inch-longer wheelbase and 1¼-inch-wider track than the prototype 7 GNO in a move to tame its twitchy manners. It was clothed in a neater body styled by Cavvy Morton — the middle-aged artist from Eye, in Suffolk, who had been introduced to Tojeiro by Ogier. Morton was a great racing enthusiast who regularly marshalled at Snetterton. As John Toj recalled: 'He would produce a perspective drawing of a car looking the way he wanted, then skilfully colour and air-brush it until it looked gorgeous. Then we would present the painting to Maurice Gomm and say "build us a body like that" . . . there were never any formal working drawings . . .'.

The new car was wire-wheeled in place of the perforated-alloy Dunlops on the prototype, and its de Dion tube was located laterally by a Watt linkage in

The third Tojeiro-Jaguar — recorded by chief mechanic Stan Sproat as 'T7' — on the starting grid for its last Ecurie Ecosse outing, driven by Flockhart in the 1959 British GP supporting race at Aintree. During the event it collided with team-mate Peter Blond's crashing Lister-Jaguar!

place of the original's sliding-block system. Ogier entered the original 7 GNO at Snetterton on March 30, 1957, where Protheroe faced Scott-Brown's sensational new Lister-Jaguar, which had set a startling pace in practice. The RAF man was second quickest alongside the new green-and-yellow car, with Peter Whitehead's Aston Martin DB3S and Peter Blond's D-Type outside him. But when the Lister defaulted on the opening lap Protheroe was not to be headed, and unleashing the Tojeiro down the straights and making best use of its experimental front anti-roll bar around the corners he completed the 15-laps at an average of 85.11mph to win handsomely, since Henry Taylor's D-Type had lost its brakes and spun Whitehead out of contention into a telegraph pole. Scott-Brown got going again near the end, and lapped at 88.69mph . . . In a Jaguar handicap to close the meeting John Ogier drove his formerly trusty XK120, which disgraced itself by setting fire to its cardboard radiator blanking!

On April 6, the British Empire Trophy races at Oulton Park saw Protheroe suffering big-end failure in practice, which entailed all-night work to fit a new crankshaft at Jaguar's Coventry works. The car was whisked back to the Cheshire circuit in time for Protheroe to start from the fifth row of the grid. He started gently in homage to the engine's new bearings, but established himself in fifth place ahead of Duncan Hamilton's borrowed HWM-Jaguar and held it off by striding away down the straights and blocking, apparently unintentionally, through the turns.

The car was placed seventh, driven again by Protheroe, at the Easter Monday Goodwood meeting, and in May, for the Stanley Sears Trophy meeting at Snetterton, the Wing-Commander settled for a safe second place behind the meteoric Scott-Brown's Lister-Jaguar.

Jack Brabham was brought in for a fee to drive the new car at Crystal Palace on Whit Monday, June 10, finishing fourth in the 10-lap unlimited sports car race behind the inevitable Scott-Brown, Graham Whitehead's Aston Martin and Les Leston's HWM-Jaguar.

For the sports car race supporting the British GP at Aintree, on July 20, Jack Brabham drove the wire-wheeled car again and Dick Steed the prototype, but both became ignominious early retirements. Ogier then gave a drive to Peter Gammon in the 1956 car alongside Steed's wire-wheeled 1957 model in the Vanwall Trophy at Snetterton the following week. Scott-Brown's Lister again won as he pleased, while Gammon and Steed swopped places all round the course with Blond's HWM and the Whitehead brothers. Gammon finally

The fourth Tojeiro-Jaguar, the ex-Le Mans car, seen with Jimmy Clark at the wheel, locking-over for Goodwood's Lavant Corner during the 1959 RAC Tourist Trophy — its last race — with Flockhart on its quarter in the team-mate D-Type. The bonnet-top bulge was to accommodate the taller 3-litre XK engine, reduced from 3.4-litres as opposed to the original unit which was enlarged from 2.4-litres.

At Goodwood, Jimmy Clark said the 'Toj' felt as though it was up on tip-toe going round Madgwick Corner. This fine Graham Gauld shot shows just how right he was.

finished second and, after taking some time to come to grips with the wire-wheeled car, Steed was fourth.

Peter Gammon, at that time the 24-year-old director of a family drapery business in Guildford, Surrey, has the most extraordinary — not to say extra-sensory — recollections of his Tojeiro-Jaguar days. After selling the Guildford business he spent some time as a marketing director for Debenham's before going off on his own as a discount trader. He told me: 'I was sufficiently mediumistic to be put into a trance by the spirit of Mike Hawthorn while I was racing. He took over my body on at least two occasions and controlled moments I had which could have been really nasty accidents . . .

'On one occasion I was testing the 'Toj' at Snetterton in the wet. The mechanic said "Warm it up", so I went out and Dickie Stoop was there in his 2-litre Frazer Nash. I took off to leave him but hit a ripple on the road and the car went up in the air with the rear wheels spinning and I went off at around 150mph. The car went about 200 yards across the grass at the hairpin and came to a halt inches from an electric fence. I just couldn't restart the engine. I found the ignition switches turned off, turned them on and it still wouldn't restart. Then I traced the wires to the master-switch under the driver's seat, and found that it had been turned off. It was the spirit of Mike Hawthorn who had saved me, he'd thrown me across into the passenger's seat when the car first took off so I wouldn't be hurt if it rolled over . . .

'I knew it was Hawthorn because I had been to a spiritualist meeting in Godalming and the medium had said there was a pilot or a farmer wanting to come through. He had a helmet and goggles and was talking about bran and hatcheries, and Druids! I realized who that was, and when the medium said he won't go away, and then said he's just said something I won't repeat in church on a Sunday, I knew for sure it was Mike . . .'.

This is an incredible story — largely because Gammon drove the Tojeiro in 1957 when Mike was very much alive and about to win the 1958 Drivers' World Championship. But quite apart from his muddled spiritualist memory, Peter Gammon recalled how the big 'Toj' could handle superbly once tied down front and rear by anti-roll bars, but in the wet was so light that it suffered runaway wheelspin. 'It was a very evenly-balanced car, perhaps too much so, because it would break away all four and slide broadside rather than spin . . . I remember making people jump over the pit counter at Snetterton when I booted it out of Coram Curve. In retrospect it's cheering that I was four seconds a lap quicker than Graham Hill in testing! I liked John Ogier, too, he was a good man . . .'.

Graham drove in the August Bank Holiday Brands Hatch meeting where the dark blue Tojeiro had a rare scrap with Blond's HWM and Graham Whitehead's DB3S to finish second, behind the inevitable Scott-Brown and the Lister . . .

September 1 saw driving rain drench the Snetterton autumn meeting, where Gammon's 7 GNO led Steed home fourth in appalling conditions behind —

guess who — Scott-Brown, Peter Whitehead and Devonian Tom Kyffin in his brand-new Lister-Jaguar HCH 736, of which we shall hear much more.

That year's Suez crisis had forced the BRDC to hold over their International Trophy meeting until September 14, and the sports car race there was again a disaster for Tojeiro as Graham Hill spun the latest car at Abbey Curve — shades of Protheroe! — and came into the pits rather pale and drawn to retire with suspension problems. Soon after his defection, Peter Gammon coasted in without oil pressure and also retired.

Two weeks later, on October 13, John Ogier took the wire-wheeled car — carrying the 7 GNO registration — out for a day's sport in his local hill-climb at Stapleford in Essex. To quote one report: 'Coming up the lower slopes at fantastic speed he got out of control on a right-hand bend and slid among the straw bales; the car flicked over and threw him some 20 feet into the air and 100 feet up the course to land heavily on the tarmac. It seemed to the horrified crowd that he must have suffered very severe injuries, but to everybody's untold relief the doctor's preliminary examination revealed nothing worse than a broken leg and possible knee-joint injuries. His crash helmet undoubtedly saved his life and being thrown out of the car was providential as it was little more than a mangled wreck . . . .'.

At about this time the original 1956 prototype 7 GNO had been sold to Frank Cantwell in New Zealand, and early in 1958 he scored immediate success only to lose control of the short-wheelbase, still very demanding motor car at Teretonga in February and somersault it. Cantwell was thrown out to find a soft landing, picked himself up and walked away with little worse than a shaking, but the 'Toj' burned briefly and was severely battered, though subsequently it was rebuilt. It passed through various New Zealand hands and was raced well

TT pitstop for the Ecosse Tojeiro-Jaguar, with Clark leaping clear as 'Wilkie' Wilkinson grabs for the fuel filler on the tail. Masten Gregory is about to take over for his — and the car's — final stint.

79

into the 'sixties, one owner being Ian Green of Christchurch, in whose hands the old car was road-registered DA5335 and painted with contrasting front wing patches and pin-striping around the panels. In 1980 the car was on its way back to Britain after 22 years down-under.

So for 1958 John Tojeiro had lost both his Jaguar-powered sports-racing cars. John Ogier's recovery from his injuries was quite a lengthy business, and as the Barkway works was deeply involved in development of a Bristol-engined Le Mans Special for the Hurlocks at AC (which won its 2-litre class in the 24-Hours race) there seemed little prospect of the programme continuing.

However, David Murray of Ecurie Ecosse had fully appreciated that his trusty D-Type Jaguars were going to become obsolescent in 1958, and he hedged his bets by ordering a Lister-Jaguar and arranging with Ogier and Tojeiro to take a new Tojeiro-Jaguar on loan to modernize his team. He had to wait until the British GP meeting at Silverstone on July 19 to debut the latest Tojeiro-Jaguar, a new 7 GNO fitted with an extraordinarily pretty Cavendish Morton-styled Gomm-built aluminium bodyshell and a D-Type dry-sump inclined XK engine.

In practice Masten Gregory had crashed the Ecosse Lister very heavily, and Murray pinned Ecurie Ecosse's hopes upon Innes Ireland in one of their ageing D-Types and Ivor Bueb in the new Tojeiro.

'Ivor the Driver' was a burly and popular 35-year-old, a director of Turk's Motors in North Place, Cheltenham, and of course a Le Mans winner in Jaguar Ds. He could, and would, drive anything, anywhere, and he took a fourth place from Bruce Halford's Lister in the race and held it to the finish, coming home behind Moss' victorious Lister-Jaguar and the Lotuses of Roy Salvadori and Cliff Allison. The latter's 1,500cc Lotus actually equalled Moss' fastest race lap in the works 3.8-litre Lister-Jaguar . . . the writing was clearly on the wall for the big cars . . .

The new 'Toj' was entered for the RAC Tourist Trophy at Goodwood in September, only to be withdrawn, and the veteran Le Mans-winning D-Type RSF 302 replaced it as Ecosse's sole representative.

Running 'Wilkie' Wilkinson's Ecurie Ecosse 3-litre XK engine enlarged from a 2.4-litre base, the 1958 Tojeiro reappeared at Goodwood on Easter Monday, March 30, 1959, entrusted to the steady Jock Lawrence, who duly placed it fifth in the 21-lap sports car race behind Bueb and Blond in Listers, Graham Whitehead's Aston Martin and Salvadori's Cooper-Maserati. Ecosse ran the Tojeiro at Oulton Park for the British Empire Trophy race and at Aintree, on April 18, for the International 200 meeting, Ron Flockhart drove the 'Toj' with a 3.8-litre engine installed. He inherited fourth place behind Salvadori's Cooper-Maserati, Graham Hill's works Lotus and his teammate Gregory in the Ecosse Lister. Flockhart drove the car again in the Silverstone May meeting, again inheriting fourth place behind Salvadori, with Moss' Aston Martin

Opposite-lock and bags of power as Gregory powers RSF 301 out of the Goodwood chicane during the TT, showing-off the car's beautifully-made Williams & Pritchard body — and the effect of high-octane fuel on temporarily painted-on race numbers!

second and Ivor Bueb's works Lister third.

Ecurie Ecosse journeyed back to Goodwood for the National meeting on Whit Monday, May 18, and there Flockhart in the 'Toj' and Jimmy Clark in the Border Reivers team's 3.4-litre Lister-Jaguar (old HCH 736) drew away from the rest of the field, Flockhart leading until he was overhauled by his young compatriot on lap 8 of the scheduled 21. But two laps later the Lister-Jaguar was slowing, the Reivers men having apparently neglected to fill its fuel tank, and Flockhart went on to win as he pleased at an average of 88.51mph. Fastest lap, however, went to John Bekaert's Lister-Jaguar, third overall, who went round at 90.19mph.

The serious business of the ADAC 1,000 Kms World Championship race at the Nurburgring followed on June 7, and there David Murray entered the Tojeiro and teamed Flockhart and Lawrence together to drive it. Ron took the start, saw teammate Gregory crash the Lister after six laps and then went off himself while dodging a backmarker. The 'Toj' was quite heavily damaged and out of the race.

Meanwhile, David Murray had commissioned Tojeiro to build him a brand-new Jaguar-powered car specifically for the 1959 Le Mans race. It was a straightforward customer deal between Tojeiro Automotive Developments Ltd and Ecurie Ecosse, and the car was completed at Barkway and fitted with a handsome aluminium bodyshell by Williams & Pritchard of Edmonton, London. It had a neat nose, D-Type-like headrest and a vestigial tailfin, and in search of maximum speed along the Mulsanne Straight, John Tojeiro faired-in its wheels. The car was to use one of 'Wilkie's 'square' 86mm x 86mm 3-litre XK engines running on Weber carburettors. The wheelbase was announced as 7ft 5½in and the track at 4ft 2½in front and 4ft 3½in rear. The new car was tested unpainted, and carefully prepared by Wilkinson's Ecosse crew. John Tojeiro recalls: 'That 1959 car was really nice-looking when first completed with what were — by the standards of the time — really good wind-cheating lines. But during testing they decided it needed improved airflow to cool the brakes and more air for the radiator, and I suppose 'Wilkie', being a practical rather than theoretical kind of chap, didn't like the wheel enclosure because it could slow down their pit stops, and so they cut it all about. I have a photograph of it at Le Mans with Ron Flockhart driving and in the background

'Dear Prudential . . .' The end of the fourth Tojeiro-Jaguar's career — lying against the Woodcote Corner bank at Goodwood after Masten Gregory's sensational catapult accident during the TT. He was flung out and landed on the far side of the bank, breaking a leg and a shoulder. The debris was unusable and the major part was scrapped.

Forza Coundley! John Coundley enjoying a brief break in filming of **The Green Helmet,** *high in the Welsh mountains early in 1960, the ex-Ecosse third Tojeiro-Jaguar being disguised for the Mille Miglia-based scenario as a Maserati, with the trident badge in the radiator air intake and a 5.05am start-time race number. Note the Italianate film extras. A D-Type is in the background.*

is one of the big Lister-Jaguars — I have to say that the Lister is better-looking'.

As prepared for Le Mans the new 'Toj' scaled around 17cwt dry, which was rather on the heavy side, and this latest — and last — Tojeiro-Jaguar was to head the Le Mans start line-up wearing Ecosse's former D-Type and Lister-Jaguar registration RSF 301. In later years the same number was applied to the Hon. Richard Wrottesley's ex-Border Reivers Lister . . . it did the rounds.

Ron Flockhart shared the car with Jock Lawrence at Le Mans, and while it was running well it lay as high as fourth completing the sixth hour's racing, and was never lower than seventh until its engine began to go off tune after 11 reliable hours. It had begun to leak water, and did so inconveniently soon after a pit stop so that the regulations forbade the adding of coolant for many laps to come. As 'Wilkie' Wilkinson remembered: 'It was a shame, really, it was going like a train until it began to leak, then eventually it just steamed-up and blew a core plug straight out. That was the finish . . .'

But Ecurie Ecosse Chief Mechanic at that time, Stan Sproat, recalled: 'The compression on that engine was far too high. When we bench-tested it on our bus garage dyno it was blowing out water. 'Wilkie' insisted it would be O.K. but it couldn't last. After it ran out of water they just drove it into the ground — its insides just melted, the head distorted, the pistons fused, the bottom-end seized . . . it was the worst-damaged engine I ever saw. Nothing was salvaged as I recall.'

After Le Mans the car was modified with a large power bulge on the bonnet to give space for a tall-block (reduced 3.4-litre) engine and in this form the car was taken to Goodwood for the RAC Tourist Trophy on September 5.

In the meantime, the first Ecosse Tojeiro-Jaguar, 7 GNO, had been repaired after its Nurburgring accident and Flockhart drove it in the British GP meeting at Aintree on July 18. Peter Blond was out in the Ecosse Lister-Jaguar and it turned out to be 'just one of those races'.

Incidents began the moment the flag fell as Moss' Cooper Monaco stalled on the line and was restarted by the Hon. Edward Greenall's Lotus shunting it hard in the tail. Ending the first lap Graham Hill's Lotus led by 4 seconds from Brabham's Cooper Monaco, Blond was fifth and Flockhart was sixth in the 'Toj'. Blond got by Halford's works Lister for fourth and then the skies darkened and heavy rain washed across the course. The small cars began to skate ahead of the heavy metal and on lap 15, with only two to run, Peter Blond spun the Ecosse Lister in the fast esses at Melling Crossing, cannoned into the straw bales and flipped back into Flockhart's path with the Tojeiro, which hit it hard. Neither driver was hurt, but shunting both cars was becoming an expensive habit . . .

The slightly revised Le Mans car, RSF 301, was to be shared by Masten Gregory and the fast-rising Scots star Jimmy Clark at Goodwood. Jimmy later told the story like this: 'In 1959 there was still keen rivalry between Ecurie Ecosse and the Reivers and therefore it seemed to be inborn with me that being a Reivers man I should never drive for the opposition. David had actually promised me a drive for some time, and during the summer of 1959 the opportunity arose. As the Reivers had not entered, he invited me to share their Tojeiro-Jaguar with Masten Gregory in the TT . . . This was a very important motor race that year for this race was virtually to decide the destiny of the World Sports Car Championship . . .

'Here I was in a highly competitive car with a really top-line driver in direct competition with the might of the Ferrari works team, the Porsche team and of course the Astons . . . any confidence I had was strained to the limit. At the same time I had this tremendous respect for Masten who, I considered, was a really great driver. The Tojeiro we drove was a long ugly-looking car and it didn't handle nearly as well as our own Reivers car (the Lister). Somehow it seemed to get up on tip-toe going through Madgwick and it was decidedly light to handle in places. It was quite twitchy through the chicane, too, and both Masten and I were having a great time sliding it round the chicane on opposite lock.

'It was a beautifully sunny day at Goodwood . . . for me the race was a turning point. Every driver goes through a number of turning points in his career, I feel, for each driver builds up images within himself. Once he has

The 'Toj' rigged as a camera car during filming of **The Green Helmet** *spinning sequences at Silverstone; John Coundley is in the driving seat with Chuck Vetter, the film's producer, by his side. The multi-tubular chassis frame is visible in the engine bay with the XK engine's exhaust manifolding wrapping over it.*

cracked one image he invents another and so progresses onwards and upwards. My particular image was Masten. During the race I found myself lapping the Tojeiro as quickly as Masten could, and in the race I realized that I might seriously compete with the idols of my schooldays. Now this may sound strange to many people, but it had a profound effect on me. I began to enjoy the race and was quite well placed . . . seventh overall actually . . . when Masten buried the 'Toj' in the bank at Woodcote Corner, completely writing off the car. Masten had arrived at the corner with steering trouble at around 90mph and just could not get through. He hit the bank so hard that the car jack-knifed and folded. Luckily Masten had started to climb out of the car before it hit the bank, and he flew through the air and almost into the crowd. He escaped with a broken shoulder, but certainly wouldn't have had an earthly chance if he had stayed in the car . . .'.

David Murray returned Ecosse's other Tojeiro-Jaguar, the 1958 car 7 GNO, to John Ogier and he brought in South African newcomer Tony Maggs to drive it, for a rental fee, at the final Silverstone meetiing of the year, on October 3, where Peter Mould's 3-litre Lister-Jaguar, YOB 575, led until the last lap of a short scratch event for unlimited sports-racers. Then Maggs and the Tojeiro 'came up with a tremendous rush, cut inside the Lister, slid right across the track on to the grass and tore past the line along the outfield . . . the judges were kind, and decided that he had, in fact, reached the end of the race but at precisely the same moment as had Peter Mould . . . official result, a dead-heat.'

At Goodwood, on September 26, Maggs was handicapped out of a Brooklands Memorial Trophy qualifying event in the big 'Toj', but set fastest lap at 84.54mph. That winter Maggs took the ageing car back home with Ogier's blessing, and campaigned it in the infant Springbok series, winning his share in a successful programme. The car returned to England to compete in some early-season 1960 events, without notable success. It appeared then in the hands of amateur driver John Coundley, who had just landed a lucrative contract to provide sports-racing cars and stunt driving for MGM's film of Jon Cleary's novel *The Green Helmet,* based upon a Mille Miglia scenario and starring Bill Travers and Sydney James.

Coundley helped MGM special-effects crews build Dexion slotted-rail frames outrigged on both ends of the Toj to carry cameras for some spectacular spinning sequences at Silverstone, and John subsequently slammed the car off the road on the Llanberis Pass, crashing through straw bales to simulate a Mille Miglia excursion. He recalled the car as 'frightening — not a pleasant thing to drive compared to the Listers which we were using at the same time . . . I was quite pleased to sell it . . .'

The car found new owners in the Lewis brothers. It was now a very rare bird, with only the rebuilt 1956 prototype 7 GNO surviving far away in New Zealand. David Lewis and his wife Vivienne used it mainly for sprints and hill-climbs, and in 1961 Mrs Lewis won her class with it in the Brighton Speed Trials. The car was well-used, covering a considerable road mileage, and in 1963, while trying to repeat her Brighton success, Mrs Lewis tragically lost control at the end of Madeira Drive and the Tojeiro-Jaguar smashed through railings to burn out in a (thankfully closed) children's playground. Mrs Lewis lost her life in this ugly accident and the car's sorry remains were bought by Paul Emery and languished behind his garage into the 'seventies, when they were acquired by Gil Dickson of Guildford, Surrey, who had been acquiring various Tojeiro bits and pieces for some time. Mo Gomm at Old Woking was commissioned to build a new body for the ex-Lewis/Coundley/Ogier-Ecosse 1958 car, and into the 'eighties the project was approaching completion . . .

One other XK120-engined Tojeiro special emerged from St. Helier, Jersey, in the mid-'seventies. It wore a D-Type-like bodyshell and was based on a very early twin-tube frame, apparently originally Lea-Francis-powered; the ex-Chris Sears car? It was owned by Anthony Taylor, of Autotune, Blackburn.

The Tojeiro-Jaguars had won themselves quite a reputation as daunting cars to drive, but they were undoubtedly quick, and one of their number was amongst the prettiest of 'fifties sports-racing cars.

6

The Lister-Jaguars

Amongst all the Jaguar-powered sports-racing cars built outside the Coventry works the Listers were, quite simply, the best. They were the most numerous and the most successful. That probably came as a surprise to anybody who believed what was written about their manufacturer at the time — lines like 'The Listers are built in a small works in Cambridge chiefly occupied by the fabrication of wrought-iron gates and railings for colleges and ancestral homes . . .'. Journalists tend to latch on to the faintly bizarre, and here they did the old-established family firm of George Lister & Sons Ltd much less than justice. In fact the company's modest factory — tucked amongst a row of residential Victorian villas in Abbey Road, Cambridge — housed a diverse engineering business rich in specialist skills. Decorative wrought ironwork was just one — sports-racing car production had become another.

Brian Lister, grandson of the company founder, was responsible for the cars which carried the family name. George Lister, Charles Flatters and Harry Branch had formed a partnership in 1890, setting-up their general engineering, blacksmith and wrought-ironwork shop in Abbey Road. As his partners retired and his sons Alfred and Horace joined the business so it became 'Geo. Lister & Sons' in 1919. Horace became sole proprietor in 1930 after the early death of his brother Alfred and then his father — George Lister himself. Horace's sons Raymond and Brian subsequently became directors, acceding to joint Managing Directorship in 1954 upon their parents' retirement. Twenty-six long years later, in 1980, Geo. Lister & Sons Ltd is still a thriving business, with Brian and Raymond Lister at its head.

In the 'twenties, Alfred Lister had briefly added the words 'and Automobile Engineers' to the company title. He was interested in motor cars and spent some time in Paris at the Renault factory, but upon his death the motor car interest had petered-out, temporarily . . .

Brian Lister, born in July 1926, followed his engineering apprenticeship with two years in the RAF, during which his own interest in automotive engineering continued to grow. In the 'forties he was a confirmed jazz fan, playing drums and vibraphone in his spare time in bands around the Cambridge area. As a member of Ken Stevens' *Downbeats Band* he twice reached the South-East Britain Finals of the National *Melody Maker* Championships — on one occasion at the Hammersmith Palais being voted S.E. Britain's outstanding drummer. In various groups he played alongside reed men like Bruce Turner — later with Humphrey Lyttleton — Percy Seeby, Peter Coe — later with Georgie Fane — and Lennie Bush, who became Britain's top bass player.

In 1948, Brian Lister — still in the RAF — began driving in competition with a Morgan 4/4. He progressed rapidly and built himself a Cooper-MG sports car. He had some help in its assembly from a like-minded Lister apprentice

Beginnings. Brian Lister, at the wheel of his fearsome Asteroid Tojeiro-JAP, taking-off in a sprint start against Don Moore's MG. With Archie Scott-Brown's driving skill they would form a fearsomely effective sports car racing combination.

named Edwin Barton and known — inevitably, from the popular radio show of the time — as 'Dick'. When John Tojeiro asked the company to fabricate some parts for his new cars Brian was intrigued, and from this relationship emerged his raucous Asteroid Tojeiro-JAP.

Motor Sport described this car at the May 17, 1952, Goodwood meeting: 'Exciting object in the paddock was B. Lister's Tojeiro-JAP, the sort of thing we have all wanted to build at some time or other — a V-twin air-cooled JAP engine with hairpin valve springs, twin Amal carburettors and twin BTH magnetos set GN-wise in a Cooper-based chassis. Alas, it did not circulate . . .'.

John Tojeiro's chassis was not Cooper-based, but KER 694, as Brian road-registered his new special, was a most exciting device once persuaded to run properly. Its Robin Jackson-tuned JAP engine drove the rear wheels through a Jowett Jupiter gearbox. 'It had phenomenal power-to-weight ratio and although it would vibrate the fillings out of your teeth it was very, very quick. I called it the Asteroid from my interest in astronomy, but when somebody suggested it would be more apt to call it the Haemorrhoid I dropped the name altogether!'

Later that season Brian 'decided I had too much imagination to make a proper racing driver, although I enjoyed driving very much' and he let a fellow Cambridge clubman take the Tojeiro's wheel. His name was William Archibald Scott-Brown — he was to become great.

Born in Paisley, Scotland, on May 13, 1927, Archie was 10 months younger than Brian Lister. He worked as a salesman for Dobie's 4-Square tobacco, he loved cars, he raced his own MG TD and he could drive like the wind.

The trio behind the Lister cars was completed by Don Moore, a mutual friend of Brian and Archie's, who ran a motor repair business in the University city. Both Lister and Scott-Brown were customers of Don's, who prepared engines for them: 'Archie and myself ran MGs and Brian a Cooper-MG before that Tojeiro-JAP. My car was a prewar P-Type. I pruned its weight down to around 9cwt and won probably 40-50 awards over a period of years. Archie drove his TD with great success, and then Brian came out with the JAP. It was a pig of an engine to work on, but it delivered tremendous torque and when Archie got his hands on it — well, it went like a rocket.'

Archie repeatedly lapped every other 1,100cc sports car at club venues across the country, but in 1953 Brian realized it was a wasted opportunity to be racing a car made by somebody else. 'We should be promoting our own company's engineering skills. I took the idea to my father, who was understandably dubious about it, but I finally persuaded him to set aside £1,500 of company money to finance a car of our own. I was given six months to get it running and to produce some success, so I had a close look at what was around and what was successful, and started from there.'

From the outset the intention was to sell replicas of the new car should its prototype prove successful. The 'Toj'-JAP had done well, like the Cooper-MG before it, 'which I had sold blown-up in the Silverstone paddock to Jack and Peter Reece' and which Jock Lawrence later drove with distinction in Scotland. The 'Toj' also went north of the border, to Peter Hughes, Technical Editor of *Top Gear* magazine and a great friend of Scott-Brown's. Brian Lister then sat down with a clean sheet of paper, and began the design and construction of his first sports-racing car, intended to carry one of Don Moore's MG XPAG-series four-cylinder engines.

The completed prototype was announced in the March 5, 1954, issue of *Autosport* magazine, the club racers' indispensible weekly. It was described as follows by John Aley:

'Although the new Lister chassis follows contemporary thought in broad outline, it has many interesting features built into its 7ft 6in wheelbase. The frame is made from 3in alloy steel tubing with two longitudinal members splayed out in the centre to provide a very low seating position, and anchorage for a full-width body. Cross-members are of similar material, and at both ends of the frame there are fabricated uprights to act as mountings for the suspension and, at the rear, to carry the differential.

'Suspension is looked after at the front by equal-length wishbones with long, threaded kingpins and helical springs enclosing direct-acting strut-type shock absorbers. The rear-end is de Dion, the main tube being located at each end by twin parallel radius arms and centrally by a sliding block assembly. Steering is by rack-and-pinion.

'Girling brakes, two leading shoe at the front, operate in Al-fin drums; the rear pair are set inboard, close to the Salisbury differential unit. MG, Bristol or

The original Lister chassis frame, as photographed for the company's first brochure, showing the kite-planform layout, front cross-member-mounted steering rack and rearward-raked 'sardine tin' rear spring pillars. De Dion rear suspension is located by twin radius-rods and a central sliding block, while the rear brakes are inboard-mounted. The pedal system, with master-cylinders beneath, was quite quickly superseded by a system in which the cylinders were pull-rod actuated and mounted in the midships cross-member for extra rigidity.

other power units to choice will be fitted, and pressed-steel wheels with 5.00 x 16in tyres or centre-lock Dunlop wire wheels mounting 5.50 x 16in tyres are optional . . .'.

The Salisbury hypoid final-drive offered a choice of three ratios, 3.73, 4.1 or 4.56:1, while the drum brakes were available in 9in diameter x 1¼in wide or 11in diameter x 1¾in wide — two-leading-shoe fronts and single-leading-shoe at the rear, the system including twin master-cylinders. Front and rear tracks were both 4ft 1¾in.

Brian designed a simple all-enveloping bodyshell unlike the spartan cycle-wing affair used on his Tojeiro. It was made for him by Wakefields of Byfleet, in Surrey, and sprayed bright mid-green. Brian hoped this shade would look less dull than the dark British Racing Green accepted by tradition, but the car still looked too sombre for his taste. He had just seen a racing stripe worn by one car in the Shell film of the Mille Miglia. In discussion with Scott-Brown and fellow club driver Dickie Stoop they decided a lengthwise yellow stripe would contrast nicely against the green. The effect was immediately pleasing — so much so that in July 1963 it was adopted by Team Lotus! Archie liked it enough to have his road-going Ford Zephyr and his crash helmet later sprayed to match.

Brian toyed with distinctive designs for a marque badge, finally adopting something like a cross between the Manx coat of arms and the Mercedes-Benz star, with three radiating arms looking rather like scimitars but unintentionally so; they were actually just a pure geometrical form. The words 'Lister — Cambridge' did the rest. The earliest badges were copper, the later ones enamelled green and yellow.

The car was tested minus body at Snetterton, where Archie had a fraught moment when a half-shaft seized at the hub and spun him harmlessly to rest. Once the bodyshell was delivered and fitted Brian registered the new car MER 303 — Dick Barton recalling Brian's story at the time: 'They said what number would you like and I said 303 — it'll go like a rifle bullet'.

Archie gave the new car its racing debut at Snetterton on April 3, 1954. In its first five-lapper for 1,500cc sports cars the 1,467cc Lister-MG won by 56 seconds from none other than Don Moore in his lightweight 939cc MG P-Type! In a 1,500cc handicap later that afternoon Archie beat Don again, by 16.2secs after overcoming a 45-second handicap off the line. Don Moore: 'I started entering my car where I knew Archie wasn't . . .'

The next day saw Archie running in a sprint at Weathersfield USAFB, but MER 303 misbehaved with fuel starvation; he was third in class. Now the big-time beckoned, and a week later, on April 10, Brian entered the Lister-MG for the British Empire Trophy race at Oulton Park. The diminutive Scott-Brown was to drive and in practice he stunned many observers by qualifying equal third in his class. But on the Friday morning both Brian and Archie were shattered as the Stewards announced he was considered unfit to drive 'owing to a disability'.

Archie Scott-Brown had been born with a malformed right arm and no proper hand, having merely a vestigial stump of a forearm with a partial palm and thumb giving a little grip. His shoulders were broad and his trunk was normal; at the dinner table he sat as tall as most men, but his legs were short. He stood barely five feet, but all who knew him recall Archie as a giant among men. He was an always friendly and cheerful extrovert without the brash irresponsibility so often connected with Mike Hawthorn or Peter Collins — two other extrovert drivers of the time. During all my researches for this story I found nobody with a bad word for him, which is rare in motor racing. He is remembered as 'a man totally without enemies' and 'the nicest bloke I ever met'. One engaging trait was his complete acceptance of what some considered to be his deformity. Cyril Posthumus, at that time Assistant Editor of *Autosport,* recalled meeting him for the first time '. . . and being a bit taken aback when he reached out with his left hand to shake hands, so I reached out automatically with my left hand to suit and it was only afterwards that I noticed he didn't have a proper right hand at all, and he'd made the first move to save *me* any embarrassment, not himself . . .'. John Bolster vividly remembered a later incident: 'Driving down to Goodwood an XK120 came blinding past and shot in front of me and I was just thinking what's this bloody fool up to when the driver waved this stump out of the window and shot away into the distance. It was Archie, he'd recognized me as he came by and waggled his arm to show me who it was. It never embarrassed him, you see, he was perfectly adjusted to the way he'd been made . . .'

Brian Lister: 'Nature always compensates, and in Archie's case I believe it

Happy days. Archie in the 1954 2-litre Lister-Bristol, the first MVE 303, sporting its broad yellow stripe and posed against the Fordson Lister transporter of the day. Brian Lister had managed to sell three of the advertising spaces on each side of the van, 'but we had to paint our own name in the fourth'.

had given him the most incredible sense of balance which is what made him such a superb driver. One of my most vivid memories is of Archie backing my Tojeiro-JAP out of its garage into the sunlight and spinning the steering wheel so fast its spokes were a blur. You couldn't possibly do that with a proper hand. He always used to say that he'd won all the slow-bicycling races at school — just by balancing there completely stationary while everybody else fell off. I never doubted it.'

Now the RAC Stewards at Oulton Park had exploded a bombshell in Archie's life, for this could be the end of all his racing ambitions. At 7 o'clock that evening, in the Blossoms Hotel at nearby Chester, Desmond Scannell of the BRDC introduced Ken Wharton — out of a drive that weekend — to Brian Lister. Wharton agreed to drive the new car on the morrow, started on the back row of the grid and ran fourth in the 1,500cc class heat, only for the engine's oil pressure to fall on the penultimate lap. He made a brief stop, was sent on and finished eighth, just failing to qualify for the final.

Gregor Grant, Editor of *Autosport,* was a Scot never averse to promoting drivers from his home country. He pressed for the restoration of Archie's licence and found a powerful ally in Earl Howe, who had been deeply impressed by Scott-Brown's driving in practice at Oulton and was shocked to discover later that it was the same young man who had been declared unfit to drive. Former 'Bentley Boy' Dr. J.D. Benjafield was another influential ally.

In the short term Brian had to find a new man, and motorcyclist Johnny Lockett and Mike Hawthorn's friend Don Beauman both tested MER 303. Then Archie suggested local man Jack Sears, who at 24 was building himself a reputation for fast and fearless driving, and Brian entrusted the car to him at Brands Hatch, Prescott and Snetterton, where Sears took a first and second on Whit-Saturday, June 5. On June 7, Whit-Monday, Scott-Brown returned to the fray, having confirmed his unrestricted driving ability to the satisfaction of an RAC medical board. Even so the Dundrod TT organizers would never accept his entry.

He drove MER 303 in the Half-Litre Club Brands Hatch meeting and was second to Peter Gammon's Lotus-MG in a hard-fought 20-lapper. Archie and

Moss in the neutral-steering Lister-Bristol during his one-off drive in the September Goodwood meeting in 1955. Testing this car later at Goodwood Alan Brown cut clean across the infield at Woodcote Corner on one fast lap. Asked later what had gone wrong he replied that he had flicked the steering as he would to make his Cooper-Bristol slide and the Lister had just turned sharp right! The Cambridge chassis handled and cornered rather well.

the Lister notched three more second places at Oulton Park and Snetterton, twice behind Gammon and once behind Colin Chapman in the invincible lightweight Lotus 6. The heavier Lister was clearly underpowered and Brian had persuaded Horace Lister to release more funds for a second car, a 2-litre using a six-cylinder Bristol engine tuned by Don Moore.

Just like the original MG-powered car, chassis BHL 1, this prototype Lister-Bristol chassis BHL 2 was based on the kite-planform twin-tube chassis with 3in diameter T45 drawn seamless steel main members. The larger 11in diameter Al-fin drum brakes were adopted, again inboard on the final-drive cheeks at the rear, while MG front suspension uprights were carried on equal-length wishbones. The de Dion rear-end employed twin radius-rods either side and vertical centre-slide location. Woodhead-Monroe telescopic dampers within co-axial coil-springs provided the suspension medium. Wheelbase was again 7ft 6in, front track 4ft 2½in and rear track 4ft 2in, and the all-up weight with a Wakefield body almost identical to the Lister-MG's was only 12cwt. Don Moore prepared the 1,971cc cross-pushrod ohv Bristol engine to deliver around 142bhp at 5,750rpm. Brian registered his new 2-litre model MVE 303 — a number to become legendary in Lister lore — and while the MG-powered car had been painted with a very narrow central yellow band along its mid-green coachwork the new Bristol-engined device carried a much more extravagant stripe more than a foot wide.

The new car made its debut at Silverstone in the British Grand Prix meeting on July 17 when two sports car races — one for 1500s, the other unlimited but including a 2-litre class — were to support the Formula 1 event. The meeting was wet, but it was televised . . .

Both sports car races used Le Mans-type starts and despite his size Archie was incredibly quick on his feet and led the small-capacity getaway, only to be hammered back into seventh place by the Lotus-MGs, a Porsche and two Connaught-engined cars before the finish.

Later in the day Archie got his own back for Lister. MVE 303 was the star of the unlimited sports car race as it soared through the field to win its class by miles and finish fifth amongst the heavy metal. Back home in Cambridge, Horace Lister watched the race spellbound on television, and Brian recalls 'he simply could not credit the number of times the company name was mentioned. From that moment on he thoroughly approved of my building racing cars'.

Initial approaches had been made to Brian from would-be customers. The latter half of that 1954 season yielded no less than five more firsts and nine second places, Archie driving every time apart from the September 25 International, when Stirling Moss handled MVE 303. Gregor Grant wrote: 'Archie was curious to see whether he (Moss) could put it across Salvadori in the Syd Greene Maserati, the Lister's rival this season in sports car events . . .

Production Lister-Bristol. The 1955 Thom Lucas-styled aerodynamic bodyshell shown off by Allan Moore at the wheel of Ormsby Issard-Davies' VPP 9 at the 1955 BRDC International Trophy meeting at Silverstone on May 7. This car was subsequently part-exchanged with Lister for the Lister-Maserati MER 303, and the frame went on to John Horridge to replace his written-off original in 1957, the Lister works retaining the original registration number for their 1958 works 'Knobbly'.

Brian looking hard-worked as Archie hops into the Lister-Maserati, MER 303, while practising a Le Mans-type start for the 1956 Silverstone May meeting. Archie was very fond of a story about his missing hand; a marshal fainted clean away as he crawled out from under his inverted sports car after a minor Silverstone shunt, convinced that Archie had lost his hand in the accident and not knowing he had been born without it.

Salvadori drove like one possessed, with the Lister ever in his mirror. Moss got everything possible out of the green and yellow car . . . The last lap was a thriller, Moss came round Woodcote right on Salvadori's tail, made a last-minute bid out of the chicane, but failed by three-fifths of a second to catch the expertly-driven Italian car . . . To Moss went fastest lap at 83.72mph'.

John Bolster tested the new car, finding it reasonably quiet, smooth and tractable, showing enormous cornering power by the standards of its time without noticeable body roll. It rode well, its springs not hard, although firmly-damped, and the body design gave stability unaffected by crosswinds. He timed its acceleration from 0-60mph in 7.6secs and 0-100mph in only 21.8secs, while maximum speed without a tonneau over the passenger's seat registered 129mph. Overall fuel consumption was around 22mpg. Brian had accepted several orders for a customer version, normally to be supplied as a bare chassis with the customer supplying his own engine and body. Had the new cars been sold complete heavy purchase tax would apply. Chassis price 'less engine, tyres and tubes' was £465, plus tax.

The Lister-Bristols raced very successfully through 1955, when Scott-Brown continued to drive the slab-bodied prototype machine MVE 303, the trouble-shooting MG-powered MER 303 having been dismantled and set aside. Customer cars were sold to Ormsby Issard-Davies for Dunstable-based Allan Moore (chassis BHL 3, Buckinghamshire-registered VPP9 in April 1955); to East Anglian enthusiast Bill Black for Jack Sears (chassis BHL 4, Essex-registered 4 CNO in March 1955); to Derby garage owner John Green for David Hampshire (BHL 5, later to carry the Derby registration HCH 736 issued in June); to Ken Eaton (thought to have been BHL 6, Warwickshire-registered SNX 590 in May); and to the Six-Mile Stable for Noel Cunningham-Reid (number uncertain, but presumably either BHL 7 or 8, Cambridgeshire-registered NVE 732 in March 1955). Another frame — Brian actually believes it to have been the first order received — went to the Murkett Bros of Cambridge, the Rover and Jaguar dealers who fitted a Rover engine to promote their dealership.

The customer cars for Issard-Davies, Sears and Green carried very futuristic-

Brian Lister was very enthusiastic about 1,500cc Formula 2 racing when the new class took effect in 1957, but his enthusiasm was not shared by his number-one driver. Here we see Brian with the prototype 1957 car outside the Abbey Road works in Cambridge and the much more sophisticated 1958 car. Contrary to contemporary reports, the original machine never ran under its own power and was scrapped, while the offset-transmission 1958 car raced only in private hands after Lister set it aside. As seen in the 1957 car, Brian and Colin Chapman dreamed-up 'Chapman strut' rear suspension almost simultaneously.

looking aerodynamic bodyshells designed by Bristolian Thom Lucas, a Cambridge graduate engineer. Lucas based his design upon wind-tunnel test models and adopted in-curled tailfins and bulged aerodynamic eyebrows above the wheelarches. The cars were constructed in a corner of the Abbey Road works and marketed through Brian Lister (Light Engineering) Ltd: 'I realized that if we went about this business the wrong way we could bring down the parent company we had set out to promote, so we made a clear division between their activities. The Le Mans catastrophe in 1955 certainly made me wary of possible liability claims should we be unlucky enough to have one of our cars do what Levegh's Mercedes had done there . . .'.

In examining the Lister story, Brian's safety-consciousness and his jealous defence of the parent company's reputation must always be remembered. At a time when other racing car constructors would sell absolutely anything of value if they could find a customer, no matter how worn-out or much-bent it might have been, Lister stood aloof — they actually scrapped worn-out components, old frames and bodies. Nothing was left to chance if it might rebound upon Geo. Lister & Sons Ltd.

Beneath the skin several changes were made to the production chassis design compared with the works prototype layout. Whereas the original chassis used almost vertical rear coil-spring/damper units reacting against angled pylons leaning rearwards from the base tubes, these 1955 frames adopted a tall vertical rear spring abutment bridge with the coil/dampers angled out to pick-up the ends of the de Dion tube. The inverted left-hand-drive Morris Minor steering rack was now mounted at hub height on the front chassis 'square' — a vertical frame created by two fabricated uprights with spring abutments at the top, standing on the tubular front chassis cross-member and braced by a top beam and two rearward stays. The prototype cars had carried the steering rack low down on that front cross-member, below hub height and creating geometrical ill-effects on lock. New Jack Turner-made finned brake drums were 12in diameter x 2¼in wide. Brian had experimented with discs, but claimed that the new drums were more than capable of stopping the car from speeds above 130mph. All Bristol engines in Lister chassis were to receive Don Moore's attention. Don converted the basic six-cylinder from chain-driven to gear-driven camshafts 'and otherwise it was basically a question of balance, porting and valve-work. I tried bigger valves, too . . .These were all three-port-head Bristols — we never had the six-port — but they went well enough to bring us a lot of success'.

In the interests of cutting manufacturing costs and to capitalize upon proven success the works Lister-Bristol MVE 303 retained its original slab-like body in preference to the new Lucas design. Archie won 13 races during that 1955 season, the customer cars adding 10 more. In April he achieved Lister's most satisfying success in the British Empire Trophy race at Oulton Park, from which he had been so insultingly excluded 12 months previously. He qualified on pole for the 2.7-litre heat, having lapped at 2minutes 2 seconds in practice, 0.2 sec faster than Sears' 4 CNO and Reg Parnell's new 2.5-litre Aston Martin. In falling drizzle Archie held an initial lead before allowing the Aston to go by and sitting happily in its wake to finish second and qualify easily for the all-important final.

In amongst the big Ferraris, Aston Martins and Jaguars for that 25-lap race the green-and-yellow car soared into third place on handicap after 13 laps and two laps later was second behind Ken McAlpine's Connaught — 35secs clear. Archie gained four seconds on each slippery lap and with four to go was on the Connaught's tail. Next time round MVE 303 was in the lead and he completed the distance victorious at 73.52 mph, 25secs clear of McAlpine and 40secs ahead of Parnell's Aston Martin.

Grant's editorial the following week read: 'Archie Scott-Brown . . . has quickly jumped to the forefront of Britain's motor racing conductors. The Lister-Bristol, made in a very small factory near (sic) Cambridge, has rapidly gained a name for itself as a first-rate sports-racing machine, and Mr Lister will be the first to admit that the careful tuning and assembly of his Bristol engines by Don Moore has been a major contribution to the success of the marque. Naturally chassis design must play a big part, and observers will have noted the exceptional roadholding qualities of what is more or less an orthodox layout, based on modern racing practice . . .'.

Archie's great rival continued to be Roy Salvadori in Syd Greene's six-cylinder twin-cam Maserati A6GCS, but when the car was withdrawn late in the year Roy drove the John Green Lister-Bristol and was third in it at Castle Combe. That car had some staying power as David Hampshire/Peter Scott-Russell were placed ninth overall and won the 2-litre class in the Goodwood 9-Hours race that August. The Allan Moore/Bill Holt-driven Issard-Davies car, VPP 9, trundled into its pit on the limited-slip diff when a half-shaft sheared and Don Moore and Dick Barton replaced it in about 35 minutes. 'Brian timed us and as the car accelerated away he said "Here, it takes you three hours to do that job in the factory, what you been playing at!" . . .'. Unlike some constructors who would have spat out every word and meant it, this was all part of the genial Lister 'kidology'. They were always a happy team.

During the latter part of that season Brian completed the design of a brand-new works car for 1956. He had always been impressed — as had Archie at closer quarters — by the Maserati A6GCS engine's evident power and torque. Now he was determined to match those attributes to his proven chassis design, which was considerably lighter than the standard Maserati's.

The car resurrected MER 303's identity, chassis BHL 1, and was the most exciting-looking Lister yet. The florid curves and fins of the Lucas body were replaced by a 'flat-iron' design based largely upon a model which Don Moore had found of Colonel Goldie Gardner's famous record-breaking MG EX 179. Brian Lister: 'We looked at this thing and thought, well, with MG's expertise and Syd Enever's grasp of high-speed aerodynamics it must be right, and so we modified the shape to fit the chassis and engine we had to use and to comply with the regulations'.

Each wheelarch humped high above the body's flat upper deck, there was a vestigial headrest behind the cockpit, and with the tail tucked-in short, the driver seated almost on the back-axle line and a long fish-mouth nose, the overall effect was of a car crouching low and poised to rush off somewhere. Frontal area was exceptionally low with an overall body width of 4ft 7in and a scuttle height of just 2ft 3in, a 20 per cent frontal area reduction from the original works body. Weight was claimed to be less than 10½ cwt, adoption of 10in diameter Girling disc brakes alone saving 40lb over the old drum system. These discs were fitted to all 1956 production Listers — which also used the flat-iron body with a different bonnet hump to accommodate the Bristol engine. The discs were carried outboard at the front and inboard on the

Silverstone, September 6, 1958, with Norman Hillwood's private-venture Lister-Jaguar 673 LMK leading Gerry Ashmore's D-Type at Copse Corner. The North London jeweller's finned special was the first Lister-Jaguar ever completed.

The great car. Brian's 1957 MVE 303 pictured immediately upon completion by the River Cam with designer and team driver in attendance. Note wrap-round screen, metal tonneau on passenger side, complete absence of front lights and five-stud bolt-on Dunlop wheel fixings, plus engine cover hump to clear the Don Moore-tuned XK engine's cam-boxes. The bridge girders in the background were a Geo. Lister & Sons Ltd product.

gearbox cheeks at the rear. Further weight-saving came from the use of aluminium interior panelling as a stressed structure in the nose to support the radiator, the hinging front body panels and all cooling ducts for the front brakes and radiator. Two 4in diameter intakes in the screen base collected cool air which was then ducted forward to the Maserati engine's air-box and rearward to the inboard brakes and diff.

Archie was to achieve only three first places with the Lister-Maserati, which for a driver and team accustomed to winning was disastrous. Don Moore: 'When the car was first completed Archie was pleased as punch and decided he'd drive it down to Snetterton for testing on the road. He hadn't gone far before the engine got itself in a terrible mess. When I pulled it all apart I found that where the oil filter mesh had been soldered into the filter body, somebody had allowed the solder to spread across the mesh itself, halving the oil flow and leaving no feed at all to the top of the engine. After a major rebuild I ran it up on the brake and decided to whip-off the cam covers to see how much oil there was up there — and there were the brand new camshafts actually wearing away before my eyes! They hadn't been hardened at the factory; they were so soft you could file them.

'Maserati were always like that. They'd send you pistons half machined and say "machine to match your engine" — liners the same, you'd open the box, unwrap the paper and there'd be a length of drainpipe and instructions to "Cut to size" . . .'. Dick Barton recalled Alf Francis, Stirling Moss' famous mechanic, advising use of a special oil to help prevent wear in that A6GCS engine.

Allan Moore and Noel Cunningham-Reid recorded consistent success in their Lister-Bristols, while later in the season John Horridge's Ecurie Bullfrog car went well. But the most successful of the Lister-Bristol privateers was Birmingham garage proprietor Austen Nurse, who had bought the ex-John Green/Hampshire/Salvadori car HCH 736. He crashed it heavily during the British Grand Prix meeting at Silverstone: 'Coming into Woodcote at something over 100mph I flicked the steering wheel to make the car slide into the corner and the wheel just twizzled round and round in my hands and I saw the bank rushing up and we hit it a hell of a clout, stopping from about 70mph I suppose in around two-foot-six . . .'. The weeklies reported that the accident was due to failure of an adaptor fitted on the steering column, a non-Lister part. The wreck was picked-clean for salvage and the surviving identity acquired by Tom Kyffin's Equipe Devone for what was to become the first serious privately-owned Lister-Jaguar late the following year. It was taken over by his mechanic Dick Walsh for Bruce Halford to drive in 1958, and went on to the Border Reivers team for a young Jim Clark in 1959. Austen Nurse: 'In later years I went to Indianapolis with Lotus and Jim Clark and he told me that he was in the crowd just the other side of the bank that I had hit at Woodcote Corner and it frightened the life out of him. He said it was the first really bad accident he'd ever seen. ''I was sure you were dead'', he said. In fact I'd cracked my ribs and had internal bleeding, but I was soon racing again and not

MVE 303 1957 details showing the cockpit tailored to Scott-Brown's needs and the final-drive and inboard rear disc brake installation. The starter motor sits on top of the gearbox ahead of the gear-lever, while on the right a bicycle bulb horn fulfilled the regulation audible warning of approach requirement — as if the XK engine's open exhausts were insufficient? At the rear the centreline-mounted diff unit carries the vertical de Dion slide on its rear, while the disc brake calipers are hung behind the axle line.

long after that Jimmy was winning all over the country in what was left of the car!'

Meanwhile, Austen had also bought a half-completed 1956 flat-iron car from John Green. 'When we first got it I had the idea of putting a Jaguar engine in for the 2½-litre class then in force. I knew Norman Dewis at Jaguar, and when Lofty England showed no interest in my suggestion Norman said he'd talk him round. But Lofty was adamant about it — he just wouldn't play.' The new car was completed with the very good Don Moore Bristol engine from 'HCH' and it took the February 1956 Derby registration JCH 888. Nurse sold it to Gil Baird, and Baird eventually sold it to hill-climber Josh Randles, and many years later it was fitted with a 2.5-litre XK engine and raced with it into 1980, Baird observing: 'What a pity, I fitted a special six-port Bristol with a Frazer Nash head developed by Bob Gerard's mechanic, which was a superb engine. I think the car would have been quicker with that six-port 2-litre Bristol any day'.

At Abbey Road the Lister men were working hard to complete their first multi-tubular racing car, a 1,500cc Climax-powered Formula 2 single-seater. It was very light, very spartan and tailored to Scott-Brown, but he was not attracted by low-powered single-seater racing and Brian's F2 ambitions were to be submerged by other things . . .

Towards the end of 1956 a North London diamond merchant and antique jeweller named Norman Hillwood entered the picture. He was proprietor of Hillwood's the Jewellers, in Edgware, North London, and had been racing and building cars since 1952. 'I really enjoyed laying out a car and building it up. Racing them once they were completed was fun, but was always secondary to me. In 1956 sports cars seemed to be the coming thing and I wanted to build another car, so I looked around. I hit on the idea of putting a Jaguar XK engine into a Lister-Bristol chassis.

'Brian Lister didn't like the idea at all, but he did sell me a chassis — for £200 for the bare frame — and I wrote direct to Sir William Lyons and got a spare wet-sump C-Type engine and gearbox. Then Brian said "send it up here and we will fit it all up", which they did. He thought about it and made me a stronger de Dion tube. Then I wanted some wheels and Dunlop said I'd need some special-design wire wheels, and when first completed the car was actually on drum brakes, C-Type drums with light-alloy backplates by Tojeiro. Because

Archie in MVE 303 at the Snetterton MRC meeting in May 1957 in which he won two races going away. This shot shows the scalloped nearside body panelling necessary to accommodate the tuned exhaust system, the car's beautifully lithe and clean build and the matching livery of car and crash helmet.

we couldn't lighten the frame much we built the rest of the car as light as possible. I designed a body with a tailfin on the headrest, modelled it in Plasticene and Mo Gomm did it for me from that in the metal. Barry Dukes, now at Heenan & Froude, worked it all out for me and engineered the car. We finished the chassis in bright yellow and the body was British Racing Green with a yellow circle round the nose. It was road-equipped and I drove it to meetings. I liked driving, but I've always been a better engineer and that car was so reliable I found myself sitting around most of the time with nothing to do. The damn car was complete and finished and nothing ever went wrong with it so I got bored. I eventually sold it so that I could get something which might be more troublesome, but which at least would keep me occupied!'

This first-off Lister-Jaguar used the kite-planform twin-tube frame of the production Lister-Bristols with the hub-height steering rack, vertical rear spring abutment towers and angled coil/damper units. Its chassis number was BHL 12 and Norman Hillwood gave it the April 1957 London registration 673 LMK.

Don Moore: 'When Norman Hillwood popped up and said he was going to fit a 3.4 Jaguar engine in a Lister-Bristol chassis Brian just about did his nut! Then along came Bryan Turle of BP and he persuaded Brian to do the same thing in the works'.

Brian Lister: 'We were contracted to BP and at that time the Shell-backed

Brian Lister's favourite photograph of Archie cornering a Lister-Jaguar, taken during a victorious drive at Goodwood on Easter Monday, 1957, with MVE 303 in a classical four-wheel drift with all four wheels pointing straight ahead and the car turning hard right through the long curve at Madgwick. Note the inboard rear brake cooling scoop added to the tail deck, in line with the rear-view mirror from this angle. Scott-Brown had an acute sense of balance and his spectacular cornering delighted crowds wherever he raced; neither did it waste him time. He was truly a brilliant little driver.

Revenge. Archie on his way to a second victory in the British Empire Trophy at Oulton Park in 1957, driving MVE 303, having won in the Lister-Bristol in 1955 to avenge his exclusion from the event first time round in 1954.

Jaguar works team had just retired from racing. BP badly needed an unlimited-capacity sports car team to combat Aston Martin and Ecurie Ecosse, who were both with Esso, and Bryan Turle talked me into doing that by developing our own chassis to accept the Jaguar engine. I wasn't so sure. I'd really set my heart on doing Formula 2, but on reflection I realized there could well be a lucrative American market for that type of car and so we approached Jaguar and bought our first 3.4 dry-sump D-Type engine from them'.

The new car was instantly successful in testing, and in March 1957 *The Autocar* described the new works Lister-Jaguar — MVE 303 — like this:

'Basically the car has a ladder-type frame built up of 3in diameter 14-gauge steel tubing; the widest part is at the level of the driver's seat, the frame tapering towards the front and, much more sharply, to the rear. One effect of this unusually wide frame has been to seat the driver about 4in lower than would have been the case with a narrower, parallel-tube frame (because he sits between the frame member and the propeller shaft), another has been the car's very low scuttle height of only 29in.

'There are three main cross-members, of the same diameter and gauge tubing as the side-members; two are placed near the points from which the tapers begin, and the third is across the forward ends of the side tubes. Particular attention has been paid to the accuracy of the joints involved, the faces of the shaped ends of the tubes being milled to obtain a 100 per cent contact area.

'The rectangular frame carrying the engine bulkhead is of 1½in tubing, with bolted-on corner gussets to allow dismantling when the engine is removed. There is a diagonal, 1½in tubular brace across one half of this, with a flanged joint for dismantling, to which is attached the top, left-hand corner of the clutch bellhousing.

'The D-Type Jaguar gearbox, in unit with the engine, is mounted on the centre main cross-member and the forward end of the engine is mounted at either side of the frame side-members, giving a three-point mounting for the engine and gearbox.

'A short length of 3in 14-gauge tube runs rearwards along the centreline of the chassis frame from the rear cross-member; this forms the lower mounting for the vertical slide that gives lateral location to the de Dion tube. The top end is attached to a rearward extension from a 1½in tubular bridge structure, which is built above the frame side tubes at the points of attachment of the rear cross-member. The top of the final-drive casing is bolted to this structure and, beneath, is held by trunnion blocks to the projecting central tube.

'Parallel radius arms, two on each side, run forward from the ends of the de Dion tube and give fore-and-aft location. Rear suspension is by Girling combined coil-springs and damper units, the top ends of which are attached to the outer ends of the bridge structure.

'Front suspension is by equal-length wishbones and Girling suspension units, the wishbones being pivoted on vertical, fabricated, box-section members, which are attached to the frame at the level of the front cross-member. Forward of these wishbone mountings and slightly below the level of the upper abutments of the Girling units is a 1½in diameter tubular structure which carries the rack-and-pinion steering. MG hubs and king-pin assemblies are used at the front, and Triumph TR3-type, Girling small-pad 11in disc brakes. The rear disc brakes, 10in in diameter, are mounted inboard of the drive-shaft. A standard D-Type Jaguar radiator block is mounted at a considerable backward slope just forward of the structure that carries the rack-and-pinion. There are no universal joints in the steering column, which runs straight from the steering wheel to the pinion.

'The fuel and oil tanks, carried in the tail of the car, are shaped to conform to the body panelling. The eight-gallon capacity of the oil tank occupies the left-hand third of the body width, and the 20-gallon fuel tank the remainder. Normally, only five gallons of oil are carried in the oil tank, the filler neck of which is connected by a small-bore pipe to the crankcase breather.

'Body panels are carried on a subsidiary framework of 1½in diameter tubing, attached by Dzus fasteners. The entire body skin can be removed in four minutes.

'The engine is a D-Type Jaguar unit, with three twin-choke Weber 45DC03 carburettors and coil ignition — an engine which, as Brian Lister says, is the finest design since the war. A large-capacity Tecalemit oil filter is mounted on the front main cross-member, and there are twin SU electric fuel pumps on the rear bridge structure. A small motorcycle-type generator is belt-driven from the nose of the final-drive and supplies the 12-volt electrical system. The battery is carried in the rear part of the passenger seat space. The engine has been carefully prepared and tuned by Don Moore — the tuning consisting largely of extremely careful assembly, matching ports and so on. The non-standard exhaust system consists of grouping 14in long pipes into two down pipes.'

The report concluded: 'The secret of the car's remarkable performance comes partly from its excellent handling and roadholding . . . and partly from (a

Appendix C trim was required at short-notice for the 1957 British GP meeting sports car race at Aintree, and Lister hastily complied by fitting MVE 303 with lights and a full-width windscreen and wipers, as seen here. Even out in the lead conditions were awful and here Archie is at Tatts Corner having pulled down his goggles for a clearer view. The rear wing-top air intake was necessary to cool the inboard discs as the full-width screen interrupted airflow to the centreline scoop.

weight of) only 17cwt 3qr — less than the dry weight of the standard D-Type Jaguar. The bhp per ton figure of the car . . . is not far short of that of the 1954 W196 Mercedes-Benz GP cars!'

Dimensions were published as: Wheelbase, 7ft 5in; front track, 4ft 2½in; rear track, 4ft 4in; overall length, 12ft 11½in; overall width, 5ft 1in; overall height (at scuttle) 2ft 5in; ground clearance (at sump) 3in. Dry weight was stated to be 1,625lb, distributed 48/52 front/rear. Transmission ratios overall were 3.54 (top), 4.52 (third), 5.82 (second) and 7.61:1 (first) with a hypoid-bevel 3.54:1 final-drive. Road speed per 1,000rpm was claimed to be 24mph in top gear on 16in diameter Dunlop light-alloy disc wheels carrying 6.50 rear tyres; 5.50s at the front.

The revived MVE 303 made its debut in the opening Snetterton meeting of that new 1957 season, on March 31. Archie already held the circuit lap record in a Formula 1 Connaught B-Type, which he had driven the previous year and after some shattering practice laps in the new Lister-Jaguar he lined-up on pole for the 15-lap main event, alongside Protheroe's Tojeiro-Jaguar 7 GNO, Peter Whitehead's Aston Martin DB3S and Peter Blond's D-Type. He scorched off the line, led into Riches Corner and promptly coasted to a stop. Brian and Don went out to investigate and found Archie fiddling with the clutch mechanism which had disengaged and jammed out. After losing six laps MVE rejoined, with Archie scorching round in the usual apparently lurid but beautifully balanced drifts and slides, unlapping himself and setting fastest lap at 88.69mph before the finish, 2.3mph faster than Blond's D-Type best later in the day. Clearly MVE 303 on this form was something very special.

Swallowing their disappointment at that early clutch problem, the team prepared for the British Empire Trophy race at Oulton Park the following Saturday. The country was still gripped by petrol rationing after the Suez débâcle, and partly to save fuel there was to be no final in the BET meeting, the Trophy going instead to the driver with the fastest race average, irrespective of heat.

Graham Hill's 1,100cc Lotus 11 won the first heat at 80.60mph and Ron Flockhart's 1,500cc version won the second at 82.55mph. For the unlimited-

Scorching at Goodwood, in September 1957, with Archie and MVE 303 at full cry into Woodcote Corner on their way to their final victory of that extraordinary season. The driver's door side-screen was omitted to allow easy entry at the Le Mans-type run-and-jump start. Note the use of knock-on hubs as opposed to the earlier bolt-on type. Knock-ons were normally used by the team in longer races where tyre-changes were a possibility.

102

capacity heat Archie had again proved the sensation of practice with MVE 303, qualifying fully 2secs faster than Salvadori's 2.5-litre Aston Martin DBR1 and 3 secs faster than Cunningham-Reid's second works Aston — a 3-litre DB3S. But whenever the brightly coloured Lister visited the pits its arrival had been accompanied by sizzling noises and the bitter smell of cooking brakes. Dick Barton and the other works mechanics rigged a large air-scoop on the car's rear deck to feed cooling air down on to the inboard discs, and they were to survive the race despite a tendency to grab near the end of the scheduled 25 laps. In fact, overheating brakes and boiling brake fluid were to become a Lister-Jaguar characteristic, and is still a problem with surviving cars today.

Archie made an uncharacteristically slow start for his heat and Salvadori led away into the country, only for MVE 303's unmistakable snout to emerge first from the woods, Scott-Brown already in the lead by 2secs. After 12 laps he was 12secs clear and he just strode away to win easily by a 10sec margin at an average of 84.21mph — good enough to take the British Empire Trophy for the second time. He had twice equalled the existing sports car lap record of 85.69mph. Jaguar were delighted and BP overjoyed — Lister were 'in'.

Easter Monday Goodwood, on April 22, featured the 21-lap Sussex Trophy sports car race, and Archie again out-qualified the works Astons in practice. One report read: 'Right from the start the Lister-Jaguar pulled ahead and began to draw steadily away from the field, Archie increasing his lead by almost precisely a second a lap, to finish 21.2 secs ahead of Roy Salvadori, setting-up a new sports car lap record of 91.33mph in the process . . . The result was a foregone conclusion . . .'

Dick Barton's personal photo collection produced this fine shot of Dick and the great little man with MVE 303 in the paddock at Auckland's Ardmore airfield circuit before the 1958 New Zealand GP. Note the temporary New Zealand registration plate — white numbers on a red background — and the car's rather battered appearance after a long and hard career, plus the surface trip down-under. There's a stone-guard in the radiator air intake.

One week later Archie and MVE 303 entertained the clubmen at Snetterton by setting FTD in the West Essex Car Club Sprint, his time of 19.64secs being 0.41sec inside John Ogier's best with the Tojeiro-Jaguar.

Yet the diminutive but so talented Scot was still encountering the occasional problem with race organizers due to his physical form. British organizers had no qualms at all, his knife-edge cornering technique delighting so many spectators, but he seemed fated never to be accepted on the Continent. The AC Milan had refused to accept him in a works Connaught for the previous year's Italian Grand Prix, and when Brian made a Lister-Jaguar entry in the GP de Spa on May 12 — a 15-lap 132-mile race for Appendix C sports cars — it was first rejected out of hand and then accepted upon his appeal, but too late for the car to be modified to Appendix C specification, complete with lights, wipers, full-width screen etc, and taken to the circuit.

Consequently, MVE 303 did not race again until May 19 at the Stanley Sears Trophy meeting at Snetterton. Archie smashed his own outright lap record in practice, despite having to negotiate tighter turns than normal in the Esses, where a newly resurfaced section had broken-up and the left-hander had to be re-aligned by moving marker tubs clear of the crumbling asphalt. Archie led from flag to flag in the race, set a new class lap record at 90.50mph and won from Protheroe's 'Toj' and Peter Whitehead's DB3S — it was Scott-Brown's Lister-Jaguar hat-trick, after just four race starts.

Whit-Monday, June 10, found the team at Crystal Palace for a 10-lap unlimited-capacity sports car race and Archie breaking the lap record in practice to qualify on pole. The Lister-Jaguar seemed equally at home on both fast circuits and slow, and Archie notched his fourth win from five starts, beating Graham Whitehead's DB3S and Leston's HWM-Jaguar. A wet track through the Glades prevented record-breaking, but Archie still set fastest lap, at 75.82mph.

July 20, 1957, was the date of the memorable British Grand Prix at Aintree in which Stirling Moss, Tony Brooks and the Vanwall won for Britain, and the meeting commenced, in pouring rain, with a 17-lap sports car race. It would appear that Aston Martin had become increasingly discomforted by repeated defeat under the wheels of the Lister-Jaguar, as Don Moore recalled: 'Old Reg Parnell used to swear: "Your bloody effing specials" he used to say, "blowing-off our proper motor cars . . ." and we did, and we enjoyed it'. Just days before the Aintree meeting, friendly Keith Challen, motoring correspondent for the *News of the World*, telephoned Brian Lister at Abbey Road and said that he thought Brian ought to know that the Aintree regs had been changed to demand Appendix C trim and equipment. It was the first Brian had heard of any such change, but upon checking with the organizing club he found it was true. MVE 303 had to be modified hastily with a full-width screen (replacing the original driver wrap-around and aluminium passenger tonneau), wipers and a full lighting set.

In practice at Aintree both Archie and Salvadori in the very fast Aston Martin DBR1/300 bettered the latter's existing sports car lap record, set the previous year at 2:08.4, 84.38mph. Archie managed 2:06.8 and Salvadori 2:08.0 and the Lister made an outstanding getaway on the streaming surface and led by 100 yards on to the Railway Straight. Scott-Brown plumed on through the rain in a growing lead — the only man not having to drive into flying spray — and by lap 10 he was 15secs clear of Salvadori and apparently unassailable. *Autosport* reported: 'The only real drama of the race occurred just three laps from the finish, when Archie began inexplicably to drop back, and at the end of the 15th tour Roy appeared round Tatt's Corner right on Archie's tail. It appears that Brian Lister had miscounted the number of laps completed and had hung out the 'take it easy' sign to Archie too soon! Fortunately, the situation was appreciated in time, Archie put his foot down once more — and there was no doubt which was the faster car!'

In fact Brian had not miscounted. Archie could not see at all through his goggles, had pulled them down and could hardly see a thing with his eyes unprotected. They were red-raw at the finish, the team suspecting that without the Appendix C windscreen he would not have been able to finish at all . . . which was ironic from Aston's viewpoint.

He won by 2secs, having averaged 78.8mph in horrible conditions, and he and Salvadori shared fastest lap in 2:11.8, 81.94mph. The Lister-Jaguar had humbled the works Aston Martins yet again in one of the most important sports car races of the British calendar.

One week later, on Sunday, July 28, Lister returned in triumph to their home circuit at Snetterton with MVE 303 still in Appendix C form, as it was to remain for the rest of its life. In the sports event Archie led from start to finish, winning at 90.72mph and setting a new sports car lap record of 92.22mph, while in the *Formule Libre* Vanwall Trophy itself he triumphed again, winning at 89.39mph from the F2 Coopers of Brian Naylor and George Wicken. His

Peter Greenslade took this fine photograph of Archie at work in MVE 303's cockpit on his way to victory in the 1958 Lady Wigram Trophy race outside Christchurch, New Zealand. Note the long steering column, Archie's spare goggles on his helmet and the grip he could apply with his right 'hand'.

fastest lap of 91.35mph was not bettered. Earlier in the day John Horridge's Lister-Bristol had collided with American Woolworth heir Lance Reventlow's 2-litre Maserati and both cars flipped. Reventlow was to 'do a Lister' and build his own Scarab sports-racing cars in California in the months to come. Horridge broke his neck in this incident and his Lister-Bristol — which wore a glass-fibre body moulded by Rochdale's from a Connaught pattern — was written-off. In 1980, running a Ford parts centre in Chorley, Lancashire, John recalled: 'I replaced it with the ex-Allan Moore Lister-Bristol chassis, which I bought from Brian Lister with a flat-iron body'. So that is where the original VPP 9 frame went to . . . Issard-Davies had part-exchanged it with Lister for the ex-works Maserati-engined MER 303, which Moore was driving for him that 1957 season.

The August Bank Holiday meeting at Brands Hatch on August 5 saw Scott-Brown driving Frank Nichols' air-cooled flat-four Elva-AJB *Sabrina* in the 1,500cc sports car race and leading handsomely until a valve dropped, then taking out MVE in the 10-lap Kingsdown Trophy and winning hands down. His 12½-minute drive netted victory at 71.79mph and yet another new lap record — 61.0secs, 73.18mph; there was simply no stopping him. Mike Anthony ran a 2-litre Lister-Bristol and retired when an oil line parted.

Immediately after the Brands Hatch meeting Archie set off for Sweden, where the organizers of the World Sports Car Championship deciding round had accepted an entry made for him by David Murray of Ecurie Ecosse. He was to share one of the Edinburgh team's D-Type Jaguars with John Lawrence. The Råbelov course at Kristianstad was a true road circuit — the first he had raced on — but after taking-over the 3.8 D-Type on lap 62, in fifth place, he charged into third behind Moss' leading Maserati 450S V8 and Collins' 4.1-litre V12 Ferrari amidst an hour-long rainstorm. Then Archie ran off into the bordering fields a couple of times, falling to fourth, regained third and handed back to Lawrence. He went off and hit a bank when an oil pipe broke, spraying him with lubricant — but the big Jaguar was still classified eighth. The 'disabled driver' had performed very well in a World Championship race on Continental soil — and this drive is too often forgotten.

He was out in the rain again at Snetterton on September 1, back this time in MVE. He started the unlimited-capacity sports car race from his customary pole position, led throughout and won at just 75mph, which demonstrates clearly the ugly conditions that day. Splashing home third was Tommy Kyffin's newly-completed Lister-Jaguar — this Mo Gomm-bodied 3.4-litre machine being based on Austen Nurse's Silverstone wreck identity of HCH 736. In the 10-lap *Formule Libre* event Archie led again for 9½ laps until an oil pipe fractured, handing victory to George Wicken's F2 Cooper, '. . . the most surprised man in Norfolk to get the chequered flag'. Geoff Richardson was fourth in his RRA — the ex-Tasman Reg Parnell Aston Martin DB3S-based single-seater fitted with a 2.5-litre XK engine. Kyffin was eighth.

The Lister equipe on the road during their New Zealand tour, with a borrowed Chevrolet pick-up truck and MVE 303 on the trailer. Len Hayden of Jaguar tends the car while Archie's unmistakable figure stands alongside. Another Dick Barton picture.

106

At this time Brian was completing a second prototype Formula 2 Lister based on the scrapped pilot car of the previous year. Whereas it had been a conventional in-line *monoposto* with the driver seated above the prop-shaft, this new version looked far more effective with its Coventry Climax FPF 1,500cc twin-cam engine inclined at 30-degrees from the vertical to offset the driveline to the nearside. The driver sat with the prop-shaft beside his left hip and the gearbox in unit with the offset final-drive. Dick Barton: 'Archie was most unhappy driving the F2 and he certainly had a 'thing' about the propshaft rotating right beside him at around 7,500rpm — with the rear gearbox, you see, it ran at engine speed'. Brian Lister: 'Archie just wasn't attracted by low-powered single-seaters — they weren't his cup of tea at all'. The car was due to make its debut in the F2 section of the BRDC International Trophy race at Silverstone — postponed to September 14 from its usual May date by the Suez crisis — but its canted engine pumped oil out through the breathers in practice and it did not start. This was not Scott-Brown's day. His Elva-AJB led the first few hundred yards of the 1,500cc sports car race only to drop a valve again, and in the touring car race his 3.4 Jaguar raced wheel-to-wheel with Mike Hawthorn's until suffering total brake failure into Copse Corner. He smashed it straight into second gear — taking the XK engine to 8,500rpm in the process — and retired unscathed having shared a new touring car lap record with the future World Champion.

In first practice for the big sports car race he had qualified fastest, a second faster than Hamilton's Jaguar and Cunningham-Reid's Aston Martin, but on the Friday Salvadori's big 3.7-litre Aston Martin at last pipped the 3.8 Lister-Jaguar for pole by 0.6sec. Salvadori and the sister 3-litre Aston of Tony Brooks led from the start with Archie hot on their heels; second time round the Lister was second, and by lap 4 it was in the lead. But even Archie's driving was never normally that hairy as MVE 303 skittered through Silverstone's open curves in

Victory. Archie and MVE 303 take the chequered flag to win the Lady Wigram Trophy from a field including Formula 1 cars. One of Dick Barton's proudest possessions is Archie's winner's sash from that race.

The team at Dunedin, where MVE 303 was sponsored by Kelvinator Jetline domestic appliances. Len Hayden is behind Archie to his left while Dick — 'I wish I'd found a comb' — stands to his right. In the street race here MVE 303's diff mounts failed.

lurid oversteering slides. Ending lap 6 Salvadori was ahead again and the race ran out with Scott-Brown and the Lister-Jaguar beaten for the first time. Post-race inspection revealed that the Lister's rear springs had settled after such a hectic season's racing and the de Dion tube was being allowed to hit its bump-stops, breaking the rear wheels' adhesion. Don Moore recalled that Archie never ever bent a valve through over-revving, but on one occasion a strip-down revealed a valve bent by an ingested stone and consequent power loss. This might well have been that occasion. The Lister team put their defeat down to experience — most others would have been proud to have finished second amongst a four-car works team from Aston Martin . . .

Two weeks later, the Goodwood International on September 28 was highlighted by Archie winning again in MVE 303 in the 21-lap Goodwood Trophy. He headed the Le Mans-type start line-up and drew away throughout to win at 88.84mph and set fastest lap at 90.38mph. This was the grand finale to a shattering first season for the works Lister-Jaguar during which Scott-Brown had driven it in 14 events, winning 11, finishing second in the 12th, retiring just once and setting fastest lap after a long delay in the other one. On every circuit upon which the duo appeared they either broke or equalled the class lap record during practice or the race.

Such a season had would-be customers beating a path to Brian's door in Abbey Road, and while he finalized plans for a production Lister-Jaguar for 1958, MVE 303 was loaned to John Bolster of *Autosport* magazine, and to Maurice Smith of *The Autocar*. Bolster wrote the most illuminating analysis reproduced in the Appendix, and in fact there had been a scheme afoot to fit the car for him with a bubble canopy and extremely high back-axle ratio and run it on the pilot motorway stretch outside Preston — hopefully for the world's first-ever 200mph magazine road test! Unfortunately, there was not enough time available for proper preparation and testing, so John sampled the car in standard form, picking it up after that final victory at Goodwood. He found the car 'a sheer delight', free of roll, smooth-riding and immensely controllable despite its fearsome performance; 0.60mph in 4.6secs, 0.80mph in 8.0secs, 0.100mph in 11.2 and 0-120mph in 15.2! Maurice Smith reported:

'The car is pleasant and easy to drive on the road. It does carry two people, rather uncomfortably if they are bigger than small, but a suit to fit someone else is likely to restrict your movements if you squeeze into it. Our Lister-Jaguar would be bespoke. Brian Lister says it would cost £2,750 basic or, without engine (so you could fit, say, a Chrysler Fire Power), £1,750 . . .'.

Archie's personal preferences had played a vital part in Brian's development of the car, as *Motor Racing* described: 'In all his development work Brian Lister depends on Scott-Brown, for and around whom his cars are built. Archie does all the test driving, and is thus able to ensure that handling characteristics are to his liking. All Listers are, in fact, built with neutral steering; under power the tail can be made to slide as required, always remaining under control — if you're an Archie, that is. Making no claims to be an engineer, Archie has complete faith in Brian Lister and Don Moore, upon whom his safety depends.

In the Lister works with the 1957 prototype Lister-Jaguar stripped-down and in apparent course of preparation immediately before its New Zealand trip, with Archie and Brian alongside. In the background is what appears to be the prototype 1958 'Knobbly' chassis with its parallel-tube section visible abaft the cockpit. The slightly canted engine mounting in MVE 303 is visible, along with the stressed-skin construction.

He considers sliding the quickest method of cornering and thus dislikes cars which understeer. Observant racegoers will probably agree with the contention — made by several of the people who follow him around the circuits — that Archie spends less time travelling with all wheels pointing straight ahead than any other driver!'.

By this time Archie had long-since left Dobie's 4-Square Tobacco — going into partnership with friends Malcolm Boston, Peter Hughes (the Haemorrhoid-JAP's second owner, remember?) and Peter Riley — another fast-developing Cambridge club racer — and opening the Autodel Garage on the Huntingdon road about five miles outside Cambridge. Archie managed it, but the Suez crisis hit business within a year of its opening and 'being situated on a stretch of road which is much too straight and fast it loses trade. Repair business is good, however, as telegraph poles seem to have an especial fascination for drivers in this area'. Poor Peter Hughes died in a road accident, and his brother Michael from Henley took over his share.

While Brian sat down to design and set-up production of his 1958 Lister-Jaguars, a winter tour to the Tasman races in New Zealand had been arranged through BP. MVE 303 in full Appendix C form with a 3.8-litre engine — just the one, no spare — was shipped from London's Victoria & Albert Docks while Archie flew-out later with Dick Barton and works Jaguar mechanic Len Hayden. The car arrived at Auckland in the North Island minus its fire extinguisher and other easily pilferable bits, but Dick and Len prepared it in time for the New Zealand GP at Auckland's Ardmore Airfield circuit on January 18, 1958. Archie was facing Jack Brabham's 2.2-litre Cooper, two Bernie Ecclestone-owned Connaughts for Roy Salvadori and Stuart Lewis-Evans, Ross Jensen's ex-Moss Maserati 250F and Ferraris for Pat Hoare, Ron Roycroft and Lex Davison — all proper single-seaters.

On that Saturday morning two 40-mile qualifying heats were held to decide the 150-mile GP's grid. Lewis-Evans won his from Scott-Brown, but Archie then led from the start of the feature race and held his advantage for three laps until Brabham scuttled by at the hairpin. Davison's Ferrari followed through,

The first private Lister-Jaguar to be produced with full works support was Tom Kyffin's HCH 736, Mo Gomm-bodied in very similar form to the works MVE 303 and seen here in the September 1957 Goodwood meeting leading a D-Type and a DB3S at the Members' Chicane. 'Old HCH' — 'The Flat-Iron Lister-Jaguar' — was to enjoy a long and noble career.

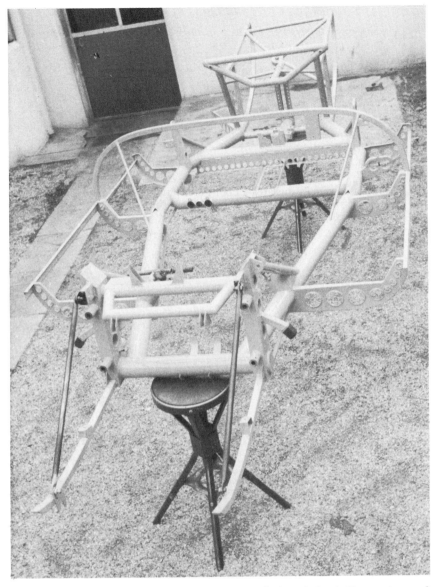

Brian Lister's chassis frame for the 1958 production 'Knobbly' cars, as shown to the press at Abbey Road upon release of the prototype car. The front 'skis' supported the radiator and oil-cooler, while the three holes in the midships cross-member carried the master-cylinders with pull-rod pedal actuation. The upturned rear frame supported the tail body section, spare wheel and fuel tank. Note the parallel tube section in the cockpit area, replacing the original kite-planform design as used up to the 1957 MVE 303.

pushing the Lister back to third, then Salvadori and Lewis-Evans chopped ahead. When Davison spun Archie regained fourth place until the Ferrari slammed past again. One Connaught dropped out, elevating MVE 303 a place, but with only three laps to go Archie roared into his pit saying he'd got a puncture. Dick Barton: 'He said it had happened when he was travelling at more than 120mph, but the tyres were all OK. We looked at the front of the car and told him that was it, he was out. He just couldn't believe it. We showed him the left-front wheel leaning in — the kingpin had fractured below the hub, and when we moved the car the whole thing just collapsed! How he'd brought it into the pits I'll never know . . .'

The 4th Lady Wigram Trophy race was held on the RNZAF airfield outside Christchurch on the east coast of the South Island the following weekend. Before taking the Bristol Freighter air ferry across the Cook Strait between islands, Dick recalled they stopped off at Levin for a minor race, Archie finishing second in the repaired Lister and winning £7 for his pains.

In first practice at Wigram on soft plugs Archie lapped in 1:26.0, 88.58mph

— 3secs inside Peter Whitehead's 1956 Ferrari lap record — then he stunned the locals by saying he'd been dropping 1,000rpm on the back straight to preserve his machinery. Next evening he cut 0.4sec off that time to take pole position, 1.1secs faster than Lewis-Evans and 1.6secs faster than Jensen.

He led from the first corner in the race, but spun on oil in the Esses on lap 8, rejoining second behind Jensen and chased by the Coopers of young Bruce McLaren and Jack Brabham. Within a lap Archie was back in the lead and next time round he set a new record of 1:23.8 to pull away. He completed the 150-miles race in a record time of 107:27.4, 83.93mph, his record lap averaging 90.8mph, having humbled the Grand Prix cars.

Some 200 miles further south, at Dunedin on February 1, MVE 303 was in trouble on the rough and dangerous street circuit. Archie qualified on row six of the grid, climbed to fifth during the race and finally retired on lap 23 when the aluminium brackets attaching the diff casing to the chassis fractured. Ross Jensen won and became the first Kiwi to win an International motor race on his native soil. Archie was sponsored by Kelvinator Refrigerators for this event, their logo being emblazoned all over the Lister and on the wee Scot's crash helmet. In a radio interview he freely admitted he had seen nothing quite like the Dunedin circuit before, and it was later reported that the Dunedin police were anxious for nobody to see racing there ever again.

The Tasman tour ended at Teretonga Park, Invercargill — the world's southernmost motor racing circuit — on February 8. There was a short sports car race run in the morning and the 60-mile *Formule Libre* International in the afternoon. Archie headed the sports car event's Le Mans-type line-up having lapped in 1:17.0, 70.2mph, in practice. He took an instant lead and as one report described, '. . . came home an easy winner having treated the crowd of 20,000 to a breathtaking demonstration of four-wheel drifts for the first time at Teretonga Park.'

After lunch the grid formed-up for the International with Jensen's 250F on pole at 1:14.2 from Brabham, McLaren and Scott-Brown. Frank Cantwell somersaulted his Tojeiro-Jaguar on the opening lap as Jensen led from MVE 303 until Brabham wrestled by to take second place. Almost immediately the Cooper flew off the road, so Archie was second again until McLaren's Cooper displaced him. 'On the 13th lap Ron Roycroft's big 4½-litre V12 Ferrari started to threaten Scott-Brown. It may have been that Scott-Brown did not like having the big Ferrari in close company, for two laps later he slightly overdid things coming into the main straight. Each time round he had used up every inch of road coming out of this bend. But this time the tail of the Lister-Jaguar went just too far and away it shot backwards into the rough and across a small ditch to end up against a sandbank. The little man was unconcerned and motored back over the ditch to rejoin the race with renewed vigour.' He eventually finished sixth, one lap down on Roycroft, the victorious Jensen and the rest.

So the New Zealand tour ended with MVE 303 having raced in seven events, winning two, finishing second twice, sixth once, and retiring twice with mechanical failures.

While Archie, Dick Barton and the Lister were away, Abbey Road was humming with activity as the first production 1958 Lister-Jaguars were completed. At this time it would appear that 20 chassis numbers had been issued, BHL 20 being the highest to have been noted by French Jaguar collector Dr Philippe Renault in his extensive researches into this subject. Not all the intermediate numbers have been traced, but now that Brian was embarking upon quite large series production and major American customers had appeared he adopted a 100-series three-digit chassis numbering system, 'partly, I suppose, to emphasize that we were no mere special-builders'.

For 1958, the international governing body's rule-makers had decreed a blanket 3-litre capacity limit on World Sports Car Championship entries. Jaguar had produced an XK engine variant to match and American millionaire sportsman Briggs Cunningham had visited Abbey Road with his team's technical director, Alfred Momo, to study Lister's product. He had immediately ordered the first two 1958 cars to be completed, to be delivered with 3-litre Jaguar engines in time for the Sebring 12-Hours World Championship round in Florida, on March 22. A third chassis was also ordered to carry a Chevrolet engine.

The first Cunningham car, chassis BHL 101, was shown to the British press at Cambridge in mid-February 1958 and created quite a sensation with its muscle-bound new body form. The 'Knobbly' Lister-Jaguar had been born.

Brian had styled this body to weave its way brilliantly through Appendix C screen-height regulations and minimize frontal area. The nose section had deeply-scalloped valleys between the wings and a central hump which enclosed the engine. At its rear-end this cam-box hump dropped sharply to a low-level scuttle from which the windscreen rose to the regulation height, an inch or so lower overall than the 1957 MVE 303's. The rear deck was level with the top of the windscreen, with flaring rear wings and a shapely headrest. Having drawn this body in elevation and section, Brian then turned his drawings over to Cavendish Morton, who produced an artist's impression perspective painting, which was put out as a 'taster' to the press before the first car was built. Williams & Pritchard in Edmonton undertook body production, Len Pritchard recalling: 'I'd done a lot of work with magnesium-elektron alloy panels during the war and I suggested that Brian could save weight by using it for some of his car bodies. It just about halved the weight of a conventional aluminium bodyshell, but doubled the price. It subsequently proved a devil to repair and we had a few panics welding it because if you were't very careful it would burst into flames. I ended-up sorry I'd ever suggested it!'

Brian mounted his new 'Knobbly' bodies in either aluminium or magnesium, to customer choice, on a redesigned twin-tube chassis. It still used the familiar 3in diameter 14-gauge seamless drawn steel main tubes, but the earlier kite-planform was modified to feature a parallel-tube section amidships, either side of the cockpit. The familiar vertical front square braced by rearward tube diagonals still provided front suspension mounts, while at the rear a round-tube bridge structure still supported the spring abutments and de Dion tube guide. The tail-frame was in lightweight square-section tube, while two square-section 'skis' projected from the front cross-member to carry the radiator and front body mounts. Perforated frames projecting outboard from the main tubes on either side carried the body sills, while the scuttle was framed by a simple square-section tubular hoop.

Front suspension was again by equal-length double wishbones carrying MG uprights and hubs, and the outboard Girling damper units still projected through the upper wishbones to pick-up on the front frame. Lister-modified Morris rack-and-pinion steering was mid-mounted ahead of the axle line, forcing the latest Girling light-alloy brake calipers behind the uprights in a violently disturbed airstream, but clasping giant new 12in diameter solid discs. At the rear Brian adopted a brand-new cast-elektron final-drive casing with a

The first-off production 1958 'Knobbly' Lister-Jaguar pictured in Abbey Road before its despatch to Briggs Cunningham in New York. The full-length-bonnet magnesium-alloy body was extremely light — and equally expensive — and it can be seen how the dropped scuttle line behind the engine bay bulge allowed a regulation-height screen to be tucked down as low as possible.

The prototype Cunningham car with its full-length bonnet removed showing how it came away complete with windscreen. Later production aluminium-bodied cars had a fixed scuttle/screen and separate opening bonnet at Williams & Pritchard's suggestion.

Salisbury hypoid crownwheel and pinion. It was mounted slightly offset to the left to increase driver space, demanding unequal-length half-shafts driving to the road wheels. A range of eight alternative final-drive ratios were available, including 2.93, 3.31, 3.54, 3.77, 4.09, 4.27, 4.55 and 4.78:1. A Powr-Lok diff was included as standard, with a ZF offered at extra charge.

Girling light-alloy calipers clasping 12in discs reappeared on the final-drive cheeks, being served with cooling air ducted from small intakes let into the leading edge of each rear wing. The calipers were mounted ahead of the rear axle line, instead of behind it as on the 1957 car.

A massive 38-gallon fuel tank was mounted high above the rear suspension to concentrate load above the rear wheels, if not doing much good to the centre of gravity. A five-gallon oil tank for the XK engine's dry-sump system slung low on the nearside rear corner, while the spare wheel slotted beneath the fuel tank, right-of-centre. The battery sat in an angled tray in the right-rear corner.

As a 'production' Appendix C sports car the new Lister-Jaguar was better appointed than the 1957 one-off with two fully upholstered seats and a padded cover for the transmission tunnel. There were shallow pockets provided in each door, but the small space outside the chassis tube to the driver's right housed twin SU electric fuel pumps with changeover taps and twin pick-ups from both

Front-quarter view showing the nose-hoop to support the slide-off bonnet section, full-length flanged lower wishbones, joint-flanged top wishbones, tall coil-spring/damper units and high-mounted anti-roll bar, vestigial roll-over protection behind the driver's head and Firestone racing tyres fitted for this American-destined car.

main and reserve supplies. The dash was fully-instrumented, carried the fuse-box readily accessible and an ignition-key starter system was used. Brian offered a choice of four engines — the XK in 3.0 or 3.8-litre form and the popular American 4.6 or 5.7-litre Chevrolet V8 for US customers. Transmission was via a standard D-Type four-speed-and-reverse gearbox with a tall central gear-change cranked forward to compensate for the far-back engine and gearbox mounting.

The 1958 car had a wheelbase of 7ft 6¾in, 1¾in longer than the 1957 works car, wider front and rear tracks of 4ft 4in and 4ft 5½in, and the overall length was 6in greater at 13ft 6in. The 1957 model's scuttle height had been 2ft 5in; the 1958 'Knobbly's' 2ft 3in while the new body's headrest peaked at 3ft 3in. Ground clearance was 4in under the sump and 4½in beneath the chassis. Turning circle was quoted as 40ft and dry weight was 15½cwt, over 160lb more than the 1957 prototype, distributed 48/52 per cent front/rear (dry, one presumes). Once again Dunlop pressed-disc 16in wheels were used, carrying 6.00 (instead of the 1957 car's 5.50) front tyres and 6.00 rears — normally Dunlop in Britain and Europe, and Firestone in the USA. Briggs Cunningham's cars were on Firestones, as worn by the prototype that sunny February day in Cambridge.

Rear-quarter view showing the high-mounted fuel tank with battery, spare wheel and oil tank mountings underneath.

The 'Knobbly' Lister-Jaguar used a slightly offset transmission line and Lister-Salisbury final-drive assembly to give the driver some extra room. This shot shows the layout in the brand-new Equipe Nationale Belge car in the paddock at Silverstone before its debut in the 1958 May meeting there. The bolt-heads reveal the offset mounting, while the brake calipers — with handbrake calipers underneath — are now mounted ahead of the axle line. Unequal-length half-shafts are used, and the 'war paint' markings on the final-drive casing are temperature paints, used to record peak running temperatures. The car's ENB ownership is revealed by its use of Dunlop R4 tyres, whereas both works cars at this meeting used the new nylon-braced carcass R5s.

What is thought to have been the prototype Briggs Cunningham team 1958 Lister-Jaguar, chassis BHL 101, being loaded on to the air-freighter before its transAtlantic flight to New York in time for the Sebring 12-Hours race. The car has yet to have its American blue stripes and its sill louvres applied. Note the deep carpet upholstery and furled regulation hood. The engine bulge top hatch saved the need for complete bonnet removal for minor work.

Brian announced that Jaguar-engined cars had been ordered, either complete or in component form, by Écurie Ecosse, by Pierre Stasse's Equipe Nationale Belge and by Peter Whitehead, while two works cars would be campaigned, one for Scott-Brown of course, and the other for a driver or drivers yet to be named. Five Chevrolet-powered cars had already been ordered from America, and the Lister works, managed by George Palmer, had installed one Chevvy engine in a frame destined for Carroll Shelby/Jim Hall — one of three American distributors Brian had adopted. This exercise allowed the works to finalize adequate engine mountings and ancillary fittings for the power unit, so that properly prepared rolling chassis could then be shipped ready for simple engine fitting in the United States. On December 17, 1957, Brian Lister (Light Engineering) Ltd had issued a press release announcing the appointment of Carroll Shelby as Lister distributor for all US States west of the Mississippi with the exception of Oregon, Washington and part of Northern California, where Tom Carstens of Seattle had the franchise, though West Coast Jaguar distributor Kjell Qvale later took an interest. Briggs Cunningham and the Momo Corporation handled the Eastern States.

That winter had also seen some important tyre developments, either side of the New Zealand tour. Don Moore: 'I recall one test session at Silverstone where we tried Dunlop, Avon and Continental back-to-back. Archie found that just putting Avons on the car was worth an instant 1-1½ secs a lap. Obviously Brian was keen to go with Avon on the strength of that and it looked to be going through when he was told: "We're sorry — we are over-extended and can't supply you". We thought Aston Martin had put the elbow on it. Avon supplied them as standard equipment on the production cars so they had a lot to lose. We had a set of Avons which Dunlop looked at, but their new R5 then appeared'. Dick Barton's 1958 log book records a Snetterton test session on March 12 at which Archie tried the new nylon-braced Dunlop RS5s and his times instantly tumbled two seconds a lap! Dunlop had produced another winner.

Cunningham's first car was collected from the air-freighter at New York on March 1, the second arrived soon after and both were Momo-prepared in time for Sebring, where Archie was to share one car with Walt Hansgen and Ed Crawford the other with Pat O'Connor.

During practice the snow-white Listers with their twin blue stripes sounded glorious and were very quick, but still no match for Moss' Aston Martin DBR1/300, which got below the lap record to head the start line-up. Archie ran fifth in the opening stages behind Moss and Salvadori in their Astons and Hawthorn and Phil Hill in Ferrari Testa Rossas, while Crawford chased two more Ferraris in eighth place.

On the fourth lap, at the hairpin, Archie's Lister slowed early and Olivier Gendebien was caught-out badly in his pursuing Ferrari, ramming the Cunningham car's tail and riding over it — his left front tyre clumping the Scot's helmet and leaving a tread mark on his shoulder! The Belgian gracelessly manhandled his car down and drove off to the pits — eventually to finish second — while a bitterly disappointed Scott-Brown was out of the race, his sudden deceleration having been caused by a piston burning out. The second Cunningham car suffered an identical failure within the first 45-minutes, followed by every other Jaguar-engined entry.

The Cunningham Lister-Jaguars were then re-engined with full 3.8-litre units and completely dominated the Sports Club of America Championship that season, and with later Listers through 1959 as well. Walt Hansgen proved virtually unbeatable and Ed Crawford played a faithful supporting role. Hansgen won his first six races of the 1958 season, at Marlboro (Maryland), Danville (Virginia), Cumberland (Maryland), Bridgehampton (New York), Lime Rock (Connecticut) and Elkhart Lake (Wisconsin), with Crawford second on his four appearances, and so it went on . . . Listers unbeatable.

Meanwhile, Archie and Dick Barton had visited Lance Reventlow's Scarab operation during their Sebring trip and back home on March 30 the British season began at Snetterton. Archie was to drive the works team's new 'Knobbly', registered VPP 9 after the Issard-Davies Lister-Bristol, which had been taken by the works in part-exchange when he bought the Maserati-powered MER 303 for Allan Moore to drive in 1957. VPP 9 had been reconstructed with a new parallel centre-section chassis and magnesium body and Archie immediately won the over-2,700cc sports car and *Formule Libre* races to celebrate his return to his home circuit. Brian Lister's thoughts,

Cunningham team cars dominated SCCA sports-racing events in 1958-59 with 'Knobbly' and Costin-bodied Lister-Jaguars, while Chevrolet V8-powered devices — in which a much more capacious bonnet bulge was necessary — became very popular. Here at Virginia International Raceway, Danville, Va, Walt Hansgen has his car's screen modified with Cunningham team technical director Alfred Momo supervizing at right. Note the sill louvring on Ed Crawford's car on the left.

however, were elsewhere, his wife José having given birth to their daughter, Nicola, at 10.15 that morning.

The serious business of the International sports car season began at Goodwood on Easter Monday, April 7, where Moss ran a works Aston DBR2, Peter Collins had the prototype Ferrari Dino 206S and Archie reappeared in VPP 9, replacing a 3.4 engine with a 3.8 after practice. Still, he had unofficially broken the lap record and for the first time there were three Lister-Jaguars on the grid; VPP 9, Peter Whitehead's brand-new car built-up from the usual kit of parts at his garage, Motorwork of Chalfont St Peter, and Bruce Halford, making his debut in Dick Walsh's Gomm-bodied HCH 736. Once again Archie led the sprint to their cars, but Moss was first away with Collins on his tail and VPP 9 slewing away in a huge power-slide third. Scott-Brown flashed past the red Dino and out-dragged the Aston Martin along Lavant Straight to lead back past the pits. But in the flurry of the Le Mans-type start Archie had trapped his seat-back cushion under his backside so he was sitting higher in the cockpit than normal with little or no back support. He struggled for four laps to shift the cushion, but there was never a spare moment in the lead with Moss on his tail. After nine laps he had slowed right down and Moss went by, Dick Barton's log-book revealing that VPP 9 'retired on the 10th lap with broken rack brackets . . .'. The extra cornering power of the new nylon-carcass Dunlop R5s had proved too much for the rack fixings. They were reinforced before the car's next appearance and Brian issued a safety bulletin to his customers recommending modification; he had George Lister & Sons Ltd's reputation at stake . . . The customers were impressed.

Le Mans-type starts were very spectacular. Here at Goodwood, on Easter Monday, 1958, Moss' Aston Martin has already departed while Peter Collins' brand-new Ferrari Dino 206S (No. 2) sets off with Archie's new works 'Knobbly', VPP 9, broadsiding wildly on the left. Once again, of course, the driver's side-door screen would have been omitted to allow him easy entry. Archie led this race before retiring when R5 tyre dynamics fractured the car's steering-rack mounts.

The following Saturday saw the British Empire Trophy at Oulton Park, run in the old manner with three capacity-class heats and a final. Archie ripped six whole seconds off his own record time of 1:56.0, averaging 90.36mph to qualify on pole. He was facing two 3.9-litre Astons for Moss and Brooks, plus the Listers of Whitehead and Halford, neither of whom had shone at Goodwood. Archie took an instant lead from Moss, Brooks and Halford again until the ninth lap, when Moss began to close noticeably before going ahead next time round. Archie had spotted the Jaguar engine's oil temperature rising ominously and opted to ease off as this was only a qualifying heat. Halford was fourth close behind Brooks, while Whitehead had retired with exhaust fumes from a broken pipe filling the cockpit.

Moss led Scott-Brown for four more laps until VPP 9 abruptly broke a steering arm at the exit from Druid's Corner — the colossal loadings induced by R5 tyres now proving too much for the basically Morris Oxford arm.

Fortunately, Archie halted the car safely. Moss and Brooks finished 1-2 in the big Astons with Halford an excellent third, while Archie had set fastest lap third time round at 1:51.0, 89.55mph. The final was due to start at 5pm and at the suggestion of Bruce Halford and Dick Walsh the works driver took over HCH 736. The Stewards were agreeable, and without time to alter the car's pedals to fit the diminutive Scott-Brown into six-footer Bruce Halford's cockpit the mechanics stuffed as many cushions behind his back as they could find. He started from row two, behind the Astons and a couple of Lotuses, and was fourth at the end of the opening lap. When Cliff Allison's 2-litre Lotus broke its engine Scott-Brown inherited a third-place finish behind the two Astons — disappointed, but in the money.

Back at Abbey Road, Brian sat down and designed a supplementary steering-arm modification to withstand the loads generated by Dunlop's new tyres and again circularized his customers to warn them of the situation. Briggs Cunningham was impressed — he had never expected such service from such a modest concern — while Stan Sproat, head mechanic of Ecurie Ecosse, who were just completing their own new Lister-Jaguar at that time, recalled: 'Lister were really excellent at keeping the customers informed. If they found a problem you heard about it straight away, and never through the jungle telegraph'.

This hectic season continued with the Aintree 200 meeting in Liverpool the following weekend, where the new magnesium-bodied Ecosse car, chassis BHL 104, Edinburgh-registered 341 SG, made its debut driven by the bass-voiced and bespectacled little Kansan, Masten Gregory. Archie blared into an instant lead in VPP 9 and on his first flying lap set a new record of 2:04.4. Gregory was haring round on his heels in the metallic dark blue Scots car, wheel-to-wheel with Salvadori and Brooks in the works Astons. Roy equalled the new Lister-Jaguar record to take a second place from Gregory, while Halford spun HCH 736 at Tatts, swiped the wall and retired with a ruptured radiator. As Salvadori came round with Gregory on his tail Masten lost control and spun on to Mrs Topham's lawns at Tatts, rejoining without losing third place. Archie knew Salvadori was close as the 3.9 Aston lapped in 2:03.6, 87.38mph, and closed within feet of the Lister's tail, but the Scot did better through back-markers and won by a few lengths. Masten Gregory had given notice he would be running amongst the favourites.

The BRDC Silverstone International followed on May 3 and there for the first time Brian Lister fielded two Jaguar-powered works cars — the usual VPP 9 for Archie and a newly-completed 1958 MVE 303, in similar magnesium-bodied trim, initially intended for Jean Behra. When the BRM driver opted-out, BP produced Wolfgang Seidel to take his place, his emphatic *Wunderbars* creating

Archie again in VPP 9 in long-bonnet magnesium-bodied form leading the 1958 British Empire Trophy at Oulton Park before strengthened steering-rack mountings transferred R5 tyre loads to the steering arms, one of which broke.

considerable amusement within the team. In practice Archie lapped at 1:43.0, 102.3mph. Gregory's Ecosse car was next up on 1:44.6, ahead of three works Astons for Brooks, Salvadori and Moss. 'That's nice', said Archie, 'two Listers in front of the Astons', but the race was to see him beaten for the first time by what was virtually a car of his own creation.

One report described it this way: 'First away was Archie with Brooks right on his tail, then Salvadori, Gregory, Halford and Moss. They screamed under the bridge and into Copse at a fantastic pace. At the end of the standing lap Archie was still in the lead, followed by Brooks, Gregory and Salvadori . . . The second works Lister-Jaguar driven by Seidel came into the pits and retired with no oil pressure. However, Archie was still in the lead in the other car and Masten Gregory was rapidly closing up on Brooks and on lap five passed him into second place.

'On lap six Brooks called at his pit . . . Brooks having got out of the way, Masten Gregory put his hoof hard down on the loud pedal and went after Scott-Brown, passing him at Copse on lap seven. This man Gregory can really drive and having passed Archie proceeded to build up a commanding lead . . . whereas at the end of five laps the race average was 97.85mph, at the end of 10 Gregory had pushed it up to 98.66mph. Faster than the old lap record!

'With 10 laps to go Gregory led at 99.21mph, Scott-Brown still second, Hawthorn (Dino) third, Salvadori fourth, Halford fifth, but about to be passed by Brooks on lap 19, whereupon poor Halford came to grief. The offside top wishbone broke and he came into the pits with his wheel almost at the horizontal. Hard luck after such a fine drive . . .

'And so they continued until the end of the 25 laps. Gregory was nearly half-a-minute ahead of Scott-Brown . . . and also set-up fastest lap in 1:44.0, 101.32mph!'

Don Moore: 'When Archie brought the car back into the paddock after the race we asked him what was wrong and he shook his head and said "There was nothing wrong, nothing at all — I drove as hard as I could but I just couldn't *win!*".'

'Wilkie' Wilkinson of Ecurie Ecosse: 'We knew a thing or two about aerodynamics and the front wings of our car were faired smoothly back into the bodyline near the cockpit, whereas the works cars' wings curved down very sharply behind the wheels and we knew that would make low pressure there and make the car's front-end liable to lift. I'd also paid a lot of attention to reducing that car's unsprung weight — it was all special bits we made ourselves.' Perhaps more objectively Stan Sproat recalled: 'I think Lister were too good to us. When we had first got our D-Types from Jaguar we were always a year behind their works cars. Lister told us everything we wanted to know, and at that time we were very close to Jaguar on engines and in fact had a corner of their service department to work in. The anti-lift fairings were a Wilkie-ism dreamed-up in the pub, I think, to make the body more like our Ds, but I think Silverstone was mainly a question of a strong engine and a very quick driver . . . Gregory could drive a bit y'know . . .'.

After his appearances in Sweden, New Zealand and the USA, Archie Scott-Brown had at last been accepted by race organizers in the heartland of Western Europe; the Belgian club organizing the G P de Spa on May 18 — the same day as Monaco — having accepted a works entry for VPP 9.

On the intervening weekend, May 11, there was a BRSCC meeting at Mallory Park which had Archie's works Lister as its star attraction. Since VPP 9 was being carefully prepared for Spa, he drove MVE 303 fresh from its brief appearance in Seidel's hands at Silverstone. Archie led all the way to win at 85.01mph from Bruce Halford in HCH 736 and set fastest lap on the way in 56.2secs, 86.48mph. Bruce appeared to be catching Archie in the turns and invariably left his braking later than anybody else. He told Gregor Grant: 'It might have looked that way but it wasn't from choice — my foot was down amongst the front suspension trying to stop!' In 1980 Bruce still recalled those terrible Lister brakes: 'We were always in trouble — at Silverstone the fluid boiled after six hard laps, and thereafter you'd be charging round with your right foot on the throttle and the left frantically pumping the brake pedal; if you didn't pump, you didn't stop, it was as simple as that'.

The Lister works, Ecurie Ecosse, Dick Walsh and Whitehead teams travelled to Spa for the following Sunday's race. Practice began there on Friday, May 16, the weather wet but mild and Scott-Brown and Gregory instantly at each other's throats, setting meteoric times around the majestic and supremely fast

Silverstone, May 1958, with the works team's brand-new 'Knobbly' MVE 303 alongside its transporter on the runway paddock with Ken Hazlewood and Dick Barton working on BHL 105, the new Equipe Nationale Belge car, alongside. Note MVE 303's regulation hood, brake-bleeding bottles and the wing of VPP 9 in the foreground.

8.8-mile road circuit high in the Ardennes. Paul Frère and Carroll Shelby were driving works Aston DBR2s, Gendebien a Ferrari V12, but the Listers were supreme. Saturday practice was dry, which suited the Listers and not the Astons. Ecosse geared their car for the long pull back up the hill from Stavelot to the La Source hairpin above the pits, rather than for maximum speed on the long Masta Straight. Wilkie recalls they used a special final-drive ratio, but Stan Sproat doubts it: 'We had a special 2.78 for Le Mans and we made up a 2.68, but the engine couldn't pull it. I'm almost certain we ran a standard 3.31 at Spa.' Gregory had more experience of this type of circuit than Scott-Brown, and he took pole with a best of 4:10.3 from Archie's 4:13.7, whose average speed for the lap was 125mph! VPP 9 practised on the lightweight bolt-on hubs used by the works team for sprint races at home in preference to the knock-offs employed whenever a tyre change was a possibility. Dick Barton was looking after the car in a garage at Stavelot while Archie, Brian, Don Moore and Archie's father, Bill, were in a hotel in the centre of Spa. To keep the hard-worked engine a little cooler three large slots were cut in the hatch and on either side of the bonnet panel behind the front wheelarches. Dick fitted the knock-off hubs for the race.

May 18 dawned grey and threatening and rain fell during the GT race beginning the afternoon. Carroll Shelby's Aston made a superb start from the second row of the grid with Paul Frère on his tail in the sister car from the front row — the Astons' five-speed gearboxes giving them an initial advantage over the Listers, which tore ahead at the end of the Masta Straight. Rain was local, affecting some parts of the course while others remained dry, and Gregory and Scott-Brown were locked in a terrific battle, leaving no margin for error.

A youthful Jimmy Clark was driving Border Reivers' D-Type in that race on his Continental debut: 'Suddenly there was an almighty howl of sound, a blast of wind, the whole car shook, and Masten went steaming past like a bat out of hell. He was well out in the lead with the Lister-Jaguar all sideways, his arms crossed-up and fighting the steering. I remember having a sudden twinge of shock and thinking: "To heck with this, if this is motor racing I'm going to

The opposition. Stan Sproat and Masten Gregory with Ecurie Ecosse's only once-raced Lister-Jaguar, BHL 104, in the Silverstone paddock at the May 1958 meeting. The anti-lift fairings rivetted into place behind 341 SG's front wing peaks are clearly visible in this Geoff Goddard shot.

give it up now". It really put me off. I didn't think anyone could drive as quickly as that . . .'.

Scott-Brown and Gregory were passing and repassing continuously around the circuit, VPP 9 already with a dented nose when Archie shot round the Clubhouse Bend before La Source and found the road slick from a rain shower, and lost it. Don Moore: 'The car grazed the Seaman Memorial there — it was where he had been killed in 1939 — glanced along the Clubhouse wall and then hit a road sign which Paul Frère had asked the organizers to remove in practice, but they hadn't bothered'. The sign stanchion snapped the car's right-side track-rod, folded the suspension back on that side and VPP 9 was beyond control. It nose-dived down the roadside slope, its tail came up and over and it rolled to rest inverted with its nose down, tail up and fuel gushing from an almost full tank. It ignited and a huge fire broke out, turning glittering white as the magnesium body caught.

Don Moore: 'I think it's right that a *gendarme* pulled Archie out. We saw him in the medical cottage in the paddock soon after. He was conscious. He said something like: "Well, I made a right bloody mess of that, didn't I?". We were waiting in the little room there, with great lumps in our throats and the doctor came out and said: "You realize, I hope, that your poor friend has the same burns as Richard Seaman in 1939; I was the doctor who took care of him then . . ." and he looked at us and we knew Archie was dying . . .'.

The much-loved little Scot died in hospital at about 4 o'clock the following afternoon, with his father at his bedside and his mother, Jeay, on her way from Cambridge. The tangle of whitened metal which was VPP 9 lay overnight where it had come to rest. Dick Barton: 'Next morning Brian, Don and myself

Beaten for the first time in what was virtually his very own type of car: Archie Scott-Brown in VPP 9 during the Silverstone race on May 3, 1958. The rounded form of the front wings is clearly visible here; note also the long-bonnet body with reinforcing rivetting around the rear wheel-arch, bolt-on hubs and oil-cooler mounting in the nose intake.

Moment of truth. Masten Gregory storms the Ecurie Ecosse Lister-Jaguar ahead of Scott-Brown at Copse Corner during the Silverstone race. The joint where the anti-lift fairings attached to the original Williams & Pritchard body's front wings is clearly visible on the Scottish car's bodywork. Note also the knock-on customer hubs.

Mallory Park, May 11, 1958. Archie's last Lister-Jaguar victory was achieved in the once-raced MVE 303 'Knobbly' as VPP 9 was lying ready for the trip to Spa. Here, MVE 303 shows off its distinctive, badly fitting driver's side door, which stayed with it throughout its life. Note also the screen cup to deflect air over the driver's head and — in the background — Bruce Halford's HCH 736.

and some others including Jack Fairman loaded it on to our transporter and I set off for home minus the customs documents which Brian had. Having realized this and wondering what sort of argument I would have with the customs — no documents and an unrecognizable car — I was caught by Bruce Halford and Dick Walsh, who had the documents with them. Then at the border I heard on the radio that Archie had died. I couldn't believe it. I never thought he was going to die . . .'. The race had been won by Gregory with Freddy Rousselle sixth in ENB's Lister-Jaguar, Whitehead ninth and Bruce having been plagued by gearbox trouble in Walsh's car.

Brian Lister: 'After Archie's death my immediate impulse was to retire from racing, but as a company we had existing contracts and commitments and one had to put one's personal feelings to one side and get on with the job.

'But after our early-season steering problems I was frightened something had failed on Archie's car. While we were with him Reg Parnell went up and had a look at the wreck and said we'd got nothing to worry about on that account, but when we got it home Fred Matthews and another RAC scrutineer came up to examine what was left just in case. They found no evidence of any failure before the impact and fire.'

The sad remains were scrapped, many years later John Harper building a new VPP 9 from some old chassis parts, including a front square carrying the number BHL 3. It may have come from a replacement VPP 9 which Brian's men built-up from the original spares to join MVE 303 in the works team. After witnessing the fire Brian swore he would not have another magnesium body,

and the rebuilt VPP 9 used an aluminium customer shell by Williams & Pritchard. These shells used fixed scuttle panelling carrying the windscreen, while the magnesium bodies had full-length bonnets sliding forward and lifting away complete with the windscreen attached.

In Britain the Lister season fell mute, but at Le Mans on June 21-22 Bruce Halford and Brian Naylor shared HCH 736 in the 24-Hours, with Brian and Dick Barton in attendance in addition to Walsh's normal crew. Equipe Nationale Belge entered their Lister-Jaguar for Claude Dubois/Freddy Rousselle, both cars using short-stroke Coventry-assembled XK engines. The Belgians' was in piston trouble early in practice and started as walking-wounded to retire almost immediately, and in the first 10 minutes Ninian Sanderson's Ecosse 3-litre D-Type also belched smoke and retired with piston failure. The writing was on the wall . . .

When the skies darkened and torrential rain fell at 6.10pm all hell broke

No quarter. Archie's VPP 9 — already with its nose dented — and Gregory's 341 SG locked in combat at the **Raidillon** early in the tragic Spa race.

Gregory locking the Ecosse car into the La Source hairpin on his way to victory at Spa after Archie's accident. This fine Andre van Bever shot shows 341 SG's anti-lift fairing, long-bonnet magnesium-alloy body. An extra Perspex panel was fitted within the standard screen and protruded 2-3 inches above it, as just visible here, to deflect air over the driver's head on this super-fast course.

loose with cars sliding and crashing all round the course. Through all the mayhem plumed old HCH 736, driven with commendable skill and calm by Halford and Naylor. Into the long wet night it lay seventh overall, only for its run to be interrupted by a broken camshaft. The crew set to work undaunted and replaced it, rebuilding the engine in 90 minutes and restarting eighth. Later that Sunday morning Brian Naylor found the gearbox jammed and pulled on to the verge after Mulsanne. Watched by a knot of photographers and spectators he struggled manfully with the transmission, aided eventually by a couple of Jaguar mechanics who had hurried to the scene. They dared not work on the car but Brian 'found' some tools on the verge — just where he had stopped! — and following the mechanics' instructions he whipped the top off the gearbox and jammed it into top gear. He managed to restart and whoop away back to the pits, having lost another hour. With four hours to survive HCH 736 trundled round jammed in top, eventually broke a brake pipe and lost its rear brakes completely, and fell back through the field, finally finishing a battered and crippled but unbowed 15th after her crew had endured troubles which would have broken lesser men.

A week later, on June 29, the Ecosse team were at Monza for the Two Worlds Trophy 500-Miles speedway race in which European cars were confronting the American Indianapolis establishment. Ecosse had run successfully in this event the previous year, using D-Type sports cars, and now Wilkinson and Sproat and the Ecosse mechanics had built-up a special single-seater based on Lister sports chassis BHL 109.

The car had been fitted with an aluminium slipper body with off-set cockpit by Williams & Pritchard and was assembled as a rolling chassis in the team's Edinburgh base at Merchiston Mews. It had been taken in the team's transporter, along with the D-Types, to the Nürburgring 1,000 Kms on June 1 and was completed in the paddock and at the BMW garage there in the week or so following the race, then went on to Monza for shakedown testing. A stronger de Dion tube, carried on a larger-diameter sliding-block pin, plus more robust wishbones, suspension arms and spring abutments were adopted to combat high G-loading on the Monza speed bowl's bankings. The track-tuned 3.8-litre

XK engine was partially offset to the nearside to give assymetric weight distribution for the left-turn-only speedway, and with triple Webers it was claimed to be giving 300bhp. The dry-sump oil tank, a small battery and the fuel pumps were relocated within the cockpit, the driver's seat being offset to the right. Dunlop produced special 17in perforated disc wheels for the front with 18in spoked wheels at the rear, carrying 7.00 x 17 and 7.00 x 18 Dunlop tyres, respectively, according to the release, although Stan Sproat's notebook quotes 6.50 x 17s being used on the front for the race, while the final-drive ratio chosen was 3.53:1 as the engine would not pull Salisbury's special 2.68. Extra-light Dunlop disc brakes were carried, without servo-assistance, and transmission was through a normal D-Type gearbox. Steering was by a modified Lister-Morris system, while special kingpins and steering arms had been made. A 30-gallon fuel tank was slung in the tail and a lightweight water radiator and oil cooler helped trim overall weight to 15cwt dry, which compared poorly with the 1957 MVE 303.

Gregory passing the works Lister fire at Spa on his way to the right-handed hairpin at La Source, the Clubhouse wall along which VPP 9 had grazed being visible to the right.

All that remained of VPP 9 was taken home and closely examined by RAC scrutineers, who found that nothing had broken on the car before impact with the Spa road sign which had robbed Archie of control. It had been a furious fire.

Denis Jenkinson took these photos of the Ecosse single-seater Lister-Jaguar BHL 109 at Monza during practice for the Two Worlds Trophy speedway race in June 1958. The middle shot shows the offset and canted engine mounting and the use of a standard broad-planform sports chassis, the upper one shows 'Wilkie' examining the rear suspension, and the third the car complete with its offset-cockpit Williams & Pritchard bodyshell. It was a failure, though a 'guid start money car'.

Jack Fairman drove this special at Monza, but its huge exposed wheels and little-changed engine power made it a poorer proposition than the standard enveloping-bodied D-Types — the extra drag of exposed wheels seeming an obvious consideration at this range. Stan recalls it as 'a good start money car'. It qualified 15th fastest of 17 starters, slower than Gregory's D-Type, and Fairman soldiered round to finish 11th in the first 63-lap heat, the Prix Esso, six laps off the pace. In the Prix Mobil, Fairman finished 10th with smoke pouring from the exhaust, and he non-started in the final Prix Shell. The car was classified 11th on aggregate, with 114 laps completed. David Murray expressed his intention to convert the car into a sports-racer to join 341 SG in a two-car Ecosse Lister team.

Back home on July 5 the works Listers re-emerged with Ivor Bueb driving MVE 303 at Crystal Palace. The car's magnesium body had been modified with additional anti-lift fairings added behind the front wheelarches like the Ecurie Ecosse car's. Bueb qualified on pole — immediately taking up where poor Archie Scott-Brown had left off — ahead of Halford's HCH 736 and Graham Whitehead's DB3S. Bruce led away from Whitehead and Bueb, but after three laps the works car was ahead and completed the 20 laps victorious by 16secs from Halford. Ivor set a new outright sports car lap record at 79.43mph, while his race average of 76.94mph was the fastest yet in a sports car event at the Palace. The works car's livery had been modified with the yellow central band now extending full-width at nose and tail in a graceful sweep. Brian Lister: 'That parallel band had become so intimately identified with Archie that I thought it was best left in his memory'.

Two weeks later, the British Grand Prix meeting was held at Silverstone and the works and Ecosse Lister-Jaguars were to meet once more. At Le Mans Brian had had dinner with the Ecosse hierarchy and as they grew merrier there had been some tasteless ribbing about his cars and about the late Scott-Brown's abilities as a driver. Brian never forgot it, and was determined to crush them at Silverstone 'for Archie'.

'I was determined to get the best driver I could, and BP — who were the most generous of sponsors — arranged for Stirling Moss to join us. He was not too expensive and he did a superb job, and if he'd wanted a fortune I'd probably have paid it just for the satisfaction of blowing-off Gregory and Ecosse. Stirling knew we had had steering problems at the start of the season and asked point blank if that was what had happened at Spa. With the RAC scrutineers' report to back me I could assure him definitely not. Then he just went out and drove'.

He was in the magnesium-bodied MVE 303, while Walt Hansgen came over from the United States to handle the replacement VPP 9 — its aluminium body featuring integral anti-lift fairings in the front wing shape. During testing with Moss it was decided to box-in the carburettor intakes and feed them with air from a bonnet-top scoop, and during practice neat inboard brake-cooling hatches appeared on both cars' rear decks and Don Moore cut an extra intake on top of MVE 303's nose to reduce under-bonnet temperature and indirectly help cool the cockpit. Meanwhile, Masten Gregory — perhaps 'psyched' by Moss' presence — lost control of Ecosse's 341 SG at Woodcote and decided to step out as the car rushed across the verge towards the bank. He was picked up with two broken ribs, a chipped shoulder blade, some cuts and severe bruising, while the car was a write-off. Stan Sproat: 'Gregory had this theory about drawing his feet up and standing on the seat once a big accident was on the way, so he would be thrown clear, and it seemed to work. That car was very severely damaged indeed, and since we insured our cars at the time it was written-off — though the frame hung about at Merchiston Mews for several months before we found a use for some of it . . .'

The race was a grid-start 25-lapper and Moss started from pole on 1:44.0 — significantly a whole second slower than Archie's time in May. Hansgen was alongside, then came the Lotuses of Salvadori and Hill; there were no works Astons. Moss led from the flag and won at 97.92mph, sharing his fastest lap of 1:46.0, 99.42mph — two seconds outside Gregory's record — with Allison.

Walt Hansgen burned-out his clutch on the line, took second place briefly, but then had to retire. Halford was an outpaced sixth in HCH 736.

The following weekend found Hansgen at Snetterton for the Vanwall Trophy meeting, joined by New Zealander Ross Jensen in the works cars. Jensen had impressed Archie and Dick Barton that winter and was now on a BP-backed tour to England. He drove MVE 303, Hansgen VPP 9, both 3.8-engined against Halford's 3.4-litre HCH 736. Hansgen walked away with the eight-lap sports car event, smashing Archie's lap record with a best of 1:42.8, 94.55mph, while Jensen just held off Halford for second place. A 10-lap *Formule Libre* event ended the day, with Hansgen again victorious, 4.8secs clear of Henry Taylor's F2 Cooper, with Jensen third and Halford fourth.

On August 4 the Bank Holiday Brands Hatch meeting saw Bueb joining Jensen in VPP 9 and MVE 303, respectively, for the Kingsdown Trophy race in

In practice for the 1958 British GP meeting at Silverstone, Stirling Moss drove MVE 303 in its new post-Scott-Brown Lister livery, this Graham Gauld shot showing the carburettor ram intake added after pre-race testing, the all-yellow plain nose and still badly-fitting driver's door. For the race (lower picture) a green surround has been painted round the radiator intake and Don Moore has opened an engine-bay cooling slot above the nose. Note also the inboard brake cooling intake on the tail deck, and anti-lift fairing joint lines on the front wings.

which they sandwiched Halford's faithful HCH 736 on the front of the grid and finished 1-2-3 — Bueb, Jensen, Halford.

The 750 Motor Club's 6-Hours relay race that month at Silverstone saw Peter Mould driving Norman Hillwood's Lister-Jaguar 673 LMK as part of the Jaguar DC team, which finished ninth on handicap. In America, the August 17 Montgomery meeting, in New York State, saw Hansgen and Crawford in Cunningham's Lister-Jaguars clash with fuel-injected Scarab-Chevrolets driven by Chuck Daigh and Lance Reventlow. Fred Windridge's Lister-Chevrolet qualified alongside Daigh and Crawford on the front row, and Daigh won after Hansgen had burst a tyre and Crawford's diff had seized. John Norwood's ex-Cunningham-Reid Lister-Bristol was fourth in the Class E Modified event at this meeting.

On September 7 the Snetterton MRC had organized a major Scott-Brown Memorial Trophy meeting — the cup being presented by Archie's mother for the 15-lap *Formule Libre* feature event. Ross Jensen won the supporting sports car race in MVE 303, while Ivor Bueb took it over for the *Libre* event and beat Jim Russell's F2 Cooper by 0.4sec. It was reported that in Jensen's race, '. . . P.Melville drove a 2½-litre Lister-Jaguar of neat appearance which finished in seventh position overall'. Pat Melville was a Scot who drove a special Lister built by Merchiston Motors — the Ecurie Ecosse-associated garage in Edinburgh — for Sir Alexander Miller, head of the Motherwell Bridge Works. The body was Williams & Pritchard-built under 'Wilkie's direction, losing the deep 'hills and valleys' of the standard 'Knobbly' and the car was Motherwell-registered GM 9639. Its chassis was BHL 111 and Miller used it gently as a road-cum-race car. It was sold subsequently to Phil Scragg, who had Lister install a 5.4 Chevy V8 in the 'sixties. He didn't like it much and sold it to Yorkshire trout farmer George Tatham, who finally sold the very decrepit Lister, minus engine, to David Ham for £1,250. Ham persuaded George Tyrrell and Colin Crisp of the original Lister works team, and still with Lister into the 'eighties, to care for the car and it became one of the most successful Lister-Jaguars in historic sports car racing, being housed in Geo. Lister & Sons Ltd's new works at Cherry Hinton, Cambridge, into which they moved from Abbey Road in 1967.

Meanwhile, on September 13, 1958, Brian had fielded both works cars in the RAC Tourist Trophy at Goodwood, and both carried massive 'snorkel' intakes to cool the rear brakes. VPP 9 was to be shared by Ivor Bueb/Bruce Halford and MVE 303 by Ross Jensen and John Bekaert, who had driven old HWM 1 so brilliantly in club events that season. Bueb qualified fourth fastest on 1:33.2 compared to Moss' Aston Martin pole time of 1:32.0; Jensen was 10th quickest

at 1:35.8. Bueb lay fourth early in the race, going great guns amongst the works Astons, but on lap 10 Salvadori slid into Eddie Greenall's Lotus at Madgwick Corner, Shelby shot by unscathed, but Ivor was forced into violent avoiding action and bounded off into the rough, damaging VPP 9's steering so badly he was forced to retire. Jensen was called in for Bueb to take over MVE 303, rejoining a lap behind the leaders, but still fourth. At the first scheduled stop Bruce Halford took over, only for an upright to fail at Woodcote, Bruce retiring on the grass at the chicane with one front wheel folded-up.

Bruce Halford: 'That was a bad weekend for kingpin breakages. During early testing I broke one below the stub-axle as I hit the brakes for Woodcote, the wheel leaned in and I limped into the pits. Brian had both cars torn apart and the kingpins were all found to be cracked. They made new wishbones with perforated stiffening webs between the tubular members, seen today on any Lister wishbone in historic racing. Brian was always honest with us. He explained what had happened and said: "It's up to you whether you race or not". Well, of course we were pros — no race, no money — so we drove and in the race I broke another kingpin, only this time above the stub-axle and the wheel folded-out.'

One week later the Oulton Park Gold Cup was run as a 125-miler for sports cars and Brian fielded just MVE 303 for Bueb, Jensen's entry being withdrawn, while Halford was back in HCH 736. Stasse's ENB team ran their luckless Le Mans Lister for André Pilette. Bueb started the 45-lap race from pole with a best lap in 2:07.0 from Halford on 2:07.6, Brian Naylor's JBW-Maserati on 2:09.2 and Pilette's 2:13.0, practice being wet so that nobody could approach Archie's April time of 1:55.0 in the ill-fated VPP 9.

Bueb led for three laps before being displaced by Salvadori's nimble 2-litre Lotus-Climax, which drew away from the heavier big-engined car at a second a lap. Salvadori lowered the late Benôit Musy's Maserati lap record from 1:56.0 to 1:55.2, 86.28mph, without troubling Scott-Brown's practice record, and Bueb was safely second despite clutch trouble. They finished that way, with Halford third and Pilette fifth. There were signs that the day of the heavy-metal sports car was drawing to its close . . .

This long British season closed on October 11 with the *Autosport* 3-Hours meeting at Snetterton, where the supporting 10-lap sports event saw Graham Hill's works 2-litre Lotus 15 beating Halford's HCH 736 by 1.6secs.

In America, the Watkins Glen GP that month gave Hansgen and Crawford another Cunningham Lister-Jaguar 1-2 success, and at Riverside the First US Grand Prix for Sports Cars saw Bill Pollack, President of the co-sponsoring California Club, driving an ex-Tom Carstens 5.7-litre Lister-Chevy, which Al Dean of Dean Van Lines had bought, engineless, for him. It boiled its brake fluid, he spun twice, rejoined and finished eighth on seven cylinders with water pumping out of the eighth stub exhaust! Cunningham's cars were absent.

During the winter of 1958-59 there were to be no foreign tours, simply hard work at Abbey Road where Brian had employed former De Havilland, Lotus and Vanwall aerodynamicist Frank Costin as body designer. Costin had been responsible for some of the brake-cooling developments on the TT cars and his new bodyshape for the 1959 Listers was shown to the press soon after the New Year. The Costin body closely resembled his earlier Lotus exercises and his one-off Maserati Le Mans coupe, with flaring front wings, thrust-forward nose and voluptuously curvaceous tail, high-decked and blending into a moulded Perspex windscreen-and-door window 'greenhouse'. The basic chassis frame was little changed from that used in the 1958 cars, retaining the parallel-tube centre-section and with body support brackets little changed from those designed to pick-up the obsolete 'Knobbly' body.

Heroine of Le Mans, 1958. Brian Naylor at speed in Dick Walsh's HCH 736, which he co-drove with Bruce Halford, and stationary in this Geoff Goddard shot taken near Mulsanne Corner as he wrestled to find a gear in the car's recalcitrant gearbox. Compare the car in this form with the picture of it as originated late in 1957 (page 110). The headlamps and radiator intake have been reprofiled in a rebuilt nose section.

This main frame was welded-up, as *Motor Racing* magazine described, on a permanent jig by Bob Gawthrop — a superb welder, still with the parent company 21 years later — and the front and rear subframes, made as sub-assemblies, were attached later. The final-drive was used to jig its own support frame and so speed production, and all engine and suspension pick-ups were carefully checked before frame despatch to Williams & Pritchard, where the body was made and fitted. Derek Watson would cut-out frame tubes to begin production of a Lister, chassis construction usually taking seven days, although it could be done in as little as four.

When the body-chassis unit returned to Cambridge from W & P in Edmonton final assembly could start in the fitting department. Dennis Belcher, Ken Hazelwood, Colin Crisp and George Tyrrell — and others in an emergency — worked in the machine shop on hubs, half-shafts, de Dion tubes and suspension parts and new modified kingpins were by now standard on all

The production-style works car VPP 9 pictured outside the Lister workshop in Priory Road, Cambridge, prior to the 1958 RAC Tourist Trophy in which its front suspension failed. This view shows clearly the inboard rear brake cooling schnorkel adopted for that race, the cockpit layout and the fixed scuttle/screen short-bonnet aluminium body-form betrayed by two joint lines ahead of the doors.

Listers. Ted Gray and Dick Bird produced tanks and ducting in the sheet metal shop. Final assembly took about two weeks as Dick Barton, Bill Noonan, Dick Martino, Dennis Adams and often some of the other lads would lend a hand to mount suspension, steering, wheels and brakes, engines, gearbox, radiator, tanks, piping and instruments. Normally just three men worked on a car at any one time, with George Palmer — a Lister man since 1947 — controlling work-flow through the shops. Wiring was completed on a Lucas-supplied loom, final connection and checking being made by the Cambridge Battery Service, nearby. Once complete, each car was taken to another Cambridge firm, Sutton & Mothersole Ltd, for spraying. Complete frames and other fabrications were made by Bob Gawthrop, Norman Smith, (the late) Derek Watson and John Knight, all 1959 car wishbones using the reinforcing webs introduced after those Goodwood TT failures.

Costin intended to use a bag-type tonneau cover — the subject of a patent application — which would inflate with air tapped from a high-pressure region within the new body and would fair-in the passenger's side of the cockpit at high speed. The high tail was intended to provide a stabilizing area in crosswinds without resort to drag-inducing separate fins. The new shell's scuttle height of 2ft 7in meant that the engine hump could be dispensed with, although overall height was little changed from the 'Knobbly' at 3ft 2in. The radiator used a ducted-air entry, but strangely no similar exit-air control, merely bleeding it away into the wheelarches and through a small port at the rear of the bonnet blister. The oil-cooler was mounted laterally on the left side beneath the bonnet, drawing cool air from a port in the body behind the front wheel, outlet air venting into the cockpit. Cox & Co (Watford) Ltd made some luxurious new seats, trimmed in hide with Bedford cord inserts. Brian had agreed with Dunlop to use their wheels, tyres and brakes, replacing the old Girling discs. The 12in discs were again mounted inboard at the rear, Costin adopting scraper wires à la Vanwall to split hot boundary air away from the disc surface into special exit ducts. In theory, cool air entered through an intake in the undertray. Another Costin duct led air around the finned rear cover of the Lister-Salisbury final-drive. The 12in Dunlop front discs mounted outboard with calipers again behind the axle line and steering ahead. Jaguar 3.0, 3.4 and 3.8-litre XK engines were specified plus the American Chevrolet V8s. The Borg & Beck three-plate six-spring hydraulic clutch was retained with the four-speed-and-reverse Jaguar D-Type gearbox. Eight final-drive ratios were again available, and a Powr-Lok LSD was standard, the ZF being extra.

Frank Costin had persuaded Brian Lister that minimizing frontal area was less important than sleek aerodynamic form, but dimensionally the new body was a gross affair, 14ft 4¾in in overall length, 5ft 7in wide, while wheelbase and track corresponded broadly with the 'Knobbly' at 7ft 6¾in, 4ft 4in (front) and 4ft 5½in (rear). One illuminating statistic was the ground clearance of 4¼in at the sump and no less than 6in beneath the chassis, 1½in more than

Ross Jensen leading the field away at Snetterton in MVE 303 in its definitive 1958 form with nose-top intake, screen cup, rivetted-on anti-lift fairings . . . and badly-fitting driver's door. On its quarter is John Bekaert in HWM 1, while the unpainted No. 68 beyond is Pat Melville's Sir Alexander Miller-owned Lister-Jaguar 2.4 GM 9639 — recently Ecosse-completed and raced with great success in Historic Sports Car events of the 'seventies and 1980 by David Ham.

the 'Knobbly'. Brian Lister: 'I really regret ever doing the Costin body. If I had my time over again I would clean up the 'Knobbly', and build lower and smaller, like the 1957 car and the Lister-Maserati'.

Works drivers were confirmed as Bueb and Halford, while Briggs Cunningham had ordered two of the new models and would again be running at Sebring. The Floridan 12-Hours was on March 21, and the Snetterton Spring meeting (opening the British season) on the following day. At Sebring, Moss shared the latest Costin-bodied Cunningham car, apparently chassis BHL 123, with Bueb while Walt Hansgen/Dick Thompson and Briggs Cunningham/Lake Underwood drove the team's older 'Knobblies'. Moss was fastest in practice at 3:33.0, while Hansgen managed 3:47.0. Bueb and Hansgen took the start in the faster Listers, running fourth and sixth early on, but after an hour's racing Hansgen lay fifth with Bueb being outpaced in the latest car. When Moss took over he elevated it to fourth place after three hours and, when the Hill/Gendebien Ferrari broke, the new Lister was third. Moss set about the two leading Ferraris and after five hours was with them. Hansgen/Thompson had a tyre burst and soon after half-distance Stirling made a refuelling stop and drove on. Then he went missing. Cunningham's crew had been churn-filling the car when Moss in his anxiety jumped aboard before the tank was full. He was about to set off when a pit marshal stopped him to have the tank officially sealed, then he boomed away, probably still 5-gallons light. The car ran out a mile short of the pits. Hansgen tried to nudge it home, but the Costin body's tail was too flimsy. Stirling hitched a lift back on a marshal's motorcycle and officialdom ruled this was 'outside assistance' and disqualified him. Brian was there: 'It was a tragedy — a perfectly healthy car in contention for the lead when it had to be abandoned. If I had been put in charge by Briggs instead of feeling I was merely there as a visitor and leaving it all to his men and Moss I feel we would never have thrown the race away like that . . . Sebring 1959 is one of my great regrets'.

Snetterton was grey and rainswept, and the meeting began with an eight-lapper for sports cars, won by Ron Flockhart in an Ecosse 3.8 Lister-Jaguar. Stan Sproat: 'That was the car using the Monza single-seater chassis. We had a body built for it by Williams & Pritchard with 'Wilkie' saying "take out that curve there and fill-in this bit here" so it was a kind of smoother 'Knobbly'. We'd been troubled by the diff overheating on both the early Lister and the Tojeiros. It made the oil-seals leak over the brakes and it was a toss-up which happened first — the brakes failed or the diff seized. On that 1959 Lister I opened-up the front of the chassis tubes, ducted air into them from the side intakes on the

The first Frank Costin-designed body installed on a Lister chassis after its arrival at Cambridge from bodybuilders Williams & Pritchard of Edmonton, London.

nose, opened a way through into the cross-member behind the cockpit, closed-off the rear section of the side tube and then welded-on mild-steel sheet ducts to blow the air on to the inboard discs and diff. You'll see there's no rear wing intakes on that body. We also fitted a big SU fuel pump, which drew oil from the diff to a cooler mounted flat under the tail. There was a switch on the dash and we warned the driver not to use the pump for at least the first three laps until the oil was so hot it had a consistency almost like petrol. Then he switched on the pump and left it circulating to cool the oil. It worked fine. Cunningham later picked it up on his light-alloy D/E. We fitted that system on both the 'Toj's and the Lister'.

The new car carried the Edinburgh registration RSF 301 inherited from a team D-Type. John Bekaert was second in Derek Wilkinson's ex-Whitehead Lister-Jaguar 'Knobbly' while Ray Brightman and John Ewer made their undistinguished debuts in two new Lister-Corvettes, thought to have been chassis BHL 125 and BHL 121, graduating from AC Aceca and Triumph TR, respectively. Flockhart and Bekaert were second and third in the 10-lap *Libre* race behind Russell's F2 Cooper.

Easter Monday Goodwood, on March 30, saw the debut of the 1959 works Lister team, their Costin-bodied 3.8 — possibly using the frame of the 'Knobbly' VPP 9, although this is very doubtful indeed — being driven by Ivor Bueb. Brian had adopted a new team livery, using a darker green and paler yellow stripe, and the cars were to run unregistered. The 21-lap Sussex Trophy was run in pouring rain. Salvadori's new C.T. Atkins-owned 2.5-litre Maserati mid-engined Cooper Monaco was handicapped by the conditions and Peter Blond led in Jonathan Sieff's brand-new Costin Lister-Jaguar from Graham Whitehead's Aston DBR1 and Bueb. Gregory lay fifth in the new Ecosse conversion, RSF 301, sandwiched by Monacos. On lap 15 Bueb took second and next time round he was in the lead, going away to win by 7secs at 78.64mph. Blond set fastest lap at 82.92mph.

On April 11 the British Empire Trophy race was run for Formula 2 cars at Oulton Park with a supporting sports car race and again it was wet. Two new works Costin-bodied Listers ran, for Bueb and Halford — both of whom had F2 rides that season in a Cooper-Borgward and a Lotus 16, respectively. Bruce lay fifth early in the race, was displaced by Graham Hill's Lotus and then plunged straight on into the lake at Cascades when a brake grabbed. He walked back to the pits to inform Brian that his cars floated well! When Don Moore, Dick Barton and the mechanics went out to retrieve the car they found a lake-bed stake driven clean through its radiator and up alongside the engine towards the

Stirling Moss at speed in Briggs Cunningham's brand-new Costin-bodied car during the Sebring 12-Hours in March 1959. The car is running one of Frank Costin's bright ideas — an aerofoil-section deflector just behind the cockpit — and it showed well in the race before an unfortunate chain of events caused it to run out of fuel when challenging strongly for the lead.

driver — and a wartime landmine surfaced in the mud as the car was hauled out! Jim Russell and Salvadori finished 1-2 in their Monacos, Hill was third, while Bueb was fifth and shared fastest lap at 80.28mph with Jack Brabham's Monaco. Jimmy Clark went well in the now Border Reivers-owned HCH 736, fitted with a 3.8-litre engine, as did Gregory in the converted single-seat Ecosse car. Don Moore recalled Jimmy at Oulton being worried because his new engine had swallowed a nut, dropped down a plug-hole: 'But it's OK, we started her up and blew it out . . .' The XK could be very strong!

One week later the circus was at Aintree for the 200 meeting, where Salvadori took pole at 2:05.6 and Gregory's RSF 301 was quickest of the big cars at 2:08.0. Halford non-started due to a practice bearing failure and Bueb retired early having run third until his car's oil pressure vanished. New steel oil-pipes had been sandblasted to remove welding scale and some of the sand had been trapped inside, turning the lubricating oil into a fair substitute for grinding paste. The engines were on loan from Jaguar, but they were very badly damaged. Gregory finished third and Clark was sixth in HCH 736.

On May 2 the BRDC International Trophy meeting at Silverstone saw a 3-litre sports car race dominated by Salvadori with Moss second in a works Aston DBR1. Bueb fought his way through the field to finish third while Gregory lay fifth early on in RSF301 until lap 14, when he tried to pass two backmarkers on the outside into Becketts Corner, lost control and stepped smartly overboard as the ex-Monza chassis smashed head-on into the safety bank. He escaped with a lacerated thigh. Blond was seventh in Sieff's car. It was quite a good day for Ivor the Driver, third in this race, second in the F2 category and winner of the touring car event in a 3.4 Jaguar saloon.

The following weekend, in Finland, the Elaintarharnajo-Djurgardsloppet race was held in Helsinki's Djurgard Park, neighbouring the 1952 Olympic Games stadium, and Pierre Stasse had entered his ENB Lister-Jaguar 'Knobbly', chassis BHL 105, for André Pilette, but he lost it in practice and virtually wrote-off the frame against a stout tree. It had never been a lucky car.

Ecurie Ecosse were also in trouble with their latest Silverstone wreck. Stan Sproat: 'David Murray was anxious to get the car repaired for another race so we took the old damaged chassis from Gregory's 1958 Silverstone shunt which had been lying around at the Mews and cut off its front frame and grafted that on to the Monza frame. What was left of the original 1958 chassis and the bent front-end of the Monza frame were then scrapped'.

Sixteen days after Silverstone, on May 18, there were two major Whit-Monday meetings in Britain. At Crystal Palace a 15-lap sports car race saw Hill's

Lotus showing the Monacos of Russell and Salvadori the way home, while Bueb finished fourth in his works Costin-bodied Lister and Bruce Halford was fifth in the veteran 'Knobbly' MVE 303, which was running unregistered on this occasion, but unmistakable with its magnesium full-length bonnet and rivetted-on anti-lift fairings.

At Goodwood that day Ecurie Ecosse's hastily repaired RSF 301 (with the main frame of BHL 109 and the front-end from 104) was driven by Peter Blond in support of Flockhart's Tojeiro-Jaguar, which won the 21-lap Whitsun Trophy as already described. Bekaert finished second in Wilkinson's ex-Whitehead 'Knobbly' and set fastest lap at 90.19mph, and Blond was third; Mike Anthony retired his Lister-Chevvy on lap 2 with fuel starvation. At Mallory Park that day Bill Jones drove his F2 Lister-Climax and finished fourth,

Costin-bodied Listers used some very smart Cox of Watford seats — 'because everybody always moaned about Lister seats' — and the cockpit layout was very neat and simple. This prototype car, photographed at Abbey Road, has yet to have its starter-motor installed, the empty mounting being visible beneath the rev-counter. The twin fuel pump mounting in the sill was carried on from the 'Knobbly' design.

eight laps behind the winner.

At the end of May a Snetterton race saw Bekaert further enhancing a burgeoning reputation in Wilkinson's NBL 660, beating Bill Moss' immaculate new Costin Lister-Jaguar, chassis BHL 126, Bedfordshire-registered as WTM 446. Brightman's 5.7 Lister-Chevvy was beaten by a newly-completed 3-litre Jaguar-engined 'Knobbly' driven by Birmingham metals founder Peter Mould. Registered YOB 575, it had been built-up for Mould by a friend named Mario Deliotti, based on probably the last 1958-style kit to leave Abbey Road.

Ecosse took their Lister and Tojeiro-Jaguar to Nürburgring for the ADAC 1,000 Kms on June 7, along with Peter Blond and Mike Taylor in the Sieff Costin car. Masten Gregory/Innes Ireland were to share the Ecosse Lister, but after only six laps the Kansan had a half-shaft UJ pull apart near Brünnchen and hit the hedgerow. The Sieff car was delayed by broken bonnet catches and then Taylor flew off the road and rolled it into a field, being lucky to emerge with just slight arm injuries.

Two weeks later, on the weekend of June 20-21, the Le Mans 24-Hours was run, towards which Brian Lister and his team had been working: 'I really regarded Le Mans as unfinished business after Archie's death and we were determined to do well there — that was one of the reasons for taking on Frank Costin to produce a really low-drag body for maximum speed along the Mulsanne Straight. We did a lot of development tailored to that race and Costin had an all-new lightweight spaceframe chassis on the stocks, but it was a long time completing'.

Dick Barton: 'One development for Le Mans was a strutted aerofoil air-brake the width of the car and about a foot in chord, which pivoted on two brackets welded to the chassis and projecting through slots in the bonnet. The intention was to operate the flap hydraulically, but we tested the idea at first light, early in the morning, on the main A11 road just before Snetterton with a manual lever under the dash. I would wait in the car at the Snetterton end of the three-mile straight for a torch signal from a chap we posted on the railway bridge at the other end, to give the all-clear. During these tests I was reaching 140-150mph, but we finally decided that the small amount of extra braking we were getting did not outweigh the disadvantage of bonnet-opening restrictions'.

The two works Listers for Le Mans were recorded in the ACO paperwork as:
1. Lister Jaguar Sports, 1959, 2996ccm

1959 Silverstone May meeting, with Ivor Bueb in the works Costin-bodied car leading Peter Blond in Sieff's customer car down Hangar Straight and into Stowe Corner.

Drivers — Bueb, Halford, McDonnell
Engine No. 1305/9
Chassis No. BHL2.59

2. Lister Jaguar Sports, 1959, 2996ccm
   Drivers — Hangsen, Blond, McDonnell
   Engine No. 1302/9
   Chassis No. BHL3.59
   Reserve engine No. EE.1304/9

The mysterious Mr. McDonnell was actually Mike MacDowell, a good friend of Ivor Bueb's and sales manager for John Coombs' Jaguar dealership in Guildford, who qualified the cars as reserve, while 'Hangsen' was of course Walt Hansgen. Both cars were the standard Costins, carefully prepared and fitted with Jaguar-prepared loan engines rather than Don Moore's own, which grieved him a little: 'I'd built some 3-litre engines from 3.4s using Jaguar's conversion kit, which made a good little engine. The works' 3-litres we had at Le Mans in 1959 had too short a stroke; half-way down the bore the con-rod angle was very acute and it was just over-stressed. I think we blew two engines in practice and Lofty England, Frank Rainbow and Ted Brookes of Jaguar helped us prepare the cars. They were a wonderful set of boys, but we had to run the works engines and they weren't quite up to it . . .'

Bruce Halford: 'In 1957 at Le Mans with old HCH 736 we'd been pulling 165mph on the Mulsanne Straight. In 1959 with the Costins we had 30 more bhp and the Costin body and a special tonneau which blew-up and changed the car's shape at high speed so it was almost like a coupe, and our top speed was still just 165, and the cockpit was impossibly hot. The whole car just felt big and uncomfortable'.

Don: 'The old Ecurie Ecosse D-Type was quicker than our cars, that old live-

The Ivor Bueb/Bruce Halford car at scrutineering for the Le Mans 24-Hours race being rolled over the minimum ground clearance 'box'. The car has a temporary stone guard to protect its radiator, while the white patches between the front wings cover slots cut for the strutted air-brake system, which was tested but not used owing to its restriction on bonnet opening during pitstops. Ivor Bueb was very indignant during practice since the Le Mans organizers had listed him as second driver to Halford. He had won the race twice and it stung the normally cheerful but very superstitious Cheltenham garage man deeply. He got to the point of refusing to drive unless the change was made publicly, even though to Brian he had always been number-one.

Peter Blond at speed in the works Lister-Jaguar, which he shared at Le Mans in 1959 with Walt Hansgen. Note the strut aperture patches on the nose, the 1959 livery styling and the inflatable Costin passenger side tonneau, duly inflated.

axle proving its worth again at Le Mans. Full fuel load in our cars put the half-shafts at a bad angle and I think we could have had some transmission power loss there to add to our frontal area and engine reliability problems. Neither did the D-Type have the ground clearance and turning circle arguments we had at scrutineering!'

Blond shunted the nose of his car on the last lap of practice, but after all these problems Ivor the Driver and Walt Hansgen were handily placed ninth and 11th after the first three hours of racing, two laps behind the leading Ferrari and Aston Martin. After some four hours and 52 laps the Hansgen/Blond car was the first to go as its engine blew apart, Don picking bits of rod and piston out of the undertray afterwards. At 9.00pm Bueb/Halford were fifth, and at the end of the seventh and eighth hours Lister-Jaguar Number 1 was fourth and with one less pit stop scheduled than the leaders. Prospects looked bright at last, if only it could last. But it could not, and the engine failed in the ninth hour after 121 laps had been completed.

Brian: 'There wasn't a lot left to race for. It was becoming more and more expensive and the returns were minimal in home events, while development work on the spaceframe car was becoming almost prohibitively expensive — it was soaking up funds like a sponge'.

In the USA Hansgen had won at Cumberland and Danville in his Cunningham Costin model and on July 5 he won again at Bridgehampton, the car running Halibrand cast-alloy wheels in a hard race against George Constantine's special 4.1-litre Aston Martin DBR1. John Fitch and Briggs himself drove the other team cars and Fred Windridge was third in Mrs Henry Clark-Bowden's 'Knobbly', thought to have been chassis BHL 114, which used a Scarab Chevrolet engine.

142

The British GP meeting was at Aintree on July 18, where Bueb qualified on row two and Halford on row three alongside Blond in the Ecosse RSF 301 and Clark in the Reivers' HCH 736, the Listers being outclassed again by 2.0 and 2.5-litre Lotuses and the Cooper Monacos. Halford was third early on followed by Stacey's works Lotus, Blond, Flockhart in the Ecosse 'Toj', Bueb, Clark and Bekaert, whose car bore the marks of a collision at Dunboyne, Eire, the previous weekend. Stacey took third from Bruce, who was also passed by Blond's Ecosse car — which must have hurt — but the race settled with the works Listers established third and fourth ahead of the other big cars. Then on lap 11 heavy rain began to fall and Bekaert dropped NBL 660 on the infield loop and emerged unhurt after a lurid roll-over, convinced that something had broken following its Irish incident. Four laps later Peter Blond spun on the puddles at Melling Crossing, flipped off the straw bales and also crawled out unhurt, although the accident had involved his team-mate's Tojeiro, so both were out of the race. Jimmy Clark made the best of the rain in old HCH 736 and finished fourth behind two Lotuses and a Monaco, with the works cars fifth and sixth.

In the weekly magazines reporting that meeting Brian Lister announced his intention to retire and sell his team equipment at the end of that season. The future of the big-engined sports-racing car was uncertain, costs were escalating and what had begun as promotion for the parent company now looked set to become a liability. Frank Costin departed and work on the spaceframe project was suspended.

The very next weekend, on July 26, the F2 race at Clermont-Ferrand saw both Ivor Bueb and Bruce Halford crashing heavily and being taken to hospital — Ivor with particularly serious internal injuries, to which he subsequently succumbed. On that day, August 1, the subdued Lister team were at Brands Hatch with Peter Blond driving one of the Costin cars in practice for the Bank

Jimmy Clark climbing into the Border Reivers' team HCH 736 at Aintree prior to the 1959 British GP supporting race, with Bruce Halford ahead of him in works Lister-Jaguar No. 4 and Peter Blond to his left in the Ecosse former Monza single-seater car, rebuilt after its May 1959 Silverstone shunt with the front part of old 341 SG's chassis from 1958. Note how HCH 736's tail had been remade with the headrest deleted when the rear cockpit bulkhead was moved back to make Clark more comfortable.

Blond's Ecosse Lister-Jaguar on the Aintree grid alongside HCH 736 and ahead of Bekaert's Derek Wilkinson-owned ex-Whitehead NBL 660 prior to the 1959 British GP supporting race in which rain soon fell and both Ecosse and Wilkinson cars were effectively written-off. The surviving body panels from the Ecosse car, BHL 109-cum-the-forepart-of-104, still carried this Aintree number 8 in 1980.

Works Listers leading Ecosse Tojeiro during that 1959 Aintree race: Bueb-leading-Halford-leading-Flockhart out of Tatts Corner and away past the Grand National horse-race grandstands towards the pits. This was the Lister works team's last race.

Holiday Monday meeting on the 3rd. He crashed heavily, but emerged unhurt, which was more than could be said for the car. Driving disconsolately home to Cambridge Brian heard of Jean Behra's death at AVUS on his car radio, then at home he received a telephone call from France to tell him that Ivor had died. There and then, Brian Lister retired his company from motor racing.

No more works entries were made, the one undamaged Costin car and the

Walt Hansgen's Costin-bodied Cunningham car — on Halibrand cast-alloy wheels — leading George Constantine's sliding 4.1-litre Aston Martin DBR1 and Cunningham team-mate Ed Crawford's 1958 'Knobbly' car at Watkins Glen in 1959. In the background, Fred Windridge is off the circuit with Mrs Henry Clark Boden's Scarab-Chevrolet-powered Lister with an unusually large radiator intake.

The post-works career for what was almost certainly the true 1958 ex-Scott-Brown/Moss/Bueb/Halford MVE 303 began here at Aintree in the August 29, 1959 BARC Members' Meeting, where Jim Diggory — a Wrexham garage proprietor — drove TUN 708, as seen here in company with Geoff Breakell's Lotus. The car was magnesium-bodied, has rivetted-on anti-lift fairings on the front wings and a works Lister-type screen cup.

Jim Diggory was also responsible for completion of the Frank Costin-designed spaceframe Lister-Jaguar, seen here outside his garage at Rhostyllen, Wrexham, before the Costin body was fitted. The design, development and construction of this car had soaked up Lister funds 'like a sponge' before it was abandoned.

Bedford transporter plus a mass of spares being advertised for sale in *Autosport* on August 21, along with the wrecked ENB car from Helsinki available 'at £700' from Brussels.

On September 7 Peter Blond/Jonathan Sieff shared the latter's Costin car in the Goodwood TT with Dick Barton in their pit, but they were forced out by a cooling-system failure which the mechanics worked long but unsuccessfully to repair.

In America Walt Hansgen won his second Lister-Jaguar SCCA Championship title; he was second after taking over Phil Forno's car at Montgomery, New York, on August 9, and won the Watkins Glen Sports Car Grand Prix at the end of September for the third time to take permanent possession of the trophy. Briggs Cunningham gave his car to Ed Crawford after the eternal second's own car retired, and he finished sixth. But Hansgen's fastest lap at the Glen with the Costin car was 91.3mph, and Crawford's in the 1958 'Knobbly' had been 92mph. That was the story of Lister's 1959 season — the new car had been at best a great leap sideways, while Lotus and Cooper had steamed ahead.

During their six years of racing the Lister marque had produced something like 56 or 57 individual cars, the vast majority assembled and completed by customers outside the Cambridge works. Unfortunately, the concern's original records were lost in two moves of factory since those far-off days in Abbey Road. In 1961-62 George Lister & Sons Ltd made chassis and suspension parts for Emeryson and then built-up the Ford V8-engined Sunbeam Tigers for Le Mans in 1964. Brian maintained an interest in racing, becoming Chairman for a year of the British Racing & Sports Car Club and into the 'eighties there is still a possibility of a new road-going Lister-Jaguar — if conditions are right. His were the ultimate in Jaguar-engined sports-racing cars, the best of the breed . . .

Later lives and Lister mysteries

After the Lister factory abandoned racing the fortunes of their cars took an immediate dive in 1960, curiously enough recovering to some extent in 1961-62 and actually returning to the international endurance-race arena in private hands in 1963-64. The big sports car class in Britain had passed through a state of flux as a new GT World Championship gained prominence. Where open-cockpit sports-racing cars were concerned it was the mid-engined Cooper Monaco and Lotus 19 which ruled the roost, using 2.0 or 2.5-litre Coventry Climax FPF power, and in comparison the front-engined Jaguar machinery looked great and gormless — clearly antiquated and over the hill.

One or two drivers did their best to disprove that theory, notably John Coundley, a property developer from Ringwood in Hampshire, who had formerly been racing a D-Type (2 CPG) very effectively. He had acquired the ex-Bill Moss Costin-bodied 1959 production Lister-Jaguar chassis BHL 126, Bedfordshire-registered as WTM 446. It performed very creditably in his hands in the early months of 1960, seldom out of the first four or five overall and at the head of its class. That season also saw John Bekaert and Peter Mould persevering in their 'Knobbly'-bodied cars, NBL 660 and YOB 575, respectively, and those two machines became perhaps the most famous of their breed, while WTM 446 became involved in one of the many Lister mysteries, wreathed in rumour and legend by the passage of years. Most of the Lister-Jaguar mysteries involve the original works team cars, however, and here we can examine the questions in some detail — if not always with a black-and-white solution.

The main question to be asked is simple. What became of the works cars? The answer is involved.

At the end of the 1958 season Brian Lister (Light Engineering) Ltd owned two works 'Knobblies', one the still magnesium-elektron-bodied original second-string car MVE 303, and the other the production aluminium short-bonnet, fixed-scuttle car VPP 9 — the replacement for the Spa wreck. In 1959 the requirement for sports-racing car road-registration was eased, and the new Costin-bodied works cars ran without the familiar numberplates — although they were still often driven on the public road under tradeplates. Bruce Halford raced a 'Knobbly' works car unregistered at Crystal Palace, on Whit-Monday, May 18, 1959. It was demonstrably MVE 303 with its full-length bonnet, nose-top air scoop, rivetted-on anti-lift fairings behind the front wings, screen cup and ill-fitting driver's door — a characteristic feature which that body never lost.

VPP 9 does not appear to have survived into 1959 as a raceworthy works 'Knobbly'. No works records survive and team memories are understandably confused at a range of 21 years, but there are three possible fates. One — it may have been scrapped. Two — it may have been sold as it stood into private hands, on either side of the Atlantic. Three — the 'Knobbly' body was removed, the frame was re-bracketed and it was fitted under a new Costin body as one of the 1959 team cars . . . which is probably the most likely.

If the 'scrapping' alternative sounds incredible, one must remember that the car would have been surplus to requirements and Brian might well have considered it unsaleable *while his team was still active* because Geo. Lister & Sons Ltd's reputation remained all-important to him and the expense in time and money of rebuilding a works car 'as new' to make it 'good enough to sell' did not appeal.

In July 1959, when Brian announced his intention to pull out of racing, disband the team and sell its cars at the end of the season, he was approached by Jim Diggory — an enthusiastic garage owner from Rhostyllen, just outside Wrexham in North Wales. Diggory — in 1980 running Cambrian Fly Fishers at Ruabon, Llangollen — recalled: 'I bought a complete ex-works 'Knobbly' less engine and got an engine for it from Don Moore. The car was unregistered, but I was told it was ex-Scott-Brown. It had an elektron body'. Having been approached 'cold' about the car he recalled its chassis number as DBL 2. Considering that a year later — in 1960 — he had run an ex-works Aston Martin, mainly for Bruce Halford, which was a DBR1 — the confusion with a BHL-series chassis number is understandable. MVE 303's original chassis number had been BHL 2 and at a range of 21 years might not pinpoint recall of such obscure detail have seemed just too perfect? Certainly MVE 303 was the only surviving works car with a magnesium-elektron body, and certainly it was the only surviving ex-Scott-Brown car, since he had raced it at Mallory Park on May 11, 1958, and both his other Lister-Jaguars had long gone. Photographs of Diggory's car — Denbighshire-registered TUN 708 — equate very closely with the 1958 works MVE 303 subject to additional louvring, which he adopted on Costin's advice to cool the fluid-boiling brakes.

During the 'seventies the story grew that long-lost TUN 708 had been an assembly of ex-works parts. This is quite possible, but the ill-fitting driver's door of MVE 303 was just as ill-fitting on TUN 708, which suggests strongly that the mag-elektron panels were hung on the self-same sub-structure, *ie*, the self-same chassis, which would have been BHL 2 (perhaps with the addition .58 as in those Le Mans records?).

Diggory also bought from Lister the unfinished Costin-designed spaceframe car, of which more shortly, and after TUN 708 had achieved a fair degree of club success driven by both Jim Diggory and Colin Escott it was set aside in 1960 as the spaceframe car was completed and the Wrexham equipe raced their big Aston. John Coundley subsequently bought the spaceframe car for 1961 and crunched it into one of Mrs Topham's substantial gate-posts at Anchor Crossing, Aintree, during the 200 meeting in April. In May Diggory again advertised TUN 708 for sale 'in pieces for £1,000'. John Coundley spent a week at Rhostyllen, re-assembled and prepared the car and won with it in a minor club race at Silverstone the following weekend, the old mag-elektron body still in grey primer. John's mechanic John Pearson subsequently painted the car black 'with a couple of tins of Valspar lacquer' and as 'The Black Lister' Coundley recalled it in 1980 as '. . . a super car. I had run the Costins the previous year — 1960 — and they were always in terrible brake problems with boiling fluid and they felt just too big. If they had sorted out the problems I believe those cars could have been great, but I greatly preferred the 'Knobbly' and the black one was the best we had. We lengthened the cooling ducts beneath the car to get cool air into the rear brakes, and cut bigger holes in the tail to let hot air out and it was really sorted in that way. It was very good indeed.'

The old car was subsequently returned to Diggory after Coundley had achieved considerable success and he completed the 1961 club season with it in the north, spinning out of the lead on one occasion at Charterhall, 'which had a surface like a relief map of Donegal'.

He subsequently sold the veteran Lister, less engine but with gearbox, to Mike Wright, a motor engineer based at Much Wenlock in Shropshire. He had been sprinting and hill-climbing an XK120 fitted with a D-Type dry-sump engine and swopped that car with Diggory, retaining the engine for TUN 708. He told the story of the old Lister's demise: 'I drove the car regularly on the road, but one night on the main road from Bridgenorth to Craven Arms something went wrong with the electrics and the headlamps went out. I knew the road like the back of my hand so drove on using the sidelights, but about four miles later they went out as well, I lost my way and hit a tree head-on on the apex of a very fast corner. It took the nearside front wheel right off and spun us round and we got quite badly knocked-about. The police couldn't shift it to clear the road, so eventually they rolled it side-over-side into the hedge, writing-off what hadn't been damaged. The insurance paid out in full, and I burned the magnesium body behind my garage — setting fire to it with a welding torch. The frame was cut-up

and the salvaged rear suspension and bits went to a chap in Weston-super-Mare. Ken Wilson had the oil tank, and that was the end of it'.

The surviving parts circulated through enthusiasts and then the trade, fetching-up with John Pearson, who in 1980 was building them into a replica TUN 708. Meanwhile, another car had been brought into England from the USA in the early-'seventies which, upon examination, was found to have similar cooling intakes to the original 1958 MVE 303's, which had been patched and filled-over, but in an aluminium body. A set of Lister works bolt-on hubs issued from the same source in America and the car's importer re-registered it MVE 303 at the Cambridge licensing office. It then went to John Harper — who has unrivalled experience of all these Jaguar-engined sports-racing cars — and he completed a lovely rebuild in late-1958 works livery for French collector Dr Philippe Renault. It forms a worthy successor to the MVE 303 image since the original car had — this author concludes — long since gone to the great scrapyard in the sky. In fact the combination of rear deck cooling intakes, aluminium body and works bolt-on hubs smells more like VPP 9/late-1958 — but intensive US research effort had drawn a blank as these pages went to press.

The 1959 Costin cars' fates are just as complex. Brian Lister recalled selling them both at Cambridge to Graham Warner of the Chequered Flag sports car dealership in Chiswick, West London. Graham confirmed his memory; 'I bought the two cars, both Costin-bodied, both road-registered and taxed, with logbooks . . . I took one for a blast up the Great West Road here'. So that's where they went — or did they?

The Chequered Flag's ads for late-1959 include just one ex-works Costin-bodied Lister-Jaguar, and their system was such that a car only received a stock number and was entered in their stock book upon its sale. Only one of the Costin Listers appears in their 1959 stock book, carrying the classical registration MVE 303 transferred from the redundant works 'Knobbly'. The customer's name is unrecorded, but the car was probably exported to the USA. Again the trail of this car goes cold. So, if the 'Flag' had sold MVE 303, what became of the second works Costin car?

Ray Fielding was, and still is at the time of writing, head of the P.S. Nicholson Ltd garage business in Forres, Scotland. He acquired 'the ex-Hansgen/Blond Le Mans Lister-Jaguar' direct from Abbey Road and also travelled to Brussels and bought the smashed ENB 'Knobbly' car — both machines having been offered in the Lister team's withdrawal advertisement in August 1959. The conclusion must be that the Costin car sold by Warner under the MVE 303 registration was the other 1959 team car, driven by Bueb and Halford

Compare these shots of what was clearly the 1958 MVE 303, racing unregistered in Bruce Halford's hands at Crystal Palace in 1959, and TUN 708, as owned and driven by Jim Diggory at Oulton Park on October 3, 1959. The author submits that they are one and the same car, although Diggory has improved rear brake cooling intakes with Frank Costin's help. See text . . . Ivor Bueb is trailing Halford at the Palace in the works Costin car after Bruce had dumped his own in the Oulton Park lake!

The ex-Bill Moss customer Costin Lister-Jaguar WTM 446 being driven to victory by John Coundley in the AMOC Martini Trophy Silverstone meeting on May 21, 1960 and leading the pack from the Le Mans-type start. Car No. 1 on the left is John Ewer's Lister-Chevrolet, which started life with a standard Costin body before being 'improved' like this. It reappeared in southern Africa in 1961.

at Le Mans, and that the Costin VPP 9 was returned to Cambridge for sale to Fielding, or that there were actually three Costin-bodied cars involved, and the second 'Flag' car went elsewhere through channels or persons unknown, and was in any case a non-works team machine.

Ray rebuilt the ENB 'Knobbly' and sold it to Ken Wilson in Wales, while the Costin VPP 9 — like the 'Flag's MVE 303 registered purely for sale — was fitted with an ex-HWM wet-sump 3.4-litre engine with D-Type mods — the car having been acquired less engine, of course, as the original works unit had been on loan from Coventry. Ray sprinted the car a couple of times, didn't like it, and sold it to David Howard, a photographer from South London. He ran into problems early in the 1960 season, and by May was advertising it for sale, the price falling through a series of anguished ads to £1,350.

Enter John Coundley, MGM and 'The Green Helmet Mystery' . . .

An MGM unit under producer Chuck Vetter was making a film of Jon Cleary's Mille Miglia-centred novel The Green Helmet, starring Bill Travers and Syd James. John Coundley had been contracted to provide cars and driving and in July that year photographs of a crumpled Costin Lister-Jaguar appeared in the specialist press, crashed during

filming. The question exercising Lister enthusiasts ever since has been, 'Which car was it?'

The answer is WTM 446, John's ex-Bill Moss car in which he had achieved some good results in the early part of the 1960 season. The car was fudged-up with glass-fibre exterior panelling to masquerade as the 'Launder', the hero's car in the film. In June the film unit was on location for Mille Miglia-type shooting on the Llanberis Pass in North Wales, when Travers' racing driver stand-in Stephen Ouvaroff took WTM 446 away from a standing start with actor Joe Wadham by his side, accelerated fiercely for some 200 yards into a mountain-side corner, promptly dropped the lot and smashed into a roadside wall. The car came to rest, right-side badly mangled, dangling over a considerable precipice. Coundley sold the wreck, less his very good D-Type engine, to Maurice Charles, City Road, Cardiff garage owner and D-Type driver.

Coundley had to replace WTM 446 rapidly to complete filming, and he acquired VPP 9 for MGM from Howard. It was disguised as the 'Launder' and once The Green Helmet had been completed it was sold to Gerrards Cross garage proprietor Roy Bloxam, of HWM-Jaguar fame. Early in 1961 it appeared at British internationals with a suitcase-sized protrusion on its tail as its new regulation luggage-space, but on Whit Monday the unfortunate 34-year-old crashed fatally at Goodwood's very fast Fordwater corner. The car caught fire and its wreckage was acquired by S.H. Richardson, the Staines-based parts and scrap dealers, who had just opened a new centre in Pease Pottage. The bits were reputedly seen there by an

Filming for **The Green Helmet** saw WTM 446 modified with fake applique panelling as the hero's Launder car. Here at the Llanberis Pass we see Steve Ouvaroff in the 'Launder' alongside Coundley's Tojeiro-Jaguar 'Maserati', and the damage sustained by poor WTM 446 in its argument with that dry-stone wall. Photographs have been published before showing the relatively undamaged nearside, but these MGM prints provided by John Coundley are, we believe, the first to be published of the car's savaged offside. Stephen Ouvaroff limps away . . .

Australian visitor named Earl Cameron. He bought enough to rebuild and took it home. He fitted a Chevrolet V8 engine from his racing boat *Nitro*, but ran the car only once, at a Castlereagh drag meeting, where its clutch disintegrated. The car was then placed in storage until Gavan Sandford-Morgan, a director of Adelaide's Birdwood Mill Museum, located it in 1969. He acquired and rebuilt it and in mid-1975 it was advertised for sale at A$19,000. It was bought by Neville Webb, who cherishes it as I write.

Maurice Charles sold the remains of WTM 446 to Nigel Moores, the ill-fated Woolworth heir, a very pleasant personality and a great competition car connoisseur. It was subsequently sold, supposedly with a straightened chassis, to John Pearson for around £900. Pearson sold it to Harper and it followed a convoluted course, Harper having to straighten the frame a second time to erase the mark of that Welsh wall. The car ended-up with Stephen Langton of Reigate, who fitted a 'Knobbly' body and raced it in his black-and-gold colours into the 'eighties. He found it 'extremely

Jimmy Clark in the Border Reivers' Lister-Jaguar, HCH 736, at Mallory Park where, first time out in 1959, he won three races in a day. Here he is leading John Dalton's Aston Martin DB3S away from Shaws Hairpin into the Devil's Elbow. In 1980 HCH 736's Italian owner-driver was kidnapped and murdered before a ransom could be paid.

exciting and very manageable, although it does tend to get the better of me now and then'.

Meanwhile, the registration WTM 446 had been transferred to the last ex-works team car — the Frank Costin-designed spaceframe which ex-Naylor mechanic Ken Wylde had completed for Jim Diggory at Rhostyllen in 1960. Diggory, Escott and Bruce Halford drove the red-painted car, Escott winning at Oulton Park (as he had in TUN 708 the previous year) and Halford a fine race at Brands Hatch where he set a new short-circuit record of 57.4secs, which stood for many years. Bruce: 'In practice there the car wouldn't rev above 4,500 or so and eventually in desperation we tore out the wires to its electronic rev-counter and, hey presto, it ran sweet as a bird! It was quite a car, it felt more compact, more of a piece than the works Costins with the twin-tube frame, very stiff and obviously it had great potential'. Jim Diggory was more emphatic: 'I believe the spaceframe Lister-Jaguar was the best-handling big sports car ever produced . . . but it lacked the Aston's power'.

As already described, Diggory sold the car to Coundley, he bent it at Aintree and John Pearson recalled their running the car Manx-tailed on one occasion. That fine D-Type engine from 2 CPG passed through the long succession of Coundley Listers and reputedly ended its life in a JCB Historic Championship race in the 'seventies, back in a

D-Jag. Coundley advertised the spaceframe car for sale in May 1962 and began to race the ex-Mould/Gerry Ashmore/Gil Baird 'Knobbly' YOB 575 in its place, a car for which his mechanic John Pearson developed a particular affection and which he was to own in later years. He ran it for *Thoroughbred & Classic Cars* magazine editor Michael Bowler in late-'seventies historic sports car events, and sold it to Ben Huisman in Holland, still with its original aluminium bodywork intact.

The spaceframe car went to Peter Sargent, with the WTM 446 registration, and he had a special Le Mans coupe bodywork conversion executed by Playfords in South London. He shared the car with Peter Lumsden on a Lister return to Le Mans in 1963, but after running steadily and well in the early stages the car was forced out after three hours when its clutch bolts sheared — they had been supplied from a bad batch, and that was the end to the Le Mans Lister story, save for the Abbey Road-built Sunbeam Tigers which contested the 1964 race.

The spaceframe coupe reverted to John Coundley, who ran it in the 1964 ADAC 1,000 Kms at Nürburgring, co-driving with former winner Jack Fairman. 'Jolly Jack' was roasted in the greenhouse cockpit, John Pearson recalling how

John Bekaert was a most popular, universally well-liked and respected racing driver who could have gone far in the sport had his level-headed approach to life not taken him into the business world. Here, in Derek Wilkinson's ex-Whitehead NBL 660, he tackles Woodcote Corner at Goodwood, on Whit-Monday, 1959.

they virtually wrung him out after a driving stint, and the car again ran strongly, if not prominently, before its rear suspension pulled apart. Jaguar Drivers Club luminary David Harvey then acquired the car, holding the Gurston Down hill-climb class record with it, a venue about as far removed from Le Mans as one can imagine. It then moved on to J.A. Pearce and Neil Corner before being cut into near-original roadster trim by Hexagon of Highgate, destroying a perfectly adequate Le Mans car in favour of a form in which the car had never achieved anything notable, beyond a Brands Hatch short-circuit record. It was driven in historic events for Hexagon by Gerry Marshall and Nick Faure, and in 1973 was sold to Barry Simpson — a long-time associate of Bruce Halford — in Devon. Barry's assessment is interesting: 'With a more advanced chassis design than the other Listers one supposes it will have equally better performance, but this hasn't been the case. It is about 1cwt heavier at 19cwt without fuel and oil, and

unfortunately its de Dion rear-end does not match up to its more sophisticated unequal-length-wishbone front. While the front-end is extremely predictable and can be placed accurately the rear-end is equally unpredictable. Driven near the limit it will break away without warning, Gerry Marshall, John Harper, David Ham, Bruce and myself all confirming this.' He improved matters with a great deal of fine tuning, but the car was never really competitive with the equally fine-tuned 'Knobblies' in historic racing — adding weight to Brian Lister's assessment of where he had gone wrong on that far-off day in 1959 . . .

Pick of the Bunch: Any series-produced competition car marque will throw up a few examples with an outstanding history. Amongst Lister-Jaguars the customer cars campaigned so effectively by Bruce Halford and Jimmy Clark, by John Bekaert and by Peter Mould instantly claim attention, while the Ecurie Ecosse-built car which David Ham raced to such effect in historic events during the 'seventies is one whose career 'as new' was a mere prelude to greater things to come. Here we can take a brief look at some of the more significant Lister-Jaguars' later lives . . .

HCH 736 — Chassis BHL 5: The heroine of Le Mans 1958 was sold by Dick Walsh to the Border Reivers team for Jimmy Clark's use in 1959, as already described in detail. By Jimmy's own account: 'The Lister taught me a great deal about racing, and I had fun with that car. It was a beast of a thing, mind you, really vicious, but it was more fun than any except maybe the Aston Martins I drove later. When we got back to Berwick we started to modify the Lister for I honestly don't know how Bruce managed to drive it. It was so

cramped in the cockpit. We managed to carve a bit out of the bulkhead behind the seats to push the driver's seat further back . . .' Perhaps this explains the ease with which Scott-Brown took over the car from Bruce — a six-footer — for the British Empire Trophy final in 1958. 'My first race with the car was at Mallory Park where I had a field day, winning three races in the Lister.

'I began to learn a lot after those first races for I found that it was a lively car. You could drive it round the corners on the throttle whereas the D-Type was all stop or all go. The Lister was very much more progressive. It taught me quite a bit about brakes, in that I couldn't rely on them. I had to nurse them and make them work, without overheating them. I remember at Aintree once going to have the tyres checked just before the race. I got up there and put my foot on the brakes and the pedal went straight to the boards. I pumped it and the pressure came back and that's how we set off for the race! That was a great day for me . . . I finished second to Graham Hill in a 2½-litre Lotus, managing to beat all (sic) the works Listers.

'The handling of the car was fabulous. For example, at Gerard's Bend at Mallory you could set the car up going into the bend hard, and get round the corner without touching the steering again. If you wanted to come out tight you just put your boot in it, the tail came round and it was a matter of driving it round on the throttle the whole way. That really taught me quite a bit about racing, particularly about controlling a car by the throttle'.

The car which taught the great Jimmy Clark so much about race driving was sold by Reivers to Gordon Lee who moved it on to the eccentric Hon. Richard Wrottesley in the early-'sixties. In his hands it used the registration RSF 301 from his badly-damaged ex-Ecosse D-Type which he was advertising for sale at the time, with the cautionary note that about £650-worth of repairs were necessary. Wrottesley drove the car hairily to quite considerable club-level success, and eventually Gordon Lee bought it back and cherished it for many years, well into historic events in the 'seventies. Robert Cooper eventually acquired the old car, upon Lee's untimely death, and it was driven by Richard Bond before passing into Italian ownership with Medici, and into the 'eighties with Fossati.

NBL 660 — Chassis BHL 103: Peter Whitehead bought this third-off production 'Knobbly' and had it assembled at his Motorwork, Chalfont St Peter garage by his long-serving mechanic Arthur Birks. It used a first-series Williams & Pritchard body with rounded front wings, distinctive for its large cooling vents set into either side of the bonnet behind the front wheelarches. The old car never adopted the anti-lift fairing fashion popularized by Ecurie Ecosse. Whitehead raced the car in his usual

consistent manner, but apparently never particularly liked it. There is a story that he felt it was rather *infra dig* to have a car with upside-down Morris Minor steering, and insisted on substituting an XK140-150 rack-and-pinion, instead. Unfortunately, since the Morris-Lister steering went ahead of the axle line and the steering on the XK140-150 was behind it, when the latter's system was fitted on the former chassis the track-rods pulled when they should have pushed, steered left when the driver steered right and there was an early collision with the garage wall . . . Believe it if you like.

But in September 1958 Peter Whitehead died when the class-leading Jaguar 3.4 saloon in which he was navigating at that moment, being driven by his half-brother Graham Whitehead, crashed over an un-parapeted bridge during the Tour de France. The Lister-Jaguar was sold for the 1959 season to Derek Wilkinson, for John Bekaert to drive. John recalled: 'Derek had an interest in Dove's of Northampton, owned an ERA, was a director of a greetings card company and wanted a modern

The Ecosse special's body was a Wilkinson-modified 'Knobbly' with many Stan Sproat tweaks, as described in the text. When Gregory crashed the car at Silverstone it was hastily repaired with the front-end from Masten Gregory's 1958 British GP practice wreck grafted on to the Monza chassis. Peter Blond then crashed the unfortunate car at the 1959 British GP meeting, after which Stan Sproat refitted the original Monza offset-single-seater body in modified form to provide hill-climber Phil Scragg with his famous cycle-winged Lister-Jaguar 254 KTU, seen here at Prescott on one of its class-winning runs.

155

racing car. We had met in 1958 when I was driving HWM 1 on a shoestring and he bought the Lister after we had tried it for a day at Snetterton. It was a marvellous car and Derek was a great chap to drive for . . . he had a full-time mechanic, Jim Abbott, to care for it and paid our expenses in travelling, picked-up all the bills and gave us a quite handsome budget — about £1,000 — for the season. We could even afford new tyres! Whitehead had raced the car with a 3-litre engine, but we had a 3.8 fitted which was prepared at the Jaguar factory by George Hodge. While the Don Moore engines were said to be up around 300-odd horsepower we settled for a reliable 292 and as always George did a marvellous job on it.

'In two seasons with the car we had 23 firsts, 12 seconds and six thirds at all levels from Club to National and International, but in mid-1959 I hit Ashmore's D-Type in the wet at Dunboyne and although we went on to win there I think it tweaked something fundamental because the following weekend at Aintree in the Grand Prix meeting I lost it for no apparent reason on the way out of Village Corner and it rolled over. It was extensively damaged. We thought we could re-use the original chassis, but Derek insisted on having a

brand-new one. I believe we had the last 'Knobbly' chassis from the works while the old one went, I believe, to Gordon Lee — and he found it was still not straight.

'Jim completely rebuilt the car around the new frame, but somehow it was just never quite the same again — it never regained its original edge. I had driven a works Lister in the 1958 TT at Goodwood and compared to our car it was a real out-and-out racer. Its performance really was phenomenal, but it rattled and banged . . . the Whitehead car in comparison was like a Rolls-Royce, a very solid, high-quality, high-performance car.'

When first raced under the Wilkinson banner the car bore the old Buckinghamshire number 832 BH, but it was soon changed to NBL 660 — an August 1956 (!) Berkshire serial — under which it became famous. It was sold to Bill de Selincourt for 1961 when he graduated from an 1100cc Lola, while the popular and talented Bekaert opted to step down to a Lola — retiring at the end of the season to set-up his own textiles business 'and make some money at last'.

From de Selincourt — for whom NBL 660 was prepared by Coundley and Pearson — it went to Allan Deacon, a Fleet Air Arm officer, who disposed of its XK engine to David Beckett for his ex-Ray Brightman Chevrolet-powered car, BHL 125, registered RB 25. In much-hacked condition old NBL 660 was loaded down with a 7-litre Ford Galaxie V8 engine and eventually sold to John

Beauty and the beasts. John Coundley's ex-Diggory spaceframe Lister-Jaguar running with the mid-engined Lotus 19s and Cooper Monacos at Aintree's Anchor Crossing in the 1960 '200' meeting. It may have been a good car, but its genre was utterly outmoded internationally by this time, and John shunted it later in this race.

Rebodied by Playfords' for Peter Lumsden and Peter Sargent, the spaceframe car inherited the WTM 446 registration and was raced at Le Mans in 1963, as seen here in the Esses, but a faulty clutch bolt set put it out of the 24-Hours.

Final international long-distance race appearance of note by any Lister-Jaguar was the spaceframe car's at the ADAC 1,000Kms, at the Nurburgring, in 1964, when it was shared by John Coundley and — driving here — Jack Fairman.

Pearson. It went on to Lister enthusiast Gordon Lee, who had it rebodied to original form by Peel's of Kingston, fitted a D-Type 3.8 engine and revised the suspension and brakes. Bert Young took on the rejuvenated car in 1973 for historic racing and in the latter-'seventies it was acquired by the German Count Hubertus Dönhoff, largely for museum display.

YOB 575 — Chassis BHL 120: This car was assembled for Peter Mould of Mould Bros (Camp Hill) Ltd, metal founders, by his long-time friend and associate Mario Deliotti. Mould had formerly raced a C-Type and the ex-Sopwith Cooper-Jaguar YPK 400. His Lister-Jaguar ran a 3-litre XK engine in original form, substituting a 3.8 in later events. Its ram-intake short-bonnet production bodywork with integral anti-lift fairings and windscreen cup

looked suspiciously like the recently-vanished works car VPP 9, apart from the lack of a rear-brake cooling hatch on the tail deck. If it was not actually VPP 9 perhaps it used the ex-works car's bonnet?

In 1980, Peter Mould Ltd was specializing in keels, skegs, etc, for boats and based in West Bromwich. As a Lloyd's-registered marine supplier Peter had to keep age-old records and they included invoices for the Lister. It was supplied in January 1959 as a basic chassis kit, costing the princely sum of £436, and authorized to take the chassis number BHL 120.

'I remember Mario and I went to Cambridge and saw two of the new Costin-bodied cars being put together with great Chevrolet lumps being dropped in for John Ewer and Ray Brightman. Mario was convinced they would never cool their

Peter Mould's 1959 'Knobbly', YOB 575, survives into 1980 as a rare Lister-Jaguar with its original body still intact. The car featured many works 1958 team characteristics, but was in fact the last 'Knobbly' short-bonnet/aluminium-bodied customer car to be sold. Here, in a Silverstone club race, Peter Mould leads John Bekaert's NBL 660 at Copse Corner.

brakes properly and were too complicated, so we opted for a 1958-style 'Knobbly' instead, against all advice. In one way they were right, and there was a terrible delay in delivery of the body panels. The frame was complete and in fact we drove it around the factory yard before the body turned up. Eventually I collected some panels from Williams & Pritchard and bought the remainder — some old sections — from Brian Lister'.

So that is why YOB 575 looked so much like VPP 9. It really *did* use its bonnet. Didn't it?

No, it did not. Peter located invoices from W&P, dated March 17, 1959, showing 'Aluminium parts supplied as Lister 1958, excluding *tail*-section'. Another undated invoice from Lister indicates simply 'Aluminium parts', presumably an old tail-section, and that was to be the only panel on YOB 575 which differed markedly from the 1958 works' car VPP 9!

Mould's own company apparently cast his engine blocks, while their wide-angle heads cost £150 each and the built-up power units 'Using parts supplied' came from Jaguar for £775 the pair; 'Special price by direction of F.R.W. England'. Salisbury provided Powr-Lok final-drives for £88 10s each, while the file also contained invoices from AFN of Isleworth for a five-speed ZF gearbox. YOB 575 was indeed a very well-found car, and with Deliotti's preparation it achieved a record of 32 awards in 39 starts driven by Peter Mould himself and occasionally by Gerry Ashmore, before being offered for sale at the end of 1960.

Peter recalled: 'It was a fabulous car with that lightweight 3-litre engine, beautifully balanced and light enough for the 3-litre to push it along. With a 3.8 later on it was heavier, but still quick of course, but it lost that original delicate feel and with the extra weight up front you couldn't place it so accurately'.

Gil Baird bought the car for a season: 'It was meant to have the best brakes of any Lister, but by gum you still had to push hard — I remember bracing my shoulders back against the seat to get enough purchase on the pedal'.

The car moved on to John Coundley for 1962, in whose hands it enjoyed considerable further success, mainly at club level. He sold it to Tom Fletcher, who also drove it very quickly and it was still in very original trim as it passed down through the years to John Pearson, for whom it was driven regularly by Michael Bowler, and then in 1979-80 on to Ben Huisman of Holland — still with its original aluminium body, a rarity among historic-class Listers.

KTU 254 — Chassis BHL 109: After Peter Blond's crash at Aintree in 1959 Ecurie Ecosse were left with what was essentially their Monza single-seater-chassised, sports-bodied RSF 301 Lister-Jaguar, with a nicely-battered bodyshell on a relatively little-damaged, still-square chassis-frame and running gear. The frame, you will recall, had the front square from the 1958 Silverstone Gregory-damaged chassis BHL 104, welded on to its fore-part after Masten's May 1959 shunt at the same circuit. The Aintree-damaged body panels were reputedly sold-off for repair by a would-be special-builder, while hill-climb and sprint enthusiast Phil Scragg contacted David Murray and bought the redundant sports-cum-single-seater chassis plus the old Monza offset single-seater bodyshell, which had been in store at Merchiston Mews since the Two Worlds Trophy race. Scragg intended to reunite them as a replacement for his HWM-Jaguar SPC 982 and Stan Sproat went down to the textile engineer's home in Macclesfield to do the job, cutting-off the wide-body mounting brackets, attaching the offset-cockpit Monza body and modifying it to provide a second seat and access doors.

Scragg's preferred cycle-mudguards were attached and the dry-sump D-Type-engined special was given the March 1960 Cheshire registration KTU 254, its log-book being issued to Ernest Philip Scragg on April 26 that year.

In Scragg's hands it became a fearsomely successful sprint and hill-climb projectile before being sold to Alan Ensoll and then to Keith Schellenberg in the North-East. It subsided into a collection of mouldering parts before being taken up by John McCartney-Filgate. The car subsequently went into good hands with Gordon Chapman and his son Martyn, being reconstructed in virtual Monza trim and raced with some success through the 'seventies and into the 'eighties, Martyn saying: 'I just love that car, it's everything you could expect it to be — the most fantastic thing I've ever driven'.

YCD 422 — Chassis BHL 130: Our final 'pick of the bunch' is this Costin-bodied car which made more impact in its later life — driven in historic events for Marsh Plant Hire Ltd of Havant, Hampshire by Gerry Marshall — than it ever managed in original form, while in fact being one of the most original Costin-bodied vehicles to survive the passage of time.

It was first registered TUF 1 on March 21, 1959, being the property of Mike Anthony and powered by a 5,555cc Chevrolet V8 engine number LMCM 5139. The car was an occasional class-winner, but in general terms proved as unimpressive as its sisters owned and driven by Ewer and Brightman. While John Ewer sold his BHL 121 to Jimmy de Villiers, in Southern Rhodesia — the car survives in Southern Africa into the 'eighties — Brightman's BHL 125 was converted to Jaguar power, raced by David Beckett, and later went through a very convoluted career, mainly in the hands of dealers, during a period when the market value of Jaguar-powered Listers was beginning to climb at a remarkable rate. (In hindsight, these cars can be seen to have been a magnificent investment, for when an E-Type Jaguar might fetch £10,000, they were still obtainable for a fraction of that sum. Not any longer!)

Meanwhile, Mike Anthony sold his car with the new registration YCD 422 and a 3.4-litre XK engine replaced the Chevvy. In the early-'sixties it achieved considerable club-racing success in the hands of Mike Pendleton, of the Grosvenor Garage, Pitch Place, Guildford, in Surrey. The author lived nearby at the time and spent long

Mike Anthony driving his Lister-Chevrolet TUF 1 in a Goodwood event during 1959. This car was modified to accept a Jaguar engine after its first season's racing and became familiar and very successful in club racing in 1962, driven by Mike Pendleton under the registration YCD 422. Into 1980 it was owned by Gerry Marshall and entered under Geoffrey Marsh's Havant-based plant hire organization's banner, to achieve considerable success. It is, perhaps, the most original surviving Costin-bodied Lister-Jaguar.

minutes gawping at this great brick-red Lister, before climbing back on to his bicycle to go fishing . . .

Pendleton disposed of the car to Dick Tindell, of Esher, in whose hands it appeared very occasionally and was seen in the first JCB Historic Championship races in 1973. Gerry Marshall bought it in 1978 and for the 1980 Lloyds & Scottish Championship the very original old car was resprayed and prepared by Geoffrey Marsh's men at Havant, and entered for Marshall by his plant hire concern. It remained probably the most original Costin-bodied car in current use, alongside Huisman's YOB 575 as the most original surviving production 'Knobbly', while Ham's special-bodied GM 9639 formed a most attractive case apart . . .

ON TEST

John Bolster, former Grand Prix driver and Technical Editor of the weekly magazine *Autosport* throughout its 30-years of publication, had the rare opportunity to test-drive an example of each of the four major Jaguar-powered sports-racing cars — Cooper, HWM, Lister and Tojeiro — at the height of their early fame. His comments, which subsequently formed the basis of four articles published by *Autosport,* provide a fascinating commentary on the character of these cars at a time when engine power invariably dominated roadholding. Motor Racing Publications Limited is most grateful to Haymarket Publishing (1980) Limited and to John Bolster for their permission to reproduce the four articles on the following pages as an Appendix to Doug Nye's book.

145·1 m.p.h.

... and 15 seconds for the standing quarter-mile — the highest figures reached in an Autosport Road Test by JOHN BOLSTER in the

H.W.M.-JAGUAR

A Successful Sports-racing Car with an Outstanding Performance

IN most of the big sports car races we are accustomed to see George Abecassis making the pace. Right up among the "unlimited" works jobs his Jaguar-engined H.W.M. is always one of the fastest cars on the course. An invitation to borrow this car was therefore accepted in great haste, and a trip was made to H.W. Motors, of Walton-

HEART OF THE MATTER: *The Jaguar power unit, H.W.M.-modified, with three twin-choke Weber carburetters.*

★

"NO APPRECIABLE ROLL" says Bolster, and demonstrates the point at Brands Hatch.

The engine of HWM 1 is a Jaguar with a 9 to 1 compression ratio. It has three twin-choke Weber carburetters, and special H.W.M. camshafts developed from those of the Formula 2 engines. The clutch is a multi-plate racing Borg and Beck, and the gearbox has C-type ratios.

An important feature is the differen-

tial unit. This is a "quick-change" rear end of the type that is used at Indianapolis. In brief, the drive shaft runs beneath the final drive, which gives a desirable lowering of the propeller shaft. At the back of the housing a pair of straight spur gears transmit the power to the spiral bevel pinion. This engages the rear of the crown wheel, and the open articulated half shafts follow normal modern practice. The whole point of the design is the readily interchangeable spur gears, which can be instantly slid off their splines after only the cover plate has been removed.

Obviously, it is an immense advantage to be able to try several ratios during practice, and thus be sure of racing with the correct "cog" in place. I decided to take advantage of this feature during my test, and started off with the 4.11 to 1 gear. This is the proper wear for short circuits, where a maximum speed of not more than 120 m.p.h. can be developed. Naturally, I took the acceleration figures with the car so equipped.

Using this relatively low ratio, the liveliness of the car is difficult to put into words. One can positively fly up hills in top gear, and the gear lever need seldom be used. When drifting along on a whiff of throttle at 100 m.p.h. a touch of the pedal gives kick-in-the-back acceleration. Like all Jaguar engines, this one is so smooth that the relatively high revs. involved are not really apparent.

The standing quarter-mile figure of

on-Thames, where John Heath and partner Abecassis operate their motor business.

The actual machine I tested differs in some details from the current production models. " My " car, the celebrated "HWM 1", was, in fact, originally developed from the successful Formula 2 single-seater chassis. It has a straight tubular frame, whereas the production version spreads out in the centre to give more body support. Furthermore, the new chassis has helical springs all round, instead of a transverse spring in front and torsion bars behind. In both cases there is I.F.S. with rack and pinion steering, and a de Dion rear end. A very considerable weight saving has been achieved in the latest model, I am informed, compared with the prototype I tried.

As the data panel shows, the Girling brakes are of great size. They are mounted at the wheel hubs, front and rear, and the knock-on wire wheels have Borrani light alloy rims.

15 seconds is the best I have ever obtained. It speaks volumes for the de Dion rear end, which ensures that the wheels get a real grip of the road. In actual fact, the clutch is somewhat fierce and my getaways were, in consequence, rather violent; however, a little rubber burning had no effect on the excellent times recorded.

After all that, a 3.48 to 1 ratio was substituted, merely by changing over the two existing gears on the driving and driven shafts. Naturally, the machine became less flexible, though it was still marvellous to drive on the road. Completely equipped, and with a full width screen in place, I recorded a mean timed speed of 145.1 m.p.h. on this gear. Once again, this was the highest speed yet achieved in an AUTOSPORT road test.

The straight-cut gears emit a high-pitched whine, but this has the same exhilarating quality as the song of a blower, and takes one back to the Alfas and Bugs of one's youth. It would become tiresome in a closed car, but for

is at all times level, and there is no appreciable roll. The bucket seats give ideal location, and the steering wheel and other controls are as well placed as one would expect. The appearance is pleasantly functional, but future cars will benefit from considerable weight saving in the body.

At first I found the steering a little odd. It has much more caster than usual, and is consequently rather on the heavy side. Once I became accustomed to it, however, I found that I could make the car do almost anything. It can be driven with one hand at nearly 150 m.p.h., and curves may be entered at this sort of velocity without any drama. One can feel the more severe bumps through the wheel, but there is no unpleasant steering wheel reaction.

If a curve is entered on a trailing

sure is required at high speeds, this does ensure that accidental locking of the wheels will not take place in an emergency.

As most racing drivers have their pet ideas, and prefer to make their own changes in the specification, the exact price of the H.W.M. cannot be quoted. Suffice it to say that this very fast sports-racing car can be acquired at an extremely competitive figure. Regarded as a dual purpose vehicle, for competition work and ordinary road motoring, it would certainly be hard to beat. The passenger's seat is just as comfortable as the driver's, and is not the "token" affair one finds in so many cars designed for the circuits.

The Jaguar engine is really one of the marvels of the century. With its twin overhead camshafts, seven main

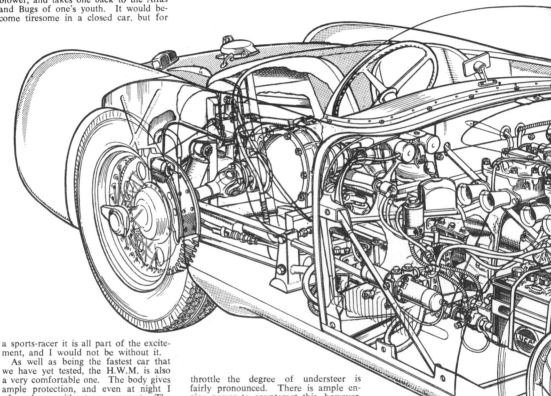

a sports-racer it is all part of the excitement, and I would not be without it.

As well as being the fastest car that we have yet tested, the H.W.M. is also a very comfortable one. The body gives ample protection, and even at night I often drove without an overcoat. The ride is fairly firm at low speeds, but

SPARE WHEEL on the H.W.M. is stowed behind a hinged panel on the offside of the body.

throttle the degree of understeer is fairly pronounced. There is ample engine power to counteract this, however, and the car corners best with plenty of use of the loud pedal. It fairly flings itself out of the faster bends, the absence of wheelspin permitting the very great urge to be fully employed. Altogether, the roadholding and suspension characteristics represent a very effective compromise. After a day or two's "ownership", I felt that I could perform the most advanced manœuvres in complete safety. Perhaps the extreme steadiness at very high speeds is the most impressive feature of all, and it is difficult to believe that the wheelbase is only 7 ft. 8 ins.

The brakes permit the full exploitation of the performance, and may be applied at the car's maximum velocity without causing any deviation. No fading is apparent, and if fairly heavy pedal pres-

NO SPACE WASTED—

every inch of the trim body

is filled with the complex

machinery and equipment required

to propel two people for long dis-

tances at a great many miles per hour.

bearings, and ultra-rigid construction, it has all the basic features of a successful competition power-unit. It deserves to be put into a small, light car, with correct suspension and steering characteristics and a genuine de Dion rear end to pin all that horse-power down to the road. That is just what John Heath and George Abecassis have done, and the result can be seen at the race meetings or on the accompanying graph. In my case the result was several days of such motoring that I was with difficulty restrained from writing this report in poetry!

JOHN V. BOLSTER.

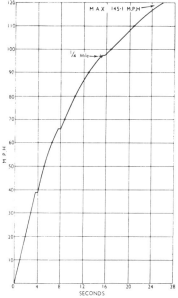

Acceleration Graph of H.W.M.-Jaguar

Specification and Performance Data

Car Tested: H.W.M. Sports 2-seater.

Engine: Six cylinders, 83 mm. x 106 mm. (3,442 c.c.). Twin overhead camshafts. 240 b.h.p. at 5,700 r.p.m. 9 to 1 compression ratio. Three twin-choke Weber carburetters. Lucas coil and distributor.

Transmission: Borg and Beck racing multi-plate clutch. Four-speed gearbox with short central remote control lever. Ratios optional with quick-change rear end. Car tested with Ratios 4.11, 4.93, 7.18, and 12.54 to 1. Also 3.48, 4.17, 6.08, and 10.09 to 1. Final drive by straight spur gears and spiral bevel. Articulated half-shafts.

Chassis: Twin tube frame with independent front suspension and de Dion rear axle. I.f.s. by transverse spring and wishbone; anti-roll torsion bar; rear suspension by torsion bars, on prototype tested. (Helical springs all round on production cars.) Girling dampers, telescopic behind, piston-type in front, with auxiliary Andre friction dampers in front.

Equipment: 12-volt lighting and starting. Rev. counter, ammeter, oil and water temperature, oil pressure and petrol pump pressure gauges.

Dimensions: Wheelbase, 7 ft. 8 ins.; track, front 4 ft. 1¼ ins., rear 4 ft. 2¼ ins. (Production cars, wheelbase 7 ft. 6 ins., track 4 ft. 3 ins.); weight approx. 1 ton (wet); Production car, 17 cwt. (wet).

Performance: Maximum speed, 145.1 m.p.h. Speeds in gears (with 4.11 rear end), 3rd 97 m.p.h., 2nd 66 m.p.h., 1st 39 m.p.h.; (3.48 rear end), 3rd 114 m.p.h., 2nd 77 m.p.h., 1st 46 m.p.h. Standing quarter mile 15 secs. Acceleration: 0-50 m.p.h., 5.2 secs.; 0-60 m.p.h., 6.5 secs.; 0-70 m.p.h., 8.8 secs.; 0-80 m.p.h., 10.6 secs.; 0-90 m.p.h., 12.8 secs.; 0-100 m.p.h., 17 secs.; 0-110 m.p.h., 20.8 secs.

Fuel Consumption: 15 m.p.g. (approx.).

THEO PAGE

HWM I

Another exclusive **AUTOSPORT** *cutaway drawing by Theo Page*

Way back in the distant past, the first 500 c.c. Cooper was built. It consisted of two secondhand Fiat 500 front ends, united by a simple, light frame. Soon afterwards, a new motor journal called AUTOSPORT tried an M.G.-engined sports Cooper for an early road test, and I still remember that little car with affection. If "Mr. Fiat" no longer made the bits, the suspension was still similar, with a transverse spring and wishbones at either end of the frame. The same design has been followed for all the Coopers built ever since.

The biggest car that the Surbiton firm has produced is the Cooper-Jaguar. There

and contains an E.N.V. nosepiece. There are short articulated half-shafts to the rear hubs, and the wheels are the racing Dunlop light alloy discs, with three-eared knock-on caps. The D-type engine is slightly inclined in the frame, and has

anything on the road.

Multi-plate racing clutches are not intended for traffic work, but this one was by no means as fierce as some. The close-ratio Jaguar gearbox was delightfully easy to handle, though the very short lever called for a little muscular effort. These big machines may consume fuel at a rate of 10 m.p.g. or so during racing, but at fast touring speeds I was agreeably surprised at the quite reasonable consumption.

What a touring car this is! The acceleration bears no relationship to any normal experience, and a touch of third speed caused the seat back to give one a real kick in the spine as one rockets past the 100 m.p.h. mark. Once under way, the independent suspension permits the full power to be used without a trace of wheelspin. The Cooper-Jaguar is, however, a very difficult car to take cleanly off the mark.

JOHN BOLSTER TRIES
A Cooper-Jaguar
Michael Head's Successful Sports-Racing Car

were, in effect, two versions of this, and Colonel Head ordered one of the later-type chassis. He bought a D-type engine from Jaguar Cars, Ltd., and incorporated some of his own experience in the machine.

In brief, the original idea was that the car was to be driven to its races, both here and on the Continent. So, it has a large detachable luggage grid to which the metal cover for the passenger's seat can be clipped. The general standards of seating comfort, ease of entry and exit, and so forth, are of a much more practical nature than one generally finds in a "sports-racer".

The basis of the vehicle is a space frame, built up of 1½ ins. steel tubes of 14 or 16 s.w.g. A massive structure encloses the gearbox and propeller shaft and forms the main backbone. The two seats are separated to some extent by this member, but the driver does not sit "outboard" as he did in the first models. For this powerful machine, the well-known Cooper suspension is modified by having tubular wishbones top and bottom, but the suspension media are still transverse springs, though these have no locating duty to perform.

The differential unit is chassis mounted.

three 45 mm. Weber twin-choke carburetters. The unit developed 252.5 b.h.p. at 6,000 r.p.m. on a 9 to 1 compression ratio, but this one now has a 10 to 1 ratio, on which it is still tractable provided that the new super-grade petrols are used.

Those of us who saw Michael Head's decisive victory at Goodwood, against very strong opposition, remarked on the roadholding of the Cooper-Jaguar. In fact, nothing very startling in the way of modifications has been carried out, but a great deal of thought and hard work has improved the handling out of all knowledge. The machine is not as light as some of its competitors, but the effective roadholding, coupled with the immense power of the servo-assisted Dunlop disc brakes, render it a highly effective racing instrument.

I collected the Cooper-Jaguar from Michael Head's charming house in Surrey. The big machine started at once on the starter, and burbled happily off through the country lanes. With a wheelbase of 7 ft. 7 ins. and a track of 4 ft. 3 ins., this is really a very small car. I found that a mere touch of the accelerator sent it flying past any opposition, and truly I had an easy mastery of literally

This is because there is a normal differential instead of one of the limited-slip variety. Thus, unless the two wheels are on a road surface of completely uniform grip, one tyre may start to spin and the getaway is ruined. It is tricky to choose between too much wheelspin on the one hand, and too few revs for the Webers to pick up cleanly on the other. I covered a standing quarter-mile in 14.8 secs., but excellent though that time is, I could certainly beat it with a little more practice, I feel.

As regards maximum speed, this is largely a question of gear ratio in a car as powerful as this. The crown wheel and pinion fitted at the time of my test were unchanged after Goodwood and Aintree and gave a road racing ratio. I quickly found that, on a long straight, it was possible to over-rev, and in fact I had to take my foot off during the timed runs. As this was a privately owned car in the middle of a racing season, I decided that about 6,000 r.p.m. would be enough, though I momentarily touched 6,100 r.p.m. as I hurriedly eased the accelerator. The result was 136.3 m.p.h., but obviously well over 150 m.p.h. could be achieved with a higher "cog".

I came to the conclusion that the Cooper-Jaguar, as modified by Micheal Head, is an extremely potent and effective sports-racing car yet has sufficient tractability and comfort to be quite acceptable for road use. I have, in the past, written many paragraphs on the superb Jaguar engine. Here, it is allied with effective four-wheel independent suspension and immensely powerful disc brakes. The result is a foregone conclusion.

horsepower to the road. One lets in the clutch at 3,000 r.p.m., and thereafter one takes the motor up to 6,200 r.p.m. in each gear with no wild sliding of the tail or smell of burning rubber.

The consequence of this quite exceptional traction, coupled with the advantageous shape of the Jaguar power curve, was that by far the best set of performance figures were recorded that have ever appeared in AUTOSPORT. The acceleration graph is somewhat spectacular, to say the least, and comparison of the figures with those of other extremely fast sports cars prove that the "Toj" is in a class of its own. A standing quarter-mile in 13.6 secs. is a breathtaking achievement, as is 0-50 m.p.h. in 3.8 secs. or 0-100 m.p.h. in 12.6 secs. I recorded these staggering times straight away, with no practice and only a brief acquaintanceship with the car. It is probable, therefore, that even these

JOHN BOLSTER TESTS

THE TOJEIRO-JAGUAR

Jaguar D-type Engine in Light Tubular Chassis with De Dion Rear Axle Gives a Sports Car of Fantastic Performance

At the risk of repeating myself, I must pay homage to the Jaguar engine. Here we have a highly efficient twin-overhead-camshaft unit which produces power, and lots of it, right through the revolution range. Yet, it is smoother, and more flexible, than the engines of many luxury limousines, even when it is in race-winning tune.

I therefore anticipate with pleasure a road test of any Jaguar-engined car. In the present case, however, the recipe was something very special. Take a D-type Jaguar power unit and insinuate it into a very small but beautifully made multi-tubular chassis. Give it independent suspension by wishbones in front, and fit a de Dion axle at the rear, on parallel trailing arms and a bronze slider block. Cover it with an aerodynamic shell, and keep the weight down to 15½ cwts. including water, oil, and four gallons of petrol, and you will have one of the most potent sports cars that has yet been built!

There has been a certain amount of correspondence about intractable sports racing cars, and I have personally met such machines which were almost undrivable on the road. In this case, though, I lunched at the Steering Wheel with John Tojeiro and John Ogier, and then took my seat in the 250 b.h.p. bomb which was to be my normal means of transport for the next week. The big machine started at once on the button, and glided into the traffic stream with only a low rumble from the exhaust to indicate its latent power.

Once out on the open road, it was

LOOKING FORWARD from the cockpit over the powerful Jaguar D-type engine, with three Weber carburetters, which gives the car a possible maximum speed of approximately 170 m.p.h.

obvious that the performance set an entirely new standard; 333 b.h.p. per ton is a startling enough figure, one must admit, but many cars of much lower potency are plagued with wheelspin and unable to make use of their full engine power. The Tojeiro has plenty of weight on the rear wheels, where it is wanted. It has a de Dion axle, and the unsprung weight is kept to a minimum by mounting the disc brakes inboard. Finally, it has a ZF limited slip differential. The result of these things is a capacity to transmit all that

stupendous figures could be bettered after further experience!

The maximum speed requires a word of explanation. The gear ratio fitted to the car was the one that had been employed on typical road circuits, where one has no room to exceed 150 m.p.h. Under test conditions, however, I speedily found that one could over-rev. on top gear, and in fact I had to ease my foot slightly for this reason when timing the machine at 152.5 m.p.h. I do not doubt that something like 170 m.p.h. would be available with a "Le

165

Mans cog" in the final drive, 150 m.p.h. is quite a fair velocity, though, and it can be attained on even relatively short straights, when the sensation of sheer speed is immense.

I was warned by John Tojeiro that he was not entirely satisfied with the road-holding of this prototype car, and was incorporating improvements in subsequent production models. The machine holds well on the straight, I found, but the cornering power is not up to the rest of the performance. It is almost impossible to maintain a genuine four-wheel drift through a corner, because the rear end is for ever breaking free. My guess is that there is insufficient rear axle movement, and that the de Dion tube is coming up against the bump stops. Much greater travel is to be allowed in future, I understand, and a torsional anti-roll bar is to be added to the front suspension. At present, one has to get the car fully straightened up after a bend before giving it full throttle.

The only other point for criticism is the brakes. These are discs without a servo, and they do not possess that reserve of power which one appreciates

on a very fast car. The D-type engine can be supplied with a servo pump, and this facility is to be employed in future. Obviously, the phenomenal traction and light weight of this car give it a far higher performance than that of any other Jaguar-engined machine. Once its cornering power and braking have received the proposed modifications, it should lap the circuits at an extremely high velocity.

Having taken my performance figures and thrashed the car round a road circuit, I used it for normal road work. Some of my passengers became highly emotional when I first pressed that little pedal on the right, for really such acceleration is a somewhat startling experience. On returning the Tojeiro, I drove it again in London's traffic, and all the time I used the same sparking plugs, nor did I have to give the machine any mechanical attention.

The Tojeiro-Jaguar is an exceptionally well-made competition car of delightfully functional appearance and electrifying performance. We shall hear more, much more, of this ultra-high-performance British machine.

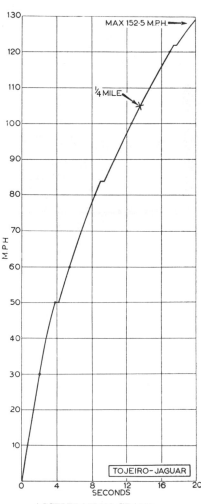

ACCELERATION GRAPH

BONNET-OFF view (above) shows the radiator, front suspension and the air-intake ducting from the nose to the carburetters.

★

CLOSE-UP (left) of the front suspension reveals helical springs, tubular wishbones and disc brakes. On future production models of the car the brakes will be servo-assisted to improve their power.

★

Specification and Performance Data

Car Tested: Tojeiro-Jaguar Mark II sports-racing two-seater.

Engine: Six cylinders, 83 mm. x 106 mm. (3,442 c.c.). Twin overhead camshafts. 250 b.h.p. at 5,750 r.p.m. 9 to 1 compression ratio. Three twin-choke Weber carburetters. Lucas coil and distributor.

Transmission: Borg and Beck racing multi-plate clutch. Four-speed gearbox with short central control lever. Ratios: 3.5, 4.2, 6.1 and 10.1 to 1 Final drive by chassis-mounted Salisbury hypoid and ZF differential.

Chassis: Multi-tube space frame. Double wishbones and rack and pinion steering in front. De Dion axle on parallel trailing arms and central bronze slide block, at rear. Armstrong piston-type dampers and helical springs all round. Disc brakes, inboard at rear. 6.00-16 ins. (front) and 6.50-16 ins. (rear) tyres on light alloy disc wheels with knock-off hub caps.

Equipment: 12-volt lighting and starting. Rev. counter, ammeter, oil pressure and water temperature gauges.

Dimensions: Wheelbase, 7 ft. 3 ins. Track, 4 ft. 2 ins. Height to top of scuttle, 2 ft. 8 ins. Weight, 15 cwt.

Performance: Maximum speed, 152.5 m.p.h. Speeds in gears: 3rd 122 m.p.h., 2nd 84 m.p.h., 1st 50 m.p.h. Standing quarter mile, 13.6 secs. Acceleration: 0-30 m.p.h. 2 secs., 0-50 m.p.h. 3.8 secs., 0-60 m.p.h. 5.4 secs., 0-80 m.p.h. 8.2 secs., 0-100 m.p.h. 12.6 secs., 0-120 m.p.h. 16.8 secs.

Fuel Consumption: 15 m.p.g. (approx.).

John Bolster Tests

The LISTER-JAGUAR

A Week-end With Britain's Fastest Sports Car

WITHOUT any doubt, the most outstanding feature of the 1957 racing season in this country has been Archie Scott-Brown's mastery of the sports-car events with the Lister-Jaguar. As the low green projectile, with its well-known yellow stripe down the middle, has taken the lead time and time again, many spectators must have wondered just what it would feel like to drive a car as fast as that. A week-end with the Lister-Jaguar must be the secret dream of the majority of enthusiasts.

I have actually realized that dream, for I have recently been using that famous car as my personal transport on the road. In the first place, Brian Lister wanted to fit a really high cog and see how nearly she would approach 200 m.p.h. Unfortunately, lack of time prevented that exciting project, and we decided that, in any case, a test with a normal road racing gear ratio would be of more general interest. The car was not specially prepared in any way. Indeed, after Archie had won the big sports car race at Goodwood with almost contemptuous ease, he stepped out of the Lister-Jaguar and I got in, and my week-end had really begun.

As regular readers are aware, I have driven many Jaguar-engined sports-racing cars. This particular one has the latest and largest Jaguar power unit in the shape of a "works" 3.8-litre, with three Weber twin-choke carburetters. There is a three-plate racing clutch and a D-type Jaguar close-ratio gearbox. This box incorporates a linkage whereby either first or second speed is positively locked until the clutch is withdrawn.

The chassis is typically Lister, and very similar to that of the Lister-Bristol which I have driven in the past. The main frame members are two large-diameter tubes, and the independent front suspension is by helical springs and wishbones with rack and pinion steering. Behind, there is a de Dion axle, again on helical springs, and the dry sump oil tank and the fuel tank are both in the tail. The disc brakes have no servo in their hydraulic system, and the rear ones are inboard-mounted. The Dunlop light alloy disc wheels have three-eared knock-on hub caps.

The car is very compact for its considerable engine capacity. One sits well down in it, the body coming right up round the shoulders. The passenger's seat is perfectly practical, and the shallow full-width Perspex screen deflects the draught sufficiently to allow fast driving without goggles if desired.

On moving off, one is at once impressed with the comparative smoothness of the clutch, which one does not normally expect from a three-plate racing assembly. First speed is much higher than usual, for it is intended to be used on sharp corners, and its engagement is consequently synchronized. Nevertheless, it gives a most stirring getaway, and the machine runs remarkably straight without correction if too much wheelspin is accidentally induced.

Once the car is on the move, the excellence of the traction is its most outstanding feature. All the power of that great engine can really be transmitted to the road, and I habitually used full throttle on all four gears on every sort of road surface. The sheer sensation of immense acceleration is difficult to put into words. The acceleration figures are the best ever recorded by AUTOSPORT. If one compares them with the times that I have achieved with other sports-racing cars, it is easy to understand the long list of Lister-Jaguar victories.

Such performance would be useless, even in the hands of Archie Scott-Brown, if there were not roadholding to match.

"IT'S MINE NOW!" says Bolster, interviewing Scott-Brown at Goodwood for B.B.C. Television, before taking over the Lister-Jaguar.

POWER-PACKED: The Lister-Jaguar with quickly detachable bodywork removed to reveal raked-back radiator and double-wishbone front suspension.

PROTOTYPE (left)
The Lister-Jaguar as
raced during 1957.

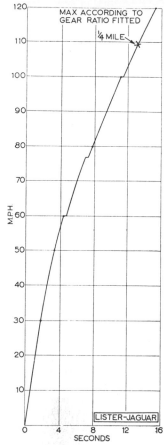

[Graph: MPH vs SECONDS]

MAX ACCORDING TO GEAR RATIO FITTED

¼ MILE

LISTER-JAGUAR

SPECIFICATION AND PERFORMANCE DATA

Car Tested: Lister-Jaguar sports-racing 2-seater.

Engine: Six-cylinders 87 mm. x 106 mm. (3,781 c.c.) 10 to 1 compression ratio, 300 b.h.p. (approx.) at 5,800 r.p.m. Twin overhead camshafts. Three twin-choke Weber carburetters. Lucas coil and distributor. Dry sump lubrication.

Transmission: Three-plate racing clutch. Four-speed gearbox with central remote control lever and synchromesh on all gears, ratios 3.73, 4.75, 6.11, and 7.99 to 1. Salisbury hypoid final drive unit with ZF differential.

Chassis: Twin-tube frame with independent front suspension by wishbones and rack and pinion steering. De Dion axle at rear. Helical springs and telescopic dampers all-round. Disc brakes, inboard at rear. Light alloy wheels with centre-lock hubs, fitted 6.00-16 ins. (front) and 7.00-16 ins. (rear) tyres.

Equipment: 12-volt lighting and starting. Rev. counter. Oil pressure, water temperature, and oil temperature gauges.

Dimensions: Wheelbase, 7 ft. 5 ins. Track (front) 4 ft. 2¼ ins., (rear) 4 ft. 4 ins. Overall length, 12 ft. 11½ ins. Width, 5 ft. 1 in. Height to scuttle, 2 ft. 5 ins. Weight (dry) 14¼ cwt.

Performance: Maximum speed 140 m.p.h. plus, according to gear ratio. Speeds in gears, 3rd 100 m.p.h., 2nd 77 m.p.h., 1st 60 m.p.h. Standing quarter-mile 13.2 secs. Acceleration 0-30 m.p.h. 2 secs. 0-50 m.p.h. 3.6 secs. 0-60 m.p.h. 4.6 secs. 0-80 m.p.h. 8 secs. 0-100 m.p.h. 11.2 secs. 0-120 m.p.h. 15.2 secs.

Fuel Consumption: Racing, 10 m.p.g. Touring, 15 m.p.g. (approx.).

In fact, the roadholding is extremely good and the cornering power very high. There is no roll, the car simply remaining level and answering perfectly to its light and accurate steering. Rear end breakaway does not occur, unless it is provoked deliberately with that immense horse-power. With a normal road-racing final drive ratio, the acceleration continues to be breathtaking right up to 140 m.p.h. or so, which comes up on any reasonably straight stretch of road. The maximum speed would be at least 190 m.p.h. with a suitable crown wheel and pinion; it is during high speed acceleration in top gear that the extra punch of the 3.8-litre engine makes itself felt.

As a road car, the Lister-Jaguar is a sheer delight. For continuous use, one would prefer rather more exhaust silencing, but I drove through several large towns without difficulty. The engine obviously prefers the open road, but by sympathetic handling it can be made to behave in quite a docile manner. I do not know whether or not the engine heat would be oppressive in summer temperatures, but for driving on a frosty autumn morning I found the warmth most comforting. The protection is so astonishingly complete that I never wore an overcoat during hundreds of miles of driving.

Used intelligently, the stupendous acceleration renders this an extremely safe car. Overtaking can be done so rapidly, and the left side of the road can be regained very quickly indeed. The disc brakes did not at first feel particularly powerful, though I was at once impressed by their absolute progressiveness. I later found that they were in fact capable of getting me out of all the difficulties in which I managed to place myself. Even during panic stops, none of the wheels tended to lock and there was no grabbing.

Archie Scott-Brown has already proved that the Lister-Jaguar is Britain's fastest sports-racing car. I have now proved that it is an admirable sports-touring car, and that all its racing virtues make it a better and safer machine, irrespective of the purpose for which it is used! I still feel, however, that the landlord of my local pub summed it up perfectly. "One moment he was here," he said, "and the next moment he wasn't!"

Boy! What a week-end!

DETAILS of (right) inboard rear brakes and de Dion axle. (Below) Driving compartment, with cranked central-change gear lever.